Leonard Withington

Solomon's Song

Translated and explained, in three parts

Leonard Withington

Solomon's Song
Translated and explained, in three parts

ISBN/EAN: 9783337318703

Printed in Europe, USA, Canada, Australia, Japan

Cover: Foto ©Thomas Meinert / pixelio.de

More available books at **www.hansebooks.com**

SOLOMON'S SONG:

TRANSLATED AND EXPLAINED,

In Three Parts.

I. THE MANUDUCTION.   II. THE VERSION.
III. THE SUPPLEMENT.

BY

LEONARD WITHINGTON,
SENIOR PASTOR OF THE FIRST CHURCH IN NEWBURY, MASS.

—ἡ σὰρξ οὐκ ὠφελεῖ οὐδέν.

BOSTON:
J. E. TILTON AND COMPANY,
161 WASHINGTON STREET.

Entered according to Act of Congress, in the year 1861, by
LEONARD WITHINGTON,
In the Clerk's Office of the District Court of the District of Massachusetts.

PREFACE.

Every new book to be profitable asks a certain degree of attention. But a reader is not always disposed to give a new book much attention; and indeed it must be allowed, on the strictest doctrine of chances and probabilities, that as an hundred are to one, so is the chance *against* the new claimant. However, here is a new book that humbly solicits attention; and let the reader remember, if it should not prove profitable, unless he gives it the requisite attention, the fault may not be wholly mine.

CONTENTS.

PART I.

THE MANUDUCTION.

		PAGE
I.	THE DESIGN	1
	THE DESIGN (CONTINUED)	17
	ADVERSE AUTHORITY	20
II.	PLACES IN SCRIPTURE WHERE DIVINE LOVE ASSUMES THE FORM OF AN EROTIC SIMILITUDE	31
	THE UNITY	40
III.	AMATORY DEVOTION IN HEATHEN LITERATURE AND IN THE CHURCH SINCE THE DAYS OF THE APOSTLES	50
	HAPPINESS	70
IV.	DIVINE LOVE AN INTELLECTUAL AND INFORMING PASSION	95
V.	THE DRAMATIC ELEMENT IN INTERPRETING THE BIBLE	133
	PARTICULAR APPLICATION	145
	THE USE OF THE IMAGINATION	166
VI.	THE DOUBLE SENSE	171
VII.	METAPHYSICS	187
	EXEMPLIFICATION	205
	THE EXAMPLE OF THE SACRED WRITERS	209

PART II.

THE VERSION	223
THE GOLDEN SONG OF SOLOMON	228

PART III.

THE SUPPLEMENT	277
THE CLAIM AND THE PROOF	304
THE CANON	313

PART I.

THE MANUDUCTION.

THE MANUDUCTION.

THE DESIGN.

ONE of the first requisites to the understanding of this mystic Song is to see the author's design,—"In every work, regard the writer's end." The Bible is too often considered by the neologist as a book of fragments, having no moral unity,—no single design, no *divine* design; and this injustice to the whole necessitates a greater injustice to all the parts,—nay, a want of perception of their import, or beauty. Every part of an arch rests on the key-stone. The history of the kingdom of God may be considered as one great drama, terminating in the triumph of grace over sin, and good over evil. "Behold the tabernacle of God is with men, and he will dwell with them, and they shall be his people, and God himself shall be with them, and be their God. And God shall wipe away all tears from their eyes; and there shall be no more death, neither sorrow, nor crying, neither shall there be any more pain; for the former things are passed away."

No book has suffered more than this Song from the

want of seeing the design. There is a twofold want. First, a want of seeing the design of the whole work of revelation; and secondly, a want of seeing the design of this particular book, and its harmony with the whole. Let us then point out, first, its probable

Historic Origin;

and this may help us to the moral design.

That the book was written by Solomon, I shall assume; for there is no end to that destructive criticism which whispers suspicions of a later origin. Even the Pentateuch itself has not escaped the daring innovators; and Aramæanisms, or later forms of Hebrew, are found in the earliest books of the Bible. The neologists prove that nothing is or can be ancient. I must be allowed to say, without depreciating any man's Oriental learning, that I cannot conceive of a degree of familiarity with any of these languages, which have been dead for many centuries, which can justify a critic in such bold censures as they undertake to pronounce.*

* Dr. Noyes, after giving several instances of alleged Aramæanism, comes to this very judicious conclusion: "From these and other instances, Gesenius, De Wette, and Umbreit have referred the Book of Job to the time of the captivity, — a period assigned to it by Le Clerc, Warburton, Heath, Garnet, and Rabbi Jochanan, among the older critics. But from the few remains of Hebrew literature that have come down to us, and our imperfect acquaintance with the history of language, it follows that it is by no means certain that the words and forms above mentioned may not have been in use in some parts of Judæa before the time of the captivity. ש, as a prefix, occurs in the Book of Judges. See vi. 17." — *Preface to Job.*

They cut here and slash there, until the whole forest of antiquity is levelled to the ground. Indeed, I cannot conceive of any language, which is not vernacular, being so critically known to a man as to justify him in upsetting all tradition, and saying he finds modernisms in every page. Dr. Bentley, in his dissertation on the Epistles of Phalaris, speaks very modestly of the modernisms he discovers in those Epistles, and places the chief evidence of their forgery on the anachronisms which he everywhere discovers. Besides, suppose there are real Aramæanisms, is recency of authorship the only way in which they can be accounted for? We are told in the sacred history, that Solomon " spake three thousand proverbs, and his songs were a thousand and five," (1 Kings iv. 32,) and why may not this be one of them? Who more likely to produce it, than he of whom it is said, there came of " all people to hear the wisdom of Solomon, from all the kings of the earth, which had heard of his wisdom"? There is no end to this learned scepticism; and truth would always be found by these sagacious divers, were she always certain to conceal herself in the bottom of a well. They are sure to miss her when she is on the surface.

Nor can I possibly agree with those who regard this book as a COLLECTION of songs. The remarks of Rosenmüller are on this point excellent. " That this book," he says, " contains one connected song, was never questioned until Richard Simon called it into doubt, by saying it was a collection of various minor poems by various authors; and since his day the same hypothesis has been adopted by distinguished critics; the book, according to these critics, is a collection of amatory songs, having no unity but the common subject, like the Book of Psalms, or the Book of Proverbs." But, as Rosenmüller says, there is no vestige in the book of this variety, — *nulla tamen tumultuariae congestionis vestigia.* It is everywhere a continued dialogue of the same speakers, in the same style, on the same subject. The unity is complete; and the man who finds this variety must do as a man who breaks a glass vase, and then complains that he only finds a collection of fragments. The only plausibility that such a theory can have must arise from a peculiarity which pervades all Hebrew poetry; namely, the rapid transitions by which a primitive people leave the reader to supply the interstices of their thoughts. The transition of such writers is always rapid; and if every break indicates a new subject and a new author, there is no end to the variety which bad taste and daring speculation may everywhere find. Following these ancient, simple writers is not like walking in the gravelled paths of a garden, trodden down by art and consolidated by the roller, but like walking over the glaciers of the Alps, where you must leap many a chasm, and where you are an unskilful traveller if the first interruption stops your way. The frost in these haggard regions will not imitate the nicety of an artist in his studio.

The want of tact in discerning the difference between a rapid transition (such as constitutes the character and beauty of primitive poetry) has led Rosenmüller himself, in that beautiful break in the nineteenth Psalm, ver. 7, to find a new subject. " Mihi tamen ea carminis pars, quae inde a versus et decurrit, parum apte cum reliqua videtur cohaerere. Ea vero in utraque rerum et verborum est dissimilitudo, ut nullus dubitem, duo diversa carmina, aut certe diversorum carminum particulas, quorum unum virtutem Jehovae ex opificio coelorum mire relucentem, alterum legum divinarum praestantiam et excellentiam celebraret, casu vel consilio in hoc uno esse conjuncta, quae proinde a nobis erunt sejungenda." But surely there never was a more beautiful unity than this Psalm presents, or a more beautiful transition. How natural that the works of God should suggest the clearer revelation of his Word, and that the same ode should present the harmony of both!

That this book should be regarded as a *collection* of fragments, is one of the most baseless visions that ever entered a mind darkened by its own ingenuity. Never was there a book that had greater unity. It is all about the same pair, Solomon and Solomitis. The style is the same; the subject is the same; and the whole impression is unique. The fragments must be made by the fragmentary mind that reads it.

The best way to discover the moral design of this

book is to consider its historical origin. We must endeavor to state to ourselves the circumstances under which its design was suggested and its form arose. It is pretty clear that most of the Psalms, and many of the prophecies, had an occasional and temporary application; and that the local event was an interpreter to the ultimate design. The analogy of one to the other was often very striking and instructive. Now this principle, sanctioned by so many examples, we propose to apply in explaining the design of this difficult poem.

We know from the sacred history, that Solomon, in his high glory, made affinity, not only with equal kings, as the king of Egypt, but also with the rural chiefs and sheiks of the tribes around him. We are told expressly (1 Kings xi.): "But King Solomon loved many strange women" (i. e. foreigners), "together with the daughter of Pharaoh, women of the Moabites, Ammonites, Edomites, Zidonians, and Hittites; of the nations concerning which the Lord said unto the children of Israel, Ye shall not go in to them, neither shall they come in unto you; for surely they will turn away your heart after their gods. Solomon clave unto these in love." Now we must remember that all these nations, except the Zidonians, were pastoral and rural nations, very much below the Israelites in the scale of civilization in the golden days of Solomon. I cannot think that the bride in this song is Pharaoh's daughter, though Lowth and other learned critics have countenanced this opinion. The Solomeith or Solomitis of this Song is everywhere a rural lass, having that mixture of rusticity and refinement which marks the daughter of some sheik, — just such qualities as would now characterize an Arab princess. " How beautiful are thy feet with shoes, O prince's daughter!" (vii. 1.) " I am black, but comely ;" that is, a handsome brunette. (i. 5.) " I am the rose of Sharon," i. e. a modest autumnal flower, and " the lily of the valley," i. e. a beautiful flower growing in a humble place. (ii. 1.) She sleeps under the trees; " our bed is green ; the beams of *our* house are cedar, and *our* rafters are fir." (i. 16, 17.) She is made keeper of a vineyard, and follows a flock, and the more polished daughters of Jerusalem are jealous of her; in a word, she speaks like a polished, rural lass. Now if we put the hints of history and of the book together, we may come to the conclusion that Solomon, in spreading his peaceful empire, made affinity with some of the Arab tribes around him. He did it from a partial wish of spreading the Hebrew empire and religion through the vicinity. He did not aim to conquer by war, but by affinity; he wished to cement a glorious empire ; it is true, that afterwards his idolatrous wives turned away his heart; but such, probably, was not his first intention. Nothing is more natural than that, when we mix too much expediency in our designs to spread religion, the evil should eat out the good. I suppose Solomon might have a mixed motive; it was one of those cases where his own wisdom might deceive him; his folly was not the folly of a fool, and I cannot imagine any other reason for his vast number of wives and concubines. "And he had seven hundred wives, princesses," (mark the word!) "and three hundred concubines: and his wives turned away his heart. For it came to pass when Solomon was old," (mark again,) "that his wives turned away his heart after other gods; and his heart was not perfect" (mark again) "with the Lord his God, as was the heart of David his father. For Solomon went after Ashtoreth, the goddess of the Zidonians, and after Milcom, the abomination of the Ammonites. And Solomon did evil in the sight of the Lord, and went not fully after the Lord, as did David his father. Then did Solomon build up an high place for Chemosh, the abomination of Moab, in the hill that is before Jerusalem, and for Molech, the abomination of the children of Ammon. And likewise did he for all his strange wives, which burnt incense and sacrificed unto their gods." (1 Kings xi. 3-8.) Several things may be here noticed. First, the vast number of his wives, beyond all the purposes of sensuality, — one thousand! — and I fancy some of them found their houses more of the convent than the seraglio. No doubt the purpose was to prepare the way for a splendid kingdom. Secondly, it will be noticed that the seven hundred wives were princesses; now the very number shows they did not belong to great kingdoms, like Egypt; they must have been princesses in the little tribes around Palestine. Thirdly, it will be noticed that Solomon is not totally condemned: "They turned away his heart; it came to pass when Solomon was old, that his wives," &c. "He went not fully after the Lord, like David his father;" "his heart was not perfect with the Lord his God," &c. It seems very probable, therefore, that at first his intention might have been good, or at least he thought so; he wished to establish a great kingdom; he was not a man of war; he must do it by other arts, — the arts of peace; he bound the rural tribes around him to himself by his multiplied affinities; — none but the best and worst men act from single motives. Solomon was a mingled character; his great wisdom sometimes marred the simplicity of his piety. Now, putting these things together, I suppose that he wooed and won some beautiful daughter of some neighboring sheik, — perhaps for the first time; the thing made a great noise in Jerusalem; the fathers were alarmed, and the daughters of Jerusalem were jealous. Sometimes he carried his rustic bride, his autumnal flower, his lily of the valley, up to Jerusalem, where she complains: "The watchmen that went about the city found me, they smote me, they wounded me: the keepers of the wall took away my veil from me." And sometimes Solomon himself went down to rusticate in her country, to spend part of the summer; the wild cliffs were as sweet to the king as the polished houses of Jerusalem were to the bride. "O my dove, that art in the clefts of the rock, in the secret place of the stairs, let me see thy countenance, let me hear thy voice; for sweet is thy voice, and thy countenance is comely. Take us the foxes, the little foxes that spoil the vines, for our vines have tender grapes." (ii. 14, 15.) These alternations are presented throughout the whole poem. Such, then, is the HISTORICAL ORIGIN of this beautiful work. King Solomon chooses some foreign bride; he deviates from the customs and laws of his country; his conduct excites great attention, and produces great commotion in Jerusalem. But a popular king has his own privileges; his intentions are for good, though not legal, and he writes this poem to show how pure his felicity, how happy his marriage with a rural bride, taken from a Pagan nation, whom, nevertheless, he brings under the influence of the true religion, and hopes to convert to the true faith, and make one of the instruments of promoting the glory of his peaceful kingdom.

But we are told in Judges xiv. 4, that, when Samson went down to Timnath, and saw a woman in Timnath of the daughters of the Philistines, and wished to have her for a wife, contrary to the wishes of her father and mother, "his father and his mother knew not that the thing was of the Lord." So in this case, the occasional song was exalted by the providence of God into a higher purpose. That purpose was mainly and primarily to foreshow the formation and union of the Gentile Church with Christ, when a more sublime and spiritual religion should be presented. Of course, in this purpose, as a unity, many constituents are involved; for example, a higher religion, a higher class of saints, the union of the soul with Christ, — all of which I consider not as separate items, but all involved in the great idea. There is to be a religion (such is the spirit of the book) which, uniting the soul with its Saviour in a nobler life, is to bring the Gentiles under its influence, and have power enough to spread through the earth. For this opinion we should adduce several reasons. First, the perfect analogy between the historical fact and the spiritual signification. If Solomon hoped to spread his kingdom by these marriages, the first bride was not only a type, but an actual specimen, of the signification looked for. Secondly, there is a perfect consonance between this view and the occasional signification of other places in the Psalms and prophecies. They often have an historical origin, and a sublime future import, as, in the seventy-second, the reign of Solomon and the kingdom of Christ. This is the general method; when the neologists say that whatever is great and splendid about temporal things in the Old Testament was applied by the later Jews to the Messiah and his kingdom, they only pervert and misuse a fact, which is the occasional signal of the great design. Thirdly, this Book would scarcely have had a place in the sacred canon, if the authors of that canon, whoever they might be, had believed it to be a mere love-song; it would have been like introducing the image of Bacchus or Silenus into their holy temple. On this point one of their own Rabbis has spoken,— Aben-Esra. "Absit, absit ut Canticum Canticorum de amore carnali agat, sed omnia figurate in eo dicantur. Nisi enim maxima ejus dignitas esset, in sacrorum librorum corpus non fuisset relatum, neque de eo ulla est controversia." To which Rosenmüller adds, that the whole character and design of the sacred books forbid the supposition that a song which sung the loves of a man and a woman should be numbered among the books of the Old Testament. When we read the following verse in the Book of Hymns by Dr. Watts, we have no hesitation, from its place, to allow its subject and design, though the words may seem ambiguous : —

> "Let my beloved come and taste
> His pleasant fruits at his own feast;
> I come, my spouse; I come, he cries,
> With love and pleasure in his eyes."

And the same reasoning applies to this book. It stands rank and file amidst the solemnities of revelation. This circumstance has in fact decided the Church, at the least the vast majority of it, to receive the book in its mystical import; and the fact is significant; it was the decision of unconscious reason, which the public mind could not resist. It is one of those conclusions that we adopt before we have analyzed its force. We do not expect the levity in a Greek chorus which we find in an Anacreontic song. But there is another reason. Fourthly, the poor, barren meaning that emerges, if the allegoric is not taken. A very peculiar choice meets us,—the great or the little; the sublime or the ridiculous; the most exalted devotion or the meanest sensuality. On this point even the comment of Grotius is instructive; he rejects the spiritual meaning, and where does he fall? He shows the melancholy consequence of not catching the note of inspiration from its celestial harp. I hardly dare to state the import which this great critic gives to this sacred book. In searching for the latent meaning of this book, we are reminded of the epitaph mentioned in Gil Blas,— "Here is interred the soul of the Licentiate Peter Garcias." The pert coxcomb laughed at the absurdity of supposing a soul interred in a grave; but his wiser companion fathomed the mystery and found the treasure.

But, fifthly, the place the book supplies in meeting the wants of a certain class of readers, perhaps I may say, in some degree, of all mankind. Who does not know that one great problem always before the awakened and anxious mind is, How shall I get the will to conquer my corruption? How shall I shake off those evil propensities, which, like iron chains, fasten my soul down to earth and transgression? To be saved I must be willing to be saved; but how shall I get that will? You tell me that religion is a cure for all sorrow and sin; that it is easy,—"the yoke is easy and the burden is light." But you contradict my experience. It is vain to tell me of the reasonableness of religion; the human passions are not reasonable,—mine are not; and I turn like a door on its hinges, and yet never get separated from my own selfishness. Such are the complaints I have heard from hundreds of sinners. Now, to such a mind how impressive, how instructive it must be to know that there is a form of religion where even the struggle is lost in the perception of celestial beauty and the free, spontaneous love which arises from it! There are attainments in religion where it ceases to be an effort,—duty is lost in delight; Christ is seen and his drawings are felt; the whole soul is borne on a new current. Let us seek an illustration. Yonder is a barge entering the harbor; the tide is against her, and the wind is contrary. How they toil at the oars, and how little is their headway! But suddenly the tide turns and the wind changes; they spread their sails, and enter the harbor with streamers flying and with triumphant speed. "I went down into the garden of nuts to see the fruits of the valley, and to see whether the vine flourished and the pomegranates budded; or ever I was aware, my soul made me like the chariots of Amminadib." (vi. 11, 12.)

To the Christian, too, the lesson is important. We begin religion in a violent struggle with our own evil propensities. It is a most discouraging combat, and our frequent failures plunge us almost into despair. Some of the strongest expressions are used in the New Testament to describe this painful conflict. It is plucking out the right eye, tearing off the right hand; it is a crucifixion; it is taking up the cross daily; it drives us to the most agonizing prayer. How delightful it must be to know that when the renovated will, feeble at first, has done its part, a time will come, when, if we are faithful in the struggle, the will must give place to the whole powers of the heart. There will be no struggle, no conflict, no cross. Indeed, the great secret in religion is, to have a clear perception of the celestial bridegroom, and to have the heart in a corresponding state. Strauss says that Christ is a principle, and I believe it. He is a principle and person too; and he is the more a principle because he is a person; and Dr. Young was more than a poet when he said:

> "Talk they of morals,—O thou bleeding Love!
> Thou Maker of new morals for mankind,
> The grand morality is love to thee."

But, sixthly, I think this must have been the origin and the signification of this song; that is, its sublime meaning grew out of its historical origin, from the fact that all the Pagan nations had similar ideas, and God, in thus signifying his will to his people, only employed the universal language. The Pagans regarded all nature as one great sympathetic system, indicating by the informing spirit future events. The flight of a bird, the motion of a serpent, the form of a cloud, the speaking of an ox, the voice of thunder, stumbling at the threshold, were all omens. Nature was everywhere sensitive and significant. We are told by Tacitus that the Germans were accustomed to set a captive of the nation with which they were at war and one of their own people at single combat, and judge by the event the fate of the war. What is this but the same principle,— a portentous incident foretelling a great result? How much more would the Jews, from their remarkable theocracy, be led to judge in the same way; and how credible is it that God should use such means to signify his will. The Bath Col— the voice among the Jews — was founded on the same principle.

Lastly, the unmistakable authority of the Apostles sanctions the same principle. But on this point we shall not at present enlarge.

THE DESIGN (Continued).

There naturally, then, grows out of the historical origin this spiritual design. As it has been forcibly remarked that the Psalms were written to show us, after reading the continual ritualism of the books of Moses, that there was a spiritual power in the old religion, so this book seems to have been written to show us the ultimate spirit of the true Church. When religion was ritual in its dress, it was sectional in its character. Circumcision, for example, confined it to the Hebrews. But the idea of an enlarged Church was connected with a refined religion. The higher spirit of religion was all-embracing. The affinity of Solomon with some Arab princes was made the occasion of showing a Gentile Church and a purer faith. The lessons of this book are, first, that there is something in religion which no words can teach. It transcends the power of language. It can be felt only by a bursting heart. It is life. "My soul breaketh for the longing it hath." Secondly, love is this transcendent spirit, — supersensual love. But, thirdly, not blind love; love arising from the perception of celestial beauty; distinct from delusion, because founded on truth. Fourthly, this passion and perception are mysteriously interlocked; we cannot say which is cause and which consequence. We

B

may say the perception of the beauty produces the love, and the love, or at least the disposition to love, produces the perception. Here is an involution which no mental analysis can unfold; and this book presents the two poles of this electric tide; to our experience they come together, but we cannot tell which is cause and which effect, which is prior either in time or in nature. Fifthly, the mystic union with Christ; what is it? Here it is shown as it must be shown in the emotional. Sixthly, there is a higher class of saints;—

> "They scorn to seek our golden toys,
>   But spend the day and share the night
> In numbering o'er the richer joys
>   That Heaven prepares for their delight;
> While wretched we, like worms and moles,
> Lie grovelling in the dust below."

Seventhly, piety, owning its origin, tends to its end. Religion begins in severe struggles; it is a period of conflict. Augustine has stated the difficulty, and in part solved the mystery. "Unde hoc monstrum, et quare istud? Imperat animus corpori et paretur statim; imperat animus sibi et resistitur. Imperat animus, ut moveatur manus, et tanta est facilitas, ut vix a servitio discernitur imperium; et animus animus est, manus autem corpus est. Imperat animus, ut velit animus, nec alter est, nec facit tamen. Unde hoc monstrum, et quare istud? Imperat, unquam ut velit, qui non imperat, nisi vellet; et non fit, quod imperat. Sed non ex toto vult; non ergo ex toto imperat." (Confess., Lib. VIII. c. 9.) " Whence this wonder, and how does it come ? The mind commands the body, and is immediately obeyed; the will commands itself, and is resisted. The mind commands the hand to move; and such is the facility of the obedience that we hardly discern the commanding from the servile power. The mind is mind, the hand is body. The mind commands according to its own will, and yet does not obey itself. Whence this wonder, and how does it arise? That power commands by its will whose whole province is to will, and yet, itself commanding itself, the deed is not done; and the reason is, the will is not entire; the command is not from the whole heart." Now, in all these struggles, it is delightful to know the higher, spontaneous state to which every successful struggle tends; and how important it is to get those perceptions by which the whole power of Christ rushes on the soul. O, there is a flame that burns up our dross, and the will has scarce anything to do; it has sunk back and is lost in governing love. Lastly, this book shows that felicity is the gratification of celestial love. When an Almighty Saviour becomes the bridegroom, heaven, earth, and sea, the stars and the sky, become the marriage-chamber, and all the works of nature glow with the consummation.

ADVERSE AUTHORITY.

Some light may be thrown on this book by considering the objections which critics of great learning and sagacity have made to its spiritual meaning.

My object in selecting some of those critics who have made the most forcible objections, is not to depreciate them, but to answer their objections. A feigned objection of an advocate of any opinion is never so forcible as one brought by a competent opponent. I shall select the learned Professor in the Divinity School at Cambridge as the impersonation of that rigid criticism which forgets almost all the glowing elements of sacred poetry in the artificial laws that surround the lecturer's chair,— laws which light the lamp to forget the sunshine. I select him only as a representative man.

Dr. Noyes says, in his Preface to the Canticles: "The decisive objection, which applies in nearly an equal degree to all these theories, is, that there is no mention, or even intimation, in the work itself, of that which they say is its great and principal subject." And again: "The only persons introduced into it are human. There is not a sentence, or part of a sentence, which, according to the common use of language, expresses any religious idea. This is the decisive consideration with me. The author has in no way indicated that he uses language in any but the obvious and usual sense."

To this I have two answers. First, conceding the fact, I should not dare to adopt the conclusion; for you must sanction this canon of criticism, that there is never an allegory or ὑπόνοια, under-meaning, but when the sacred writers expressly reveal the literal. Now it is nowhere said, in Old Testament or New, that the tempter in Eden was the Devil, and yet the analogy is so perfect to the after-revealed character of the Devil, and the history is so mean and childish without this supposition, that all ages have concluded to adopt the indicated meaning. We shake the whole grandeur of revelation, the whole framework of divine truth, unless we say the concealed meaning is the true one. So with regard to the sacrifices of the Law, it is nowhere said in the Old Testament that they point to Christ. But, as the author of Hebrews says, "the Law is a shadow of good things to come." We adopt the necessary conclusion. We take the sublimer view. Sometimes a sentiment is expressed by an unexplained figure, as in Job iv. 10, 11: "Rugitus leonis ejusque fremitus obmutuit et dentes leonum excussi sunt. Periit leo praedae inopia ejusque catuli sunt dispersi"; that is, the strongest human power is often dispersed and broken. In the last chapters of Ezekiel, the building of the visionary temple, and in the whole book of Revelation, we are left to solve by our sagacity imagery which the author has nowhere explained; so that if we were to grant that in Solomon's Song the principal subject, as understood by the allegorist, does not appear, it would not follow from Biblical usage that it did not exist.

But, secondly, *is* there no intimation of the under-meaning? I must contend that there is. It is intentionally shown under the veil. In the fourth verse, "The upright love thee,"—*Probi te amant.* What can this mean but the literal? The author wavers from his allegory. So in iv. 4,—

> "Thy neck is like the tower of David,
> Built for an armory;
> In which there hang a thousand bucklers,
> All shields of mighty men,"—

and in v. 13–15, and in vii. 2–7, the comparison is too extravagant for a literal personage. It intimates its deeper meaning. As in Psalm lxxii. the magnificence of the imagery teaches to look beyond Solomon, to a Divine Saviour and a spiritual kingdom, so in this imagery the author seems to hint at more than a mortal lover. We must charge him with the greatest extravagance, or we must own his high design. But the passage which seems to me the clearest, considered as an intentional clew to the under-meaning, is in the eighth chapter, verses

8 – 11. The passage is introduced by describing the nature of a sublime and unchangeable love. "Many waters cannot quench love, neither can the floods drown it; if a man would give all his substance for love, it would utterly be contemned." Dr. Noyes translates it: —

> "Many waters cannot quench love,
> Nor can the floods drown it;
> Would a man give all the wealth of his house for love,
> It would be utterly contemned."

And in the previous verse (sixth), what our translators have rendered "the coals thereof are coals of fire, which hath a most vehement flame," he is still stronger: —

> "Its flames are flames of fire, —
> The fire of Jehovah."

Dathè has it: —

> "Nam potens est, uti mors, amor
> Inexorabilis, uti inferus, amoris fides;
> Ardor ejus est ardor igneus, flamma divina.
> Aquarum multitudo non potest extinguere amorem
> Flumina eum non inundant.
> Si quis omnes suas facultates ob amorem vellet insumere
> Contemptim eum rident."

Now let the reader, in interpreting these remarkable words, remember two things: — First, that in religion, as in music, there is something that neither by precept nor doctrine nor example can ever be taught, — it is A GIFT. Secondly, in the following words let him remember the riddling spirit of antiquity. Kings sent riddles to each other. Solomon, according to Josephus, was renowned for his sagacity in solving riddles; Daniel was an untier of knots. Remember Samson's riddles, and remember Jotham's parable, fable, or riddle, whatever you please to call it, Judges ix. 7-15; and also that of Jehoash, 2 Kings xiv. 9: "There passed by a wild beast that was in Lebanon, and trod down the thistle." Let him recollect the riddles of pastoral poetry, — of Theocritus, of Virgil (and Solomon's Song may be regarded as a semi-pastoral, i. e. a pastoral in its ruder form in an earlier nation). Let him recollect the riddles in Herodotus, and then consider the design of the following words, placed at the close of the poem, as a clew to the whole (viii. 8-10): "We have a little sister, and she hath no breasts: what shall we do for our sister in the day when she shall be spoken for? If she be a wall, we will build upon her a palace of silver: and if she be a door, we will enclose her with boards of cedar. I am a wall, and my breasts like towers: then was I in his eyes as one that found favor." What mean these excessive comparisons but an indication that the subject for which they are used is not literal? What possible resemblance can there be between an Arab girl and a wall, or a tower, or a door, or cedar? Recollect, too, that the

Church, old or new, Jewish or Christian, is often an edifice, a holy, heavenly building; and from this remarkable language, so senseless on every other construction, and giving a gleam of light on ours, I must conclude that it is a help to guessing the riddle. It is written, not, to be sure, to supersede our ingenuity, but to help us to the hidden design. It is the very spirit of antiquity; the first discipline of civilized sagacity.

The book, then, *has* many indications of its being a continued allegory (concealed, perhaps), to call forth the discernment and taste of a class of readers which have always existed, and have always fallen into a similar line of thought, — the disciples of an ardent and mystic piety. Grotius could not understand this book; he had not one congenial string in the whole web-work of his heart. Learning could only lead such a man astray; and Swedenborg could not understand it, for such a book would have driven him mad, if he had not been so before. But Augustine, Pascal, Fénélon, Leighton, were the men to feel its power and relish its beauties. Let them have their morsel; and when they ask for bread in the name of an all-developing God, do not give them a stone.

I grant that, if some poetic seer were to bring me Shenstone's pastorals and say there was a spiritual under-meaning; that divine love was figured under human images; that Phillada was the human soul and Paradel was a heretic, etc., etc., — I should allow that his invention was not supported by his wisdom; or rather that it was supported by *his* wisdom *alone*. But every principle that would lead me to call such a construction false, applied to Shenstone, would lead me to consider it as true when applied to this Song. Consider the difference;—one ancient, the other modern; one belonging to a sacred nation, the other a Briton; the purpose of the one to hide the better to reveal, the purpose of the other to be clear;—the taste of the Jews leaning one way, the taste of the English the other; the one standing in the line of inspiration, the other copying a whole host of poetic lovers; the one having a very gross, sensual meaning (if you take away his spiritual object), and the other the more ingenious and beautiful as he is found to be more simple and clear. Surely, there is a vast difference; and common sense, as well as pious veneration, leads to an opposite conclusion.

"But, after all," says Dr. Noyes, "the great objection remains to any conclusion from the pantheistic mystic poets, whether of Persia or India, whether Mahometans or Hindoos; namely, that their productions are founded on a religion and philosophy entirely different from the Jewish. The Canticles are productions of a different country, and separated from any of the songs of the Sufi poets by an interval of nearly two thousand years. The Jewish religion has nothing in common with the pantheistic mysticism on which those songs are founded. There is nothing in the Old Testament of a similar character." These remarks, it seems to me, have let the main questions slip. "Pantheistic mysticism" is not the only foundation of this imagery, nor are "the Sufi poets" the only example. It is probable that the school that is separated by nearly two thousand years from the age of Solomon is only a faint reflection of a more ancient example; at any rate, we know, from about all the literature that has come to our knowledge, that there was a philosophy which personified nature into two parts, discord and concord,— the modern attraction and repulsion,— and a poetry founded on it, which, allowing a personal God, arrayed divine love in a human dress. The Bible recognizes both these principles. Moses describes the original chaos, and the Spirit of God flutters over it; and Paul himself soberly tells us: "The husband is the head of the wife, even as Christ is the head of the Church; and he is the Saviour of the body. Therefore, as the Church is subject unto Christ, so let the wives be to their own husbands in everything. Husbands, love your wives, even as Christ loved the Church and gave himself for it, that he might sanctify and cleanse it with the washing of water by the word: that he might present it to himself a glorious Church, not having spot or wrinkle, or any such thing; but that it should be holy, without blemish. So ought men to love their wives as their own bodies. He that loveth his wife loveth himself. . . . . . For this cause shall a man leave father and mother, and shall be joined unto his wife, and they two shall be one flesh. *This is a great mystery: but I speak concerning Christ and his Church.*" May we not paraphrase these words as follows? "I have digressed from my avowed object, to touch upon an important hidden meaning. It was impossible for me to think of the wonderful union in marriage, begun in Eden and continued when Eden was lost, without glancing at what it was designed to represent. There is a deeper sense, as there is a higher love and a more lasting union. Christ is the heavenly bridegroom; his Church is united to him by a celestial wedlock. He has loved her with the purest passion; she should love him with a corresponding return. And I know nothing in the whole round of nature that so equally represents this reciprocal affection, as human love sanctified and secured in the marriage union." You may write this as the obvious moral at the bottom of the last verse of the Canticles.

Dr. Noyes says of this book: "If it be regarded as a specimen of the erotic poetry of the Hebrews, it will be treated with indifference by most readers, and consequently do them no harm." This is surprising! Who would not cry out here: Οὐκ εὐφημήσεις; Think of being reduced to the necessity of treating a part of the Word of God with indifference, in order to escape the harm it may do us! I know that the writer does not allow the book to be the word of God; but is there not some danger of assuming a very bold conclusion in order to support the argument? It is found in our sacred collection. There is a construction of it which to some minds has made it appear a profitable portion of divine instruction. A great majority of the Church have so regarded it; they have perused it with that subduing veneration which made it the voice of their Saviour and their God; and now — what a fall! — it is only erotic poison, from which the best protection is a knowledge of its character and indifference to its effects!!

If I were to survey a vernal sunset, blazing behind verdant hills and blooming groves, painting the skies with beauty, and an instructor were to bring me a smoked glass, darkened over a fire of birch-bark, and by holding it before the scene were to turn the sun into darkness and all the trees into black demons, the transformation would be equally valuable, but not greater. In such a case, a man is justified in saying, My remembrance is better than my perception.

Thus I have endeavored to answer these objections to the spiritual design of the book, though, I must confess, not one of them would ever have occurred to me had I been left to my original veneration for the sacred volume. To me, they are all imported.

II.

PLACES IN SCRIPTURE WHERE DIVINE LOVE ASSUMES THE FORM OF AN EROTIC SIMILITUDE.

IF this Song were the only place where this imagery is used, the difficulty of deciding would be greatly increased. But it is the favorite figure. God is perpetually the husband of his people. As a king he is also a bridegroom; and his inauguration on his throne is his marriage with his people. The imagery is carried out; he is a jealous God; he is jealous of his people. They go a *whoring* from him by idolatry; and some of the most daring pantomimes are acted by the holy prophets to impress these Oriental views. "The Lord said to Hosea, Go take unto thee a wife of whoredoms and children of whoredoms; for the land hath committed great whoredom, departing from the Lord. So he went and took Gomer, the daughter of Diblaim, who conceived and bare him a son. And the Lord said unto him, Call his name Jezreel; for yet a little while and I will avenge the blood of Jezreel upon the house of Jehu, and will cause to cease the kingdom of the house of Israel." (Hosea i. 2–4.)

Now, whether we regard this narrative as an historical fact, or as a scenic illustration, it shows that God's relation to his people is painted by this imagery. I am inclined to think that this narrative is a scenic illustration. First, because such actings out of a representation were common to an early age, and are incidental to a primitive language. The more we are fettered by words, the more we must be helped by action. Secondly, it does not seem suitable that a holy prophet should be forced to such a strange action. Thirdly, all the power of an illustration is found in the scenic act more than in the real one; that is, we gain nothing by making it real. Fourthly, a scenic act, or doing the deed in pantomime, is only a more vivid extension of the common figure of vision: "I seem to see this noble city committed to the flames; Catiline revelling, Cethegus," etc., etc. It was natural in the progress of refinement that such pantomimic representations should precede, and pave the way for, the figure which rhetoricians call vision. And, lastly, it seems scarcely possible, if the act was real, that the representation should have any force; for if an audience must wait for the prophet to marry and have two children, their expectation would cool, and the subject be forgotten, and the comparison fail of its purpose. The same remark applies to the command to Ezekiel to lie upon his right side three hundred and ninety days, and forty days on his left side; certainly in such a time the people would disperse and the whole subject be forgotten. The probability is, that the same necessity which forced a people to have recourse to hieroglyphics to express themselves in one degree of development in language, might urge them to mimic action in another degree of development. This was probably the state of the Hebrew language at that time. But however we interpret the prophet's conduct, it is certain that God is represented as the husband of his people. "Thou shalt no more be termed Forsaken; neither shall thy land any more be termed Desolate: but thou shalt be called Hephzi-bah, and thy land Beulah; for the Lord delighteth in thee, and thy land shall be married." (Isaiah lxii. 4.) So in Isaiah liv. 5: "For thy Maker is thine husband: the Lord of hosts is his name." So prevalent is this imagery, that it passes from their poetry into their laws: God is a jealous God, and the logical Paul says, that he has espoused the Church as a chaste virgin to Christ. The forty-fifth Psalm has often been quoted as a parallel example. The recondite meaning is so manifest, that one is curious to see how a learned critic can get rid of it. Rosenmüller says it cannot be written of an Israelitish king, but must have been composed during the captivity, and apply to some Persian monarch. "Persici contra regni veteris formae et institutis hoc ita congruit, ut ego nullus dubitem, carmen nostrum ab illorum Judaeorum, qui sub Persici imperii ditione viverent, poeta aliquo, novo cuidam Persicarum regi oblatum fuisse." Astonishing!! that a man should have no doubt on the positive side, when no other mortal can have any doubt on the other. A German critic, in espousing an opinion, considers nothing but the difficulty of defending it. The Jews were so prone to see national glory out of their own domains; to exult in the prosperity of idolatrous nations; to think a power would be eternal that perpetuated their own dishonorable captivity; it is so *perfectly natural* that they should wish some Persian emperor to be glorified — (Ahasuerus, perhaps, who consented to murder them all) : " Gird thy sword upon thy thigh, O most mighty, with thy glory and majesty, and in thy majesty ride prosperously, because of truth and meekness ; " — and after having been accustomed to apply this Psalm to Christ, it seems so sublime and glorious to apply it to some miscreant that sat on the Persian throne, that we say the happy thought shall be left to illustrate the fertile invention which could engender it. Rosenmüller allows that this Psalm was applied by the Jewish writers to the expected Messiah long before our Saviour's birth. He lays down this critical law: "Ut vero, quaecunque antiquitus scripta erant, a posteris collecta et sine discrimine pro divinis effatis accepta sunt; ita et haec consecrarunt posteri, cultui sacro dedicarunt, et, ne offenderentur lectores, abjecto proprio sensu, alium carminibus dederunt, allegoricum mysticum, et altissima mysteria spirantem." It will be noticed here that he allows the double meaning; that its prevalence was universal among the Jews, and that it arose from the locality of the first application of the prophecy, or ode, and the sublime end culminating in a great Messiah being superinduced on the locality. Now, surely, the alternative meets us; in a selected nation, a nation under the immediate superintendence of God, there was a reason or no reason for this prevalent opinion; and in a nation enjoying a real revelation, such an opinion must have been founded on fact, and not on fiction.

It is curious, however, to see how all critics meet the double sense, whatever path they choose to take.

Such, then, being the obviousness of a double sense, that even the destructive critic is obliged to confess it, and such being the barren meaning which those are driven to who do not apply the ὑπόνοια to Christ, the believer in real revelation regards the Psalmist as here predicting the glories of the Messiah. The imagery is abundantly of the erotic kind. "Thou lovest righteousness, and hatest wickedness: therefore God, thy God, hath anointed thee with the oil of gladness above thy fellows," i. e. all other kings. "All thy garments smell of myrrh, and aloes, and cassia, out of the ivory palaces, whereby they have made thee glad. King's daughters were among thy honorable women; upon thy right hand did stand the queen in gold of Ophir. Hearken, O daughter, and consider, and incline thine ear; forget also thine own people, and thy father's house; so shall the king greatly desire thy beauty: for he is thy Lord, and worship thou him." This is the same luxuriant imagery that is to be found in the Canticles, — the scented garments, the myrrh, the cassia, and the foreign bride that is to forget her father's house; and it is sealed to the Messiah in the same way, not by an explicit interpretation, but by the magnificent promise in the last verse. "I will make thy name to be remembered in all generations; therefore shall the people praise thee for ever and ever."

We have the same imagery in the sixteenth chapter of Ezekiel, a little varied. The Israelites are compared to a wretched infant forsaken of its mother, and found in the open field. "Thou wast cast out in the open field, to the loathing of thy person, in the day that thou wast born." But God spared and cherished the wretched infant, and afterwards espoused it. "I have caused thee to multiply as the bud of the field, and thou hast increased and waxen great, and thou hast come to excellent ornaments: thy breasts are fashioned, and thine hair is grown. Now when I passed by thee, and looked upon thee, behold, thy time was the time of love: and I spread my skirt over thee. . . . . Thou wast exceeding beautiful, and thou didst prosper into a kingdom. . . . . But thou didst trust in thine own beauty, and playedst the harlot," etc. The allegory is continued through the chapter. It is true the prophet dwells on the outward relation rather than the internal love; but the one implies the other; and in all the varieties the sacred writers seem to be guided by the same taste and spirit. " Therefore, behold, I will hedge up thy way with thorns, and make a wall, that she shall not find her paths. And she shall follow after her lovers, but she shall not overtake them; and she shall seek them, but shall not find them; then shall she say, I will go and return to my first husband; for then was it better with me than now. For she did not know that I gave her corn and wine and oil, and multiplied her silver and gold which they prepared for Baal. Therefore will I return and take away my corn in the time thereof, and my wine in the season thereof, and will recover my wool and my flax given to cover her nakedness. And now will I discover her lewdness in the sight of her lovers, and none shall deliver her out of mine hand." (Hosea ii. 7 – 10.) This passage shows the spirit of idolatry, just sinking into the love of sensual good, and then seeking it from such gods as seem willing to give it. But, as idolatry degrades divine love into earthly, so the true worship exalts the sensual into the divine.

The passage in Isaiah v. 1–5, looks toward the same principle. *There is a vineyard,* a lover, voluptuous delight, and a latent spiritual signification, as we are expressly told in the seventh verse. The sin was the want of the corresponding passion in one of the parties. So in Jeremiah ii. 2: "Go and cry in the ears of Jerusalem, saying, Thus saith the Lord: I remember thee, the kindness of thy youth, the love of thine espousals, when thou wentest after me in the wilderness, in a land that was not sown. Israel was holiness to the Lord." So in the third chapter of the same prophet: "They say, If a man put away his wife, and she go from him and become another man's, shall he return unto her again? Shall not that land be greatly polluted? But thou hast played the harlot with many lovers: yet return again to me, saith the Lord."

In the New Testament the same imagery is renewed. Indeed, the same mystic way of representing transcendental truth is used where the amatory form is not adopted. The fact is, the teachers have a difficult task to convey supersensual conceptions to the most sensual minds; to conduct sunbeams to the darkest corners of the subterranean cave; and it is instructive to see how they conquer the difficulty. For example, union with Christ,— the union which is accomplished by perfect love producing a perfect similitude. We are crucified with him; we are ingrafted into him;

we are dead with him; we are alive with him. The Lord's Supper itself — the wine and the bread, the eating and the drinking — is a material act, to signify the most sublime conception. The words of our Saviour correspond: "Then Jesus sayeth unto them, Verily, verily, I say unto you, except ye eat the flesh of the Son of Man, and drink his blood, ye have no life in you. Whoso eateth my flesh and drinketh my blood hath eternal life; and I will raise him up at the last day. For my flesh is meat indeed, and my blood is drink indeed. He that eateth my flesh, and drinketh my blood, dwelleth in me, and I in him." (John vi. 53-56.) So in another place: "In the last day, the great day of the feast, Jesus stood and cried, saying, If any man thirst, let him come unto me and drink. He that believeth on me, as the Scripture hath said, out of his belly shall flow rivers of living water." (John vii. 37, 38.) And again: "I am the true vine," etc. "The branch cannot bear fruit," etc. (John xv. 1 and 4.) Now we cannot say that this is the same imagery, but it indicates the same taste and looks to the same design.* It is a mystic veil, employed to magnify a great conception. Accordingly, it is said in Revelation xx. 9: "I will show thee the bride, the Lamb's wife."

But the most remarkable passage bearing on this subject is in Ephesians v. 32. The Apostle is talking

---

* See Gale's "Court of the Gentiles," Part IV. p. 88.

plain prose, and he seems to be giving the exponent of this imagery. It is, therefore, a very important passage, — a classic place. He is discussing the question of literal marriages, and he turns aside to say: "This is a great mystery; but I speak" (in saying it is a great mystery) "concerning Christ and his Church." Now, would it be putting too much on the Apostle's important parenthesis to say his meaning is this: Marriage is a union most wonderful, far more significant than it at first appears. In a happy marriage, two hearts are made one, — one in interest, in reputation, in affection, — in their children and in their human destiny; and it is the only instance on earth — in this respect it stands alone — to shadow forth, however inadequately, the everlasting union between Christ and his people, the soul and its Saviour. If we abandon this illustration, where shall we find another? This is at once a hint what marriage ought to be, and of what the union with Christ always is.

THE UNITY.

It is a maxim in philosophy that no part of a system can be comprehended without some view of the whole. It is so with regard to the Bible. It has suffered amazingly by being regarded as a fragmentary book, whose parts have not been collected into one whole. It must be allowed that there is a great superficial diversity. What can seem more different than the ritualism of Moses and the spiritualism of Christ, — that absence of a future state under the Law, and the life and immortality brought to light in the Gospel, — the prudential maxims of Solomon, and the total disregard to worldly success which seems to be inculcated by Christ? But yet, notwithstanding this apparent discrepancy, there is a golden thread that runs through all the varieties of revelation. It is one body in a changing dress. The variety arises from the GROWING IDEA. The orbicular shape of the sun cannot be seen when he is half risen; and the word of God is as "a shining light, which shines more and more unto the perfect day." (Prov. iv. 18.)

Now the chief mistakes which are made in interpreting the Bible arise from not seeing the unity which runs through all its parts. It is a complex drama, in which no scene is superfluous, and no speech made at random. Perhaps the uniting idea — the central thought which pervades the whole book — is suggested by the name of Jesus, and the name of the system which he preached. Our Lord was called Jesus because he was to "save his people from their sins;" and his system was to be called the Gospel, because it was to be good news to people whose natural condition reported nothing but darkness and despair. Now this redemptive system, implying a previously lost condition, is the central idea around which all the facts and principles of revelation turn. All are compact parts; preparations or accomplishments. Hence the history begins with Eden. The creation shows God's right to command, and man's obligation to obey; and, whereas it has been said that creation itself, without benevolence in the creating power, would give no right to command, behold how all the elements of right meet in God,—creation, benevolence, wisdom, worth. Here is the prime idea. God's right shows the foundation of our duty, and what sin is. Then comes the primitive innocence and the fall of man; which is the exponent of a fallen world, and lays the foundation of the great redemption. Then comes the first form of religion,—a glimmering Gospel. Sin, supplication, repentance, sacrifices. Promises are made. The Israelites are redeemed from Egypt, and the Mosaic dispensation is given; the Law has a shadow of good things to come. The multiplied sacrifices point to one ulterior. I know that difficulties may be raised. It may be asked, if the sacrifice of Christ was pictured by the old offerings, why the picture was not more simple; why they were so amazingly multiplied; why we are lost in confusion in contemplating the variety. Perhaps it was best that the simplicity should come with the culminating point; that Christ should be the only exponent, because he was the majestic centre. At any rate, we learn in all the complex examples, that "without the shedding of blood there is no remission."

It would be long to go through all the examples of this centralizing diversity. The Bible proposes one great fact, and presents one great design. Ruin and Recovery are its watchwords. Sin and an atonement; alienation from God and reconciliation; a sinner justified in his person and purified in his heart. The divine image lost and restored. All in the Old Testament is preparation; all in the New is accomplishment. As Pascal says: "Les deux Testaments regardent Jesus Christ, l'ancien comme son attente, le nouveau comme son module; tous deux comme leur centre."

The Psalms may be regarded as surpassing pictures of Christian emotion; the more striking, as shining out amid the general ritualism of the Hebrew worship. The prophecies grow brighter as the kingdom decays. They are not merely minute specifications of a literal fulfilment, as they are too often regarded, and still less a fore-plan of chronological exactness; but they are a general outline of a great restoration founded on the GREAT SECRET of God finally revealed. They are full of hope, and hope springing in the midst of outward despair. Isaiah is almost an anticipated Gospel; — its central fact, its glorious result, its predominating spirit.

But in order to show the unity in the remotest

elements, let us take a book hardest to be reconciled to its general plan, — the Book of Job, for example. A good man falls into calamity, and his friends come to comfort him, and a long discussion follows, in which all parties seem to say about the same things; and it is hard to tell where they join issue, and no result seems to follow. Now, what connection has this book with the great design of the Hebrew Scriptures? The whole trouble of the contestants in this book seems to arise from the want of a few truths which the Gospel makes very plain. The future state is hardly a positive idea with them, though they occasionally have dim anticipations of it. Of course, the design of life is not clearly seen, — its discipline, the original guilt of man, sin as a principle, the redemption and the purification. Of course their discussion is at random, and the great design of the book is revealed in the last chapters, when God is brought in upon the stage, rebuking their presumption and showing their ignorance. Compare this book with the Phædo of Plato. How striking the resemblance! how instructive the contrast! Socrates feels his way like an honest man, without a celestial guide; he is very respectable in his scepticism, and he is very instructive even in his dogmatism. He shows the best that human nature could do in his condition. But Job is met by a better guide, who teaches him his own ignorance; and the substance of the Divine sermon seems to be, Wait for better light.

The book of Ecclesiastes shows the vanity of this world as a scene of enjoyment. This is an important preparation for religion; it takes the most dangerous weight out of the opposite scale.

But it may be asked how this book (Solomon's Song) corresponds with this wonderful unity. Here is a love-song, full of ardor, with the most sensual and luscious imagery, and we are required to give it a place among the preparations for the purest system of religion ever offered to the world. I would remark, only once admit that the book is an allegory, and all the rest follows of course. We have abundance of descriptions in the Old Testament of the outward splendor of Christ's kingdom; here is its interior, — the joys and the transports it is to impart to the regenerate heart. It teaches us that there is something in religion which no words can adequately express, — the union of the soul with its Saviour, the transports and the joys of the divine life. There is one question which meets almost every sinner in his struggles with his own soul: How shall I get the will? How shall I form the purpose of obeying God? I am told that the duties of religion are easy to him who once has a disposition; but how shall I get that disposition? How shall I conquer my own heart?

Now, this book answers that question as far it can be answered. It shows there is revealed to the regenerate heart a new passion; a love stronger than death, which makes all duty easy. Self-denial is lost in the voluntary sacrifice. The soul, divorced from its grovelling passions, is devoted to the heavenly bridegroom. It is borne on by the whole of its new nature to a delightful obedience. The beauty of Christ being revealed to the soul, the corresponding passion springs up in the heart, and, like a resistless stream, draws every faculty and power into its channel. It cannot disobey; the love of Christ constrains it.

It was very important that this highest point of Christianity, like the summit of some sunny mountain, should glitter in the distance, and show the soul of the system which was yet to be revealed.

I cannot but think that this absorbing whole, this totality of revelation, explains some things in the sacred history which otherwise would seem strange. Let us look at two examples. When Jacob fled from his father-in-law, and was expecting to meet in the wilderness his indignant brother, we are told: " Jacob was left alone; and there wrestled a man with him until the breaking of the day. And when he saw that he prevailed not against him, he touched the hollow of his thigh; and the hollow of Jacob's thigh was out of joint as he wrestled with him. And He said, Let me go, for the day breaketh. And he said, I will not let thee go, except thou bless me. And He said unto him, What is thy name? And he said, Jacob. And He said, Thy name shall no more be called Jacob, but Israel; for as a prince hast thou power with God and with men, and hast prevailed. And Jacob said, Tell me, I pray thee, thy name. And He said, Wherefore is it that thou dost ask after my name? And He blessed him there. And Jacob called the name of the place Peniel; for I have seen God face to face, and my life is preserved." Here, then, is a wonderful story, on which different readers put different constructions. The neologist says it is an old wives' tale, a dream, the innocent invention of a mistaken mind; it stands rank and file with a hundred other myths in the Pagan pages. Our venerable fathers, without recognizing any difficulty, talked of wrestling with God in prayer, and brought the example of Jacob with no other design than to conform their faith, without analyzing the features of the story. But may we not say, without violating any critical rule, that, from the general design of the Old Testament, it was intended to prepare the mind of Jacob, and, through him, all the expectants, for the great doctrine of the incarnation? He meets a wonderful man; he wrestles with him; he feels the force of his bones and sinews; he carries away in his own body proofs of his materiality; and yet he says, "I have seen God face to face." Take the passage in connection with the final development, and does it not prepare the way for the great conviction? God was manifest in the flesh, and it would be vain here to start the objection, that Christ was not yet born, and his body not yet formed; for it might suit the Divine purpose to work an anticipatory miracle, and to assume a prototype of what was afterwards to be. (Genesis xxxii. 24 – 30.)

The other passage is in Exodus xxxii. 7 – 35. The whole transaction is remarkable. Nothing but a clear perception of the general design of the old economy can reconcile us to the representation. If I were a neologist, what work should I make of it? The people sin; they make a golden calf, under the very mountain blazing with the terrors of the true God. God is angry; he threatens to destroy them; he is with great difficulty turned from his purpose; and he offers to blot out the whole nation, and make of the posterity of Moses a still greater one. What an astonishing representation! Is a man more merciful than God? Does the wisdom of Moses surpass that of Jehovah? Is God, by a feeble suggestion, turned from his eternal counsels, and is there not danger that the love and gratitude of the delivered should turn from the Creator to the creature? The only rational explanation is, that the very paradox of the incident is its solution. It was permitted to illustrate a great principle, — that Divine mercy is a precious gift, because it is a victory over opposing principles. Why did Christ arise a great while before day, and go to the mountain apart to pray? Why is an atonement necessary? Why is any prayer necessary? Why is forgiveness a tardy gift, wrung from a reluctant God? All these things centre on one point. To show that the Divine Mind, in looking on all conditions and consequences, has selected these means to assure us that our salvation is a higher favor than our finite minds can well conceive. Difficulties conquered, bars removed, we must seek it with strong cries and tears; others must seek it for us; and, above all, the great Intercessor must plead the merits of his atoning blood. I will not say that Moses was a type of Christ; but I will say his prayer is a precedent, — it illustrates the great principle.

But the Bible not only has a unity itself, but it is the only book that gives an instructive unity to the world's history, — to the great design of nature. When we trace the laws of nature, we suppose a design, — an end and an aim by which all its laws must be interpreted, since it presents a culminating point to which they all tend.

III.

AMATORY DEVOTION IN HEATHEN LITERATURE AND IN THE CHURCH SINCE THE DAYS OF THE APOSTLES.

It is certain, then, that the Israelitish nation set forth the purest passion under the most sensual imagery. Divine love expressed its glowing sentiments in amatory verse. But the question may be started whether other nations adopted the same language, and fell into the same train of thought. Greece and Rome are the objects of Western admiration. From these two people we derive our literature, our language, our poetry, our grammar, and our laws. We look up to them as patterns of civilization; and from their remains we derive our wisdom. Their writers ran through almost every form of human thought. The question comes, then, What light does their literature throw on this mode of thought and expression?

And here we may at once detect two causes which must diminish our expectation of finding parallels of this peculiar poetry among them. First, they were polytheists, and had not the concentrated devotion of the Hebrews; and, secondly, they were of a colder temperament, and far less meditative. Yet I think we can find fragments and sparklings of the same taste and turn of expression. They laid the foundation of such ardent devotion in their philosophy, and, though the fire burned fainter, yet the fuel was more intellectually supplied.

They at least laid a foundation for this poetry. I imagine it began in the fact that they regarded nature as existing in two parts, — the active and the passive, — the power and the object of that power. Cicero has given us the philosophical view of nature: " De natura autem (id enim sequebatur) ita dicebant, ut eam dividerent in res duas: ut altera efficiens, altera autem, quasi huic se praebens, ea, quae efficeretur aliquid. In eo quod efficeret, vim esse censebant: in eo autem, quod efficeretur, materiam quandam: in utroque tamen utrumque. Neque enim materiam ipsam cohaerere potuisse, si nulla vi contineretur, neque vim sine aliqua materia." — " The Academics say that nature is divided into two parts; the one efficient, the other yielding itself to this efficiency until it is formed into something. In that which acts, there is power; in that which is acted on, there is the material. Neither exists alone; for the material cannot cohere without the power that contains it, nor can the power act without the material." (Cicero Academicorum, Lib. I. Sect. 6.)

In a word, there is an active and passive nature, and one step in personification would make the one male and the other female. This step was taken; and perhaps it preceded the philosophic view,—for poetry is before philosophy; personification precedes analysis.* We find spread over all early civilization, especially in Hindostan, in Egypt, in Greece, certain emblems, not intended to be obscene (though now seeming so), of the productive powers of nature. The phallic emblem in Egypt, and similar ones in the East, and in polished Greece, show that in the most sensual form of love they saw something higher and nobler. All nature was actuated by it; it engendered and continued the world. An old philosopher had said: Εἰς ἔρωτα μεταβλῆθαι τὸν Δία μέλλοντα δημιουργεῖν, that when God was about to build the world, he transformed himself into love. Hesiod has made love a principle; and Aristotle says: "One would suspect that Hesiod, and if there be any other who made love or desire a principle of things in the universe, arrived at this very thing (namely, the settling another active principle beside matter); for Parmenides, describing the generation of the

---

* Lactantius, speaking of heat and moisture, says: "Alterum enim quasi masculinum elementum est, alterum quasi femininum, alterum activum, alterum patibile. Ideo a veteribus institutum est, ut sacramento ignis et aquae nuptiarum foedera sanciantur, quod foetus animantium calore et humore corporentur atque animentur ad vitam." (Lact. Inst. Lib. II. Sect. 9.)

universe, makes Love to be the senior of all the gods; and Hesiod, after he had mentioned chaos, introduced Love as the supreme deity. As intimating herein, that, besides matter, there ought to be another cause or principle, which should be the original of motion and activity, and also hold and join all things together. But how these two principles are to be ordered, and which of them was to be placed first,—whether Love or Chaos,—may be judged of afterwards. (Cudworth's Intellectual System, Vol. I. p. 122.)

Plato, in his Symposium, has made love to be a general principle, the attraction and harmony of the natural and moral universe; in its lowest form, in all the sensualities of life, the degraded and perverted manifestation of a higher good. The material manifestation is always the shadow of something higher; hence Sir William Jones says, with regard to the offensive images in the Hindoo temples: "It never seems to have entered the heads of the legislators of the people that anything natural could be offensively obscene; a singularity which pervades all their writings and conversation, but is no proof of depravity in their morals." (As quoted in Crawford's Researches.) There is a profound remark of Constant, quoted and sanctioned by Milman: "These indecent rites (i. e. the worship of Priapus) may be practised by a religious people with great purity of heart. But when infidelity corrupts them, these rites become the cover and the cause of the most revolting corruption." Just so. I can easily imagine a simple people, with a primitive imagination, brought to worship the symbols of the most wonderful power in nature, the cause of its existence, and certainly its preservation, without lingering on the sign, but rising to the general power, which is now found to pervade all the animal and vegetable creation, which keeps the inorganic world together, and which is not without its vestiges in the mental, moral, and spiritual world; all nature subsists by the meeting of a giving and receptive power, οἷον ἂν ποιῇ τὸ ποιοῦν, τοιοῦτον τὸ πάσχον πάσχειν. (Gorgias of Plato, 476. D.) In religion, objective truth must come clothed in beauty, and that beauty must act on a receptive heart. As the Scripture says: "Break up your fallow ground, and sow not among thorns." (Jeremiah iv. 3.) I am not sure, that, in the highest sense, the second and third persons in the ever-blessed Trinity are not the acting and receptive parts of the Divine nature. It is certain that THE WORD meets the heart as a motive power, and the Holy Ghost makes it receptive. Thus a sensual people saw Divine love only in its grossest semblances.

In the Symposium of Plato, we have the philosophy, or the didactic foundation, on which this ardent poetry rests. Love, according to Plato, is neither a god nor a man, but an intermediate demon; not beautiful, but desiring beauty; always seeking, always supplied. We must begin by seeing the beauty in a single body; we must discover that the beauty in one body is twin-brother to that in another. We must rise from the individual to the species, and from the species to the genus. We must ascend from the material to the mental, the beauty of the mind, of study, of knowledge, of virtue, until we reach the perception of that great sea of beauty which makes us pour out words, but which no words can express; we must grasp that eternal idea which is not *born*, but *is;* not coming and going, but existing; not increasing and decaying, but ever fixed; not now deformed and now more fair; not comparatively beautiful; not a quality in other things, or different things; not fancied in a cheek, a hand, a shape, or a foot, but one great totality; not even an expression, or representative thought; but itself by itself, simple, uncompounded, self-seen; borrowing nothing from other things, but giving beauty to all. It is being ravished with this ETERNAL BEAUTY that awakens true love and gives true virtue; and it is implied in this scheme that this beauty must be impersonated in some competent Being, since it is a mental beauty, and is the objective cause of love, which is a mental passion, and since the beauty spread over material things, whether seen in the rose's bloom or the virgin's smile, originates in mind.

Thus, we see, a foundation was laid in philosophy for the Hebrew poem. The coincidence is remarkable. In Solomon's Song, virtue is a passion; it is love; and the cause of that love is the perception of beauty; a perception of Divine beauty awakening Divine love, and both capable of lower similitudes; and, what is still more remarkable, neither Plato nor the inspired writer attempts to explain that ETERNAL SECRET, whether the perception is the parent of the passion, or the passion produces the perception. They are simultaneous in time, and reciprocally cause and effect.

Lord Shaftesbury was a writer free from all enthusiasm, and especially all religious enthusiasm; and he seems to think that wit and good-humor are the best prerequisites to find our way among the solemnities of religion. And yet he got hold of something like Plato's idea. "The admirers," says he, "of beauty in the fair sex, would laugh, perhaps, to hear of a *moral part* in their amours; yet what a stir is made about a heart! What curious search of sentiments and tender thoughts! What praises of a humor, a sense, a *je-ne-sçai-quoi* of wit, and all those graces of a mind which those virtuoso-lovers delight to celebrate! Let them settle this matter among themselves, and regulate, as they think fit, the proportions which these different beauties hold to one another; they must allow still that there is a beauty of *the mind;* and such as is essential in the case. Why else is the very air of foolishness enough to cloy a lover at first sight? Why does an idiot-look and manner destroy the effect of those outward charms, and rob the fair one of her power, though regularly armed and in all the exactness of feature and complexion? We may imagine what we please of a substantial, solid part of beauty; but, were the subject to be criticised, we should find, perhaps, that what we most admired, even in the turn of *outward* features, was only a mysterious expression and a kind of shadow of something *inward* in the temper; and that when we were struck with a majestic air, a sprightly look, an Amazon bold grace, or a contrary soft and gentle one, it was chiefly the fancy of these characters or qualities which wrought on us; our imaginations being busied in forming beauteous shapes and images of this rational kind, which entertained the mind and held it in admiration; whilst other passions of a lower species were employed another way." (Essay on the Freedom of Wit and Humor, Part IV. Sect. 2.)

There is another form of love alluded to in Plato's Symposium, which I mention with great reluctance, and which is one of the most inexplicable enigmas of antiquity. I allude to the love of beautiful boys, and the views which the gravest men entertained of it. The classical reader will understand what I mean, by the speech of Alcibiades at the close of the above-mentioned dialogue. It is a part of their system of the influence of beauty on love, and love on the heart. They generalized the passion and its cause, and supposed that we might ascend from the beauty of the flower to the First supremely Fair, — the Great First Cause and Last End of all things. I must confess that no phenomenon in ancient history has appeared to me so astounding as the toleration and even laudatory view which Socrates and Plato take of a passion which modern decency hardly permits us to name. But the train of thinking which led these virtuous men to this amazing result was this. It is well known, I believe, and it is certain, that when two passions resemble each other, and yet differ, where the resemblance is innocent, and the difference in one of them is perfectly horrible, that to make the resemblance prevail at the expense and to the expulsion of the horrible, must seem in both ways to be the triumph of virtue. The mind shows her choice by a double selection. Thus the old monks must have supposed there was some resemblance between Divine and human love; and he that abated the higher to gratify the lower passion became a worse man; but he that gave up the lower to the higher, by a contrary rule, became celestial, angelic. Now the ancients were aware that the unnatural passion, as we call it, was a sinful one, and of course the conquering it must be virtuous; and, as the beauty of the object bore some resemblance to the great celestial beauty, both the *existence* and the *governing* of the passion must be a complex act of virtue. It was dreadful if you sunk to sensuality, but glorious if you rose to the sublime. The Aphrodite πανδήμος must yield to the true Urania. Hence Socrates thought the ambiguous passion was to be cherished in a free community; it was to be suppressed in despotic lands. It was refining when the love was fixed on the beauty of the mind. In Ionia, the passion was forbidden, for in a despotic country no enthusiasm could be tolerated, no elevation could be expected (see Symposium, page 182, B); and this passion in its conflict and victory was supposed to be connected with enthusiasm, valor, enterprise, the love of liberty, — indeed, all that makes men enterprising and free. A band of such lovers was supposed to be invincible. Hence Philip is represented as saying, when he saw the relics of the sacred band of the three hundred Thebans that fell at the battle of Chæronea: "Let them perish who suspect that these men either suffered, or did anything base."

From the fact that nature seems to be divided into two great powers, — the active and passive — together with the vivid disposition to personification in the ancient mind, it is probable that the pagans got their Jupiter and Juno, the male and female deities of Heaven.

> "Tum pater omnipotens fecundis imbribus Æther
> Conjugis in gremium laetae descendit, et omnes
> Magnus alit, magno commixtus corpore, foetus."

> "Æther, great lord of life, his wings extends,
> And on the bosom of his bride descends."
>
> SOUTHEBY.

Or according to a fragment of Æschylus:

> Ἐρᾷ μὲν ἁγνός οὐρανὸς τρῶσαι χθόνα.
> Ἔρως δὲ γαῖαν λαμβάνει γάμου τυχεῖν.
> Ὄμβρος δ' ἀπ' εὐνάζοντος οὐρανοῦ πεσὼν
> Ἔδυσε γαῖαν· ἡ δὲ τίκτεται Βροτοῖς
> Μήλων τε Βόσκας καὶ Βίαν Δημήτριον,
> Δένδρων δέ τις ὅρος ἐκ νοτίζοντος γάμου
> Τελειός ἐστι. τῶνδ' ἐγὼ παραίτιος.

(VENUS.)

> "Heaven loves, though pure, earth's bosom to invade,
> And keep the wondrous nuptials nature made;
> Showers from the covering sky bedew the ground,
> And spread the apples and the corn around;
> Each tree, each plant, from me perfection draws;
> Of all that blooms, I, Venus, am the cause."

The outlines of this system may be traced in the sacred Scriptures. Baal and Ashtaroth, or Astarte, the sun and the moon; or, as later critics say, the male and female star of fortune. In Isaiah lxv. 11 it is said: "Ye are they that forsake the Lord, that forget my holy mountain, that prepare a table for that troop, and furnish a drink-offering unto that number." Our translation hardly reaches the thought: Ye prepare a table for Baal-Gad, and furnish a drink-offering to Meni, — the male and female powers of fortune. We read in Scripture of Moloch and the Queen of Heaven, which are but repetitions of the same idea. The words translated "grove" (Deuteronomy xvi. 21, Judges vi. 25 and 28, 1 Kings xv. 12 and xvi. 33) are generally names of the female idol, Astarte, Ashtaroth, the Queen of Heaven, — the female power in nature personified. The Greeks also inherited this idea, and ripened it into a poetic perfection. Prometheus, when he is bound to the rock, consoles himself, amidst his sorrows, that he has seen two dynasties tumbled from Heaven, and he shall yet see a third revolution in the fall of Jupiter and Juno from their thrones; on which the scholiast remarks, that "there first reigned in Heaven Ophion and Eurynome; after that, Saturn and Rhea; and, still later, Jupiter and Juno; and others go still higher, and say that Uranus and Ge (i. e. Heaven and Earth) reigned first, — the one male, the other female; in all these changes they conceived a male and female power, though sometimes discordant, yet essentially bound together in love." (Rosenmüller on Isaiah, Vol. III. p. 105.) Of course the love of gods must be peculiar.

The same idea is carried out by Homer more

poetically in the fourteenth book of the Iliad. Juno suspects that her celestial husband is partial to the Trojans. She wishes to put him to sleep, that Neptune, during his repose, may give victory to the Greeks. She borrows the cestus of Venus, and adorns herself with every grace, and takes Sleep with her to the top of Ida, that her design may succeed. She goes; Jupiter is struck with her charms, and invites her to repose on the top of the mountain, the throne of their united power. The arguments by which he courts his wife are extraordinary, and such as in an earthly wife would be fitted to move indignation. He enumerates his former amours, and tells her he was never so smitten before: —

> "To whom the sovereign of the boundless air,
> Juno! thy journey thither may be made
> Hereafter. Let us turn to dalliance now.
> For never goddess poured, nor woman yet,
> So full a tide of love into my breast;
> I never loved Ixion's consort thus,
> Who bore Pirithous, wise as we in Heaven;
> Nor sweet Acrisian Danaë, from whom
> Sprang Perseus, noblest of the race of men;
> Nor Phœnix' daughter fair, of whom were born
> Minos, unmatched but by the powers above,
> And Rhadamanthus; nor yet Semele,
> Nor yet Alcmena, who in Thebes produced
> The valiant Hercules; and though my son
> By Semele were Bacchus, joy of man;
> Nor Ceres, nor Latona, nor — thyself,

> As now I love thee, and my soul perceive
> O'erwhelmed with sweetness of intense desire."
>
> Iliad, Book XIV., Cowper's Trans.

Here we must notice several things. First, it is love, celestial love, that burns in the bosom of Jove; secondly, it is inspired by celestial beauty; thirdly, the love of Jove has before been shown to individuals; this love gave birth to heroes and lawgivers,— Hercules, Minos, Rhadamanthus, etc.; fourthly, it is cemented on Ida,— the throne of celestial power; and, lastly, all nature rejoices and flourishes under its influence. Now, surely, the sensual part is only a figure,— the poetic vestment of the divine idea. The love of Jove to Ixion's consort, to Semele, Alcmena, Ceres, Latona, must be the divine love manifested to individuals,— the love between the individual soul and God.

The critics have been shocked that a husband should enumerate his amours to his wife on such an occasion to conciliate her favor. To be sure, if the literal and human is to predominate in the story, nothing can be more absurd; but certainly the poet gives every indication that the narrative is not literal,— the scene, the actors, the deed, the effects. It is an expression of God's general love to all creatures, and his special love to individuals,— the chosen of Heaven,— in the examples of Semele, Alcmena, etc. Nor is it necessary to suppose that the poet himself nicely analyzed his own narrative, or clearly saw his own design. He doubtless followed some poetic tradition, originating in the laws of ancient thought; and, like nature, which felt the influence of the divine wedlock of his gods on Olympus, though she saw them not, wrapped in their golden cloud, so his mind felt the influence of an early speculation which it had never unfolded. We are often governed by conceptions of which we are only half conscious.

The same diffusion of beauty and love through all creation is taught in the hymn to Venus, which passes under Homer's name: —

>Μοῦσα μοι ἔννεπε ἔργα πολυχρύσου Ἀφροδίτης
>Κύπριδος, ἥτε θεοῖσιν ἐπὶ γλυκὺν ἵμερον ὦρσεν,
>Καί τ' ἐδαμάσσατο φῦλα καταθνητῶν ἀνθρώπων,
>οἰωνούς τε Διϊπετέας καὶ θερία πάντα,
>ἠμὲν ὅσ' ἤπειρος πολλὰ τέρφει ἠδ' ὅσα πόντος.
>πᾶσιν δ' ἔργα μέμηλεν ἐϋστεφάνου Κυθερείης.

Which is imitated by Lucretius (Liber I.):

> "Æriae primum volucres te, diva, tuumque
> Significant initium percussae corda tua vi."

Which Dryden thus translates:

> "Delight of human kind and gods above,
> Parent of Rome, propitious queen of love,
> Whose vital power air, earth, and sea supplies,
> And breeds whate'er is born beneath the rolling skies!
> For every kind, by thy prolific might,
> Springs and beholds the regions of the light;

Thee, goddess, thee the clouds and tempests fear,
And at thy pleasing presence disappear:
For thee the land in fragrant flowers is drest,
For thee the ocean smiles and smoothes her wavy breast,
And heaven itself with more serene and purer light is blest.
For when the rising spring adorns the mead,
And a new scene of nature stands displayed,
When teeming buds and cheerful greens appear,
And western gales unlock the lazy year,
The joyous birds thy welcome first express,
Whose native songs thy genial fire confess;
Then savage beasts bound o'er their slighted food,
Struck with thy darts, and tempt the raging flood;
All Nature is thy gift; earth, air, and sea,
Of all that breathes, the various progeny,
Stung with delight, is goaded on by thee.
O'er barren mountains, o'er the flowing plain,
The leafy forest and the liquid main,
Extends thy uncontrolled and boundless reign.

In the third Georgic, Virgil has copied the same sentiment:—

"Thus all that wings the air and cleaves the flood,
Herds that or graze the plain or haunt the wood,
Rush to like flames when kindred passions move,
And man and brute obey the power of love."

Southeby's Translation.

Perhaps the address of Æneas to his goddess-mother, in the first book of the Æneid, comes still nearer to this complex passion. It is true the sexes are reversed, — the male-mortal loves the female-divine, and the dress is maternal instead of conjugal; but still the spirit and the design seem to be the same: —

> "Dixit, et avertens rosea cervice refulsit,
> Ambrosiaeque comae divinum vertice odorem
> Spiravere ; pedes vestis defluxit ad imos,
> Et vera incessu patuit dea. Ille, ubi matrem
> Agnovit, tali fugientem est voce secutus :
> Quid natum toties, crudelis tu quoque, falsis
> Ludis imaginibus ? cur dextrae jungere dextram
> Non datur, ac veras audire et reddere voces ? "

In Catullus's poem on the marriage of Peleus to Thetis, something similar is shadowed out: —

> "Tum Thetidis Peleus incensus fertur amore:
> Tum Thetis humanos non dispexit hymaneos :
> Tum Thetidi pater ipse jugandum Pelea sensit."

We see in all these passages a great conception laboring for its birth. We must remember that Polytheism was an outward and political religion. Grecian wisdom was essentially sceptical; the Greeks questioned all things, and held fast nothing. "The Greeks," says the Apostle, "seek after wisdom:" of course they never find it; and their poetry is less enthusiastic than the fervid children of the East. They recognized the principle that love was the reigning power of nature; but their colder devotion seldom addressed the Deity in such fervent language.

We have, however, in Roman literature, one production which comes nearer to this mystic style. The fable of the Golden Ass, by Apuleius, is supposed by Warburton to be itself a mystic allegory. "Apuleius of Madaura," says he (Divine Legation, Vol. II. Book IV. Sect. 4), "in Africa, was a determined Platonist; and, like the Platonist of that age, an inveterate enemy of Christianity." The object of this fable, therefore, by which the hero was transformed into an ass, and restored, was to show that vice brutalizes the mind, and the pagan religion — without Christianity — had a power to renew and restore it. The word *renatus*, or born again, is applied to the initiated pagan. But, however it may be with the general story, most critics, I believe, agree that the particular episode of Cupid and Psyche, in the fifth and sixth books, is allegorical. "There was no man," says Warburton, "though he considered the Golden Ass only as a work of mere amusement, but saw the fable of Cupid and Psyche to be a philosophical allegory of the progress of the soul to perfection, in the possession of Divine love and the reward of immortality." (Divine Legation.) The story is this. In a certain city lived a king and a queen, who had three daughters, the youngest of whom was named Psyche, or human soul. The two eldest were handsome, but the youngest excelled all modes of beauty, — all bounds of praise. Everybody that saw her was struck dumb with admiration, until finally she seemed to draw away the devotion from Venus herself. No one went to Paphos; no one to Cnidus, nor even to Cythera. Her temples were deserted, her statues without chaplets, and her forsaken altars covered with cold ashes, and all men's adoration paid to this usurping virgin. Venus was incensed, and resolved to punish this rival beauty. In the mean time, Psyche, when her sisters were married, got no husband. She had no lovers. They admired, no doubt, her divine beauty; but then they admired it as they would a statue exquisitely wrought. It is not necessary to go into the whole detail. An oracle says that she must be placed on a lofty mountain; she must not expect a mortal spouse; but Jupiter would provide. She is finally snatched away from her parents, and placed in a splendid palace at the foot of the mountain, and is wedded to an invisible husband, who meets her every night, and is invisible during the day. She finds at last it is Cupid; and, as soon as she sees him, as she does clandestinely one night, she is in love with Love himself. She several times, however, betrays important trusts, and provokes the anger of Venus and her sisters; has awful tasks assigned her by the goddess, the last of which is to descend to hell through a dark, infernal avenue; and she has more minute directions given her than Æneas had when he went down to the infernal regions.

She goes to get a portion of the beauty of Proserpine, which she is to bring up in a box, and deliver to Venus, but this box she is not to open. But female curiosity prevails, and she does open it; and she is on the verge of everlasting destruction. But she is rescued by Cupid, whom she has wounded, and who has recovered of his wounds. Then all is prosperous and happy. A sumptuous wedding-supper was prepared. The husband, reclining at the upper end of the table, embraced Psyche in his bosom; in like manner Jupiter was seated with Juno, and, after them, the other gods and goddesses in their proper order. Then Jupiter was presented with a bowl of nectar,— the wine of the gods,— by the rustic youth Ganymede, his cup-bearer; but Bacchus supplied the rest. Vulcan prepared the supper; the Hours empurpled everything with roses and other fragrant flowers; the Graces scattered balsam; the Muses sang melodiously; Apollo accompanied the lyre with his voice; and beautiful Venus danced with steps in unison with the delightful music. The order, too, of the entertainment was, that the Muses should sing the chorus, Satyrus should play on the flute, and Paniscus on the pipe. Thus Psyche came lawfully into the hands of Cupid; and at length a daughter was born to them, whom we denominate

HAPPINESS.

Remember, now, the names,— Psyche and Cupid, soul and love. Consider her wanderings, her sufferings and sorrows, her deliverance by a bleeding god, whom she had wounded, but who has recovered from his wounds,— consider the long conflict and final triumph,— and who does not see a deeper import unfolded, in a confused and complex manner, under all this mythology? The soul becomes wretched by falling into grosser love; it must be restored by recovered purity and consequent bliss.

I may be accused of being fanciful; but I cannot help suspecting that in the minute directions which the TOWER gives to Psyche in her descent to the infernal regions, I see a common impression of the necessity of revelation to us weak mortals when we deal with the sublime subjects of religion. "You ought not," says this wonderful tower, " to pass through those shades with empty hands, but should take a sop of barley-bread, soaked in hydromel, in each hand, and in your mouth two pieces of money. And when you have accomplished a good part of your deadly journey, you will meet a lame ass, laden with wood, and a driver as lame as himself, who will ask you to reach him certain cords to fasten the burden which has fallen from the ass; but be careful that you pass by him in silence."

And again: "The poor man dying ought to prepare his viaticum; but if he has no money at hand, will no one suffer him to expire? To this squalid old man give one of the pieces of money which you carry with you, yet in such a manner that he may take it with his own hand from your mouth. While you are passing over the sluggish river, a certain dead old man, floating on its surface, and raising his putrid hand, will entreat you to take him into the boat. Beware, however, of yielding to an impulse of unlawful pity. Having passed over the river, and proceeding to a little distance beyond it, you will see certain old women, weaving a web, who will request you to lend them a helping hand; but it is not lawful for you to touch the web. For all these, and many other particulars, are snares prepared by Venus, that you may drop one of the sops out of your hands. But do not suppose that this would be a trifling loss; since the want of only one of those sops would prevent your return to light." Now, while I allow that these minute directions, for which we can see no natural reason, are skilful touches of mysticism, by which we are taught to wonder and shudder at the laws of the unseen world, yet they also show that the heathen had an impression, that, in dealing with these mysteries, man could not be left safely to his own direction. The spiritual powers must teach us the conditions on which spiritual benefits must be obtained. In a word, it was a distorted confession that man needs a divine revelation.

Something, I think, of this mode of indicating is found in the Bible. Why was man separated from the tree of life, lest he should taste and live forever? (Genesis iii. 22.) Why does the Saviour say that a certain kind of unclean spirits goeth not out but by fasting and prayer? (Matthew xvii. 21.) Why does Peter so darkly intimate that Christ went and preached to the spirits in prison? (1 Peter iii. 19.) It is, perhaps, to show us how utterly hopeless is any analysis of ours of these divine secrets, and that we must leave to God his own purposes, and the degree of light in which they must be shown.

Something of this turn of thinking is found in the earliest history of Rome. Numa was inspired by a celestial bride. "Deorum metum injiciendum ratus est qui quum descendere ad animos sine aliquo commento miraculi non posset, simulat sibi quum dea Egeria congressus nocturnos esse." And even the cold and philosophic Cicero, catching a gleam of enthusiasm from Plato, confesses: "Formam quidem ipsam, Marce fili, et tanquam faciem honesti vides: quae si oculis cerneretur, mirabiles amores (ut ait Plato) excitaret sapientiae." (De Officiis, Lib. I. Sect. 5.) And again: "Oculorum, inquit Plato, est in nobis sensus acerrimus: quibus sapientiam non cernimus. Quam illa ardentes amores excitaret sui, si videretur." (De Finibus, Lib. II. Sect. 16.) This same love to an object half personified is taught in that remarkable book, the WISDOM OF SOLOMON, found in our Apocrypha; a book which has a Platonic tinge, and uses this soft and beautiful coloring. Speaking of wisdom the author says: Ἀτμὶς γάρ ἐστι τῆς τοῦ θεοῦ δυνάμεως, καὶ ἀπόῤῥοια τῆς τοῦ παντοκράτερος δόξης εἰλικρινής· διὰ τοῦτο οὐδὲν μεμιαμένον εἰς αὐτὴν παρεμπίπτει· Ἀπαύγασμα γάρ ἐστι φωτὸς ἀϊδίου καὶ ἔσοπτρον ἀκηλίδωτον τῆς τοῦ Θεοῦ ἐνεργείας καὶ εἰκὼν τῆς ἀγαθότητος αὐτοῦ,—"For she is the invisible emanation of the power of God, a pure efflux from his all-potent glory; therefore nothing contaminating can fall into her; she is a radiance from eternal light, the unspotted mirror of God's energy, an image of his goodness;" and therefore in the next chapter he says (verse second): Ταύτην ἐφίλησα καὶ ἐξεζήτησα ἐκ νεότητός μου, καὶ ἐζήτησα νύμφην ἀγαγέσθαι ἐμαυτῷ καὶ ἐραστὴς ἐγενόμην τοῦ κάλλους αὐτῆς,—"I loved her, and sought her out from her youth; I sought to lead her as bride, and was the lover of her beauty."

If we pass to the Eastern world,—to those "souls made of fire and children of the sun,"—we shall find that this form of devotion is very common. I shall not go into detail, nor repeat the quotations from Sir William Jones and others; all travellers tell us, all scholars agree, that to these ardent people such language has become familiar. "They believe," says Sir William (i. e. these Eastern people), "that the Deity pervades the universe; that he alone is perfect benevolence, truth, and beauty; that all the beauties of nature are faint resemblances only — like images in a mirror — of the divine charms; that we must beware of attachment to such phantoms, and attach ourselves exclusively to God, who truly exists in us, and we exist solely in him; that we retain, even in this forlorn state of separation from our Beloved, the idea of heavenly beauty and the remembrance of our primeval vows; that sweet music, gentle breezes, fragrant flowers, perpetually renew the primary idea, refreshing our fading memory, and melt us with tender affections; and, by abstracting our soul from vanity, that is, from all but God, approximate to his essence in our final union, with which will consist our supreme beatitude." The later Platonists have copied all this. Plotinus was four times in his life united to God, not only by power, but by ineffable energy. In his sixty-eighth year God beamed into his heart, — not having any form or idea, but seated above thought, above intelligence. (See Bale's Dict., Art. *Plotinus*, note K.) They were *inebriated* with Divine love, — an expression which Augustine uses in his Confessions. Lady Montague and Lord Byron have noticed the Turkish love-song, The Nightingale and the Rose: "The nightingale now wanders in the vines; her passion is to seek roses. I went down to admire the beauty of the vines; the sweetness of your charms hath ravished my soul."

> "For there the Rose o'er crag or vale,
>   Sultana of the Nightingale,
>   The maid for whom this melody
>   His thousand songs are heard on high,
>   Blooms, blushing to her lover's tale,
>   His queen, his garden queen, his Rose,
>   Unbent by winds, unchilled by snows,
>   Far from the winters of the West,
>   By every breeze and season blest,
>   Returns the sweets by nature given
>   In softest incense back to heaven;
>   And grateful yields that smiling sky
>   Her fairest hue and fragrant sigh."
>   The Giaour.

Respecting the Persian poet, we have the testimony of Sir John Malcolm. "Hafiz, said Khan Sahib, has the singular good fortune of being alike praised by saints and sinners. His odes are sung by the young and the joyous, who, by taking them in their literal sense, find nothing but excitement to pass the spring of life in the enjoyment of the world's luxuries; while the contemplative sage, considering this poet as a religious enthusiast, attaches a mystical meaning to every line, and repeats his odes as he would an orison. At the time of his death, continued my friend, there were many who deemed his works sinful and impious. These went so far as to arrest the procession of his funeral. The dispute rose high, and the parties were likely to come to blows, when it was agreed that a *fàl*, or lot, should be taken from his book. If it was favorable to religion, his friends were to proceed; but if calculated to promote vice, they promised not to carry his body to the sacred ground appropriated for his reception.

"The volume of odes was produced, and it was opened by a person whose eyes were bound; seven pages were counted back, when the heaven-directed finger pointed to one of his inspired stanzas:

'Withdraw not your steps from the obsequies of Hafiz;
Though immersed in sin, he will rise into Paradise.'

"The admirers of the poet shouted with delight, and those who had doubted joined in carrying his remains to a shrine near Shiraz, where, from that day to this, his tomb is visited by pilgrims of all classes and ages.

"I found that my friend, Khan Sahib, however partial from his habits to a literal interpretation, dwelt upon others which he deemed mystical, with all the rapture of a Sofee." (Sketches of Persia, Vol. II. 1827, London.)

I am aware that Dr. Noyes objects that the mystic poetry of Persia and Hindostan is founded on a philosophy different from the Jewish. They were Pantheistic mystics. But I cannot feel the force of his objection. The difference he alleges seems to me hardly to touch the point. I suppose in all countries and all ages love and devotion exist, and that it is natural to express them by the language of the one and the ardor of the other. It should be remembered that the language of love is in antagonism to pantheism; and that both Jew and Gentile struggled and were obliged to struggle to approximate the divine nature by anthropopathic terminology.*

If we pass to the Christian writers the examples are abundant. There have always been a class of Christians whose glowing love has sought to express itself in the only language which it found proportionate in the least degree to its inexpressible emotions. This style of speaking and writing began early and continued long. The famous expression of Ignatius, in his Epistle to the Romans, chap. iii. 3, "MY LOVE IS CRUCIFIED," is, no doubt, susceptible of a double meaning, the objective and the subjective. My Love, my heavenly bridegroom, was literally crucified for my redemption; and through his atonement, my love, my carnal love of the world, is crucified mystically in my heart. For he goes on to say, "and the fire that is within me does not desire

---

* ἀνθρωποπαθῶς μὲν λέγονται, θεοπρεπῶς δὲ νοοῦνται. — Athanasius.

any water; but, being alive, and springing within me, says, Come to the Father." Or, if we should take another reading, πῦρ φιλόϋλον, it comes to the same thing. The writer is using the same language which Paul does: "But God forbid that I should glory, save in the cross of our Lord Jesus Christ, by whom the world is crucified unto me and I unto the world." The real always implies the mystic crucifixion in the heart of a believer, and Christ is called his love as an expressive figure of the most grateful affection. Something of this taste appears in the Shepherd of Hermas, especially in his first vision, where he sees the same woman addressing him from Heaven whom he had before beheld washing in the Tiber, and who now accuses him of his former love; intimating, no doubt, that human passion should be supplanted by the divine. Tertullian counsels the women in his day (with some hard metaphors, it must be owned) to have their eyes painted with chastity; the word of God inserted into their ears; Christ's yoke tied to their hair; to subject themselves to their husbands. If they would do so, they should be comely enough, clothe themselves with the silk of sanctity, damask of devotion, purple of piety and chastity, and so painted, they shall have God himself to be a suitor. "Oculos depictos verecundia, inserentes in aures sermonem Dei, annectentes crinibus jugum Christi, caput maritis subjicientes, sic facile et satis ornatae: vestite vos serico probitatis, byssino sanctitatis, purpura pudicitiae; taliter pigmentatae Deum habebitis amatorem." (De Cultu Mulierum.) Those holy virgins of old, "quae Christo spiritualiter nubunt," were considered as consecrated in this way, even before the establishment of regular monasteries and convents. Each one was called Sponsa Christi. Jerome, in writing to Eustochium, says he may well call her My Lady, as she is entitled to be called the spouse of his Master. The language of Augustine is colored by the expressions of love and the wine-table. "Quis mihi dabit adquescere in te? Quis mihi dabit, ut venias in cor meum, et inebries illud ut obliviscar mala mea, et unum bonum meum amplectar te?" (Confessions, Lib. I. c. 5.) "O that thou wouldst give me to rest in thee! O that thou wouldst grant me the favor to enter my heart and intoxicate it with thy love, that I might forget my sorrows and embrace thee, my sole, sufficient good!" And again: "O, thou highest, best, most powerful, most omnipotent, most compassionate, most just, most secret, most seen, most beautiful, most brave, stable, incomprehensible; immutable, yet changing all things, never new, never old; innovating and bringing the proud to decay; always acting, always quiet; collecting, but wanting not; bearing and filling and protecting, creating, cherishing, and maturing; seeking, when nothing is deficient in thee! Thou lovest, but art never in commotion; thou art jealous, but calm; thou repentest without sorrow, and changest thy works, though thy counsels never change," — *opera mutas, nec mutas consilium*, etc. He then calls the object of his passion "my God, my life, my holy sweetness." (Confessions, Lib. I. Sect. 4.) Again, in the Third Book, sixth section, after observing that the beauty of created things is not the beauty of God, he goes on to say: "We see these things with carnal eyes, in common with the flocks and birds; yet certius imaginamur ea, quam ex eis suspicamur alia grandia et infinita, quae omnino nulla sunt, qualibus ego tunc pascebar inanibus; et non pascebar. At tu, meus amor, in quem deficio, ut fortis sim, nec ista corpora es, quae videmus, quamquam in coelo, nec ea es, quae non videmus ibi, quia tu ista condidisti, nec in summis tuis conditionibus habes." Again, in the Fourth Book, he paves the way to this imagery by his previous philosophy: "Num amamus aliquid nisi pulchrum? Quod est ergo pulchrum? et quid est pulchritudo? Quid est, quod nos adlicit, et conciliat rebus quas amamus? Nisi enim esset in eis decus et species, nullo modo nos ad se moverent. Et animadvertebam et videbam in ipsis corporibus aliud esse quasi totum et ideo pulchrum; aliud autem, quod ideo deceret, quoniam apte adcommodaretur alicui, sicut pars corporis ad universum suum, aut calceamentum ad pedem et similia." — "Do we love anything unless it is beautiful? What, then, is this beautiful thing, and what is beauty itself? What is it that attracts and conciliates us to things we love? For if there were not a grace and fairness in these things, they would by no means draw us to themselves. Now, I observed and saw in bodies themselves another totality, which was therefore beautiful; another grace, which, owing to the fitness of its parts, was therefore becoming; as a part of the body to the whole, or a slipper to the foot, or any similar correspondence of a part to the whole." Once more (Book X. Sect. 27): "Sero te amavi, pulchritudo tam antiqua et tam nova, sero te amavi. Et ecce intus eras et ego foris et ibi te quaerebam; et in ista formosa, quae fecisti, deformis irruebam. Mecum eras, et tecum non eram. Ea me tenebant longe a te, quae, si in te non essent, non essent. Vocasti et clamasti et rupisti surditatem meam. Coruscasti, splenduisti et fugasti caecitatem meam. Fragrasti et duxi spiritum, et anhelo tibi. Gustavi et esurio et sitio. Tetigisti me et exarsi in pacem tuam." The ancient interpreters generally considered this book — Solomon's Song — as the expression of inexpressible love; teaching, as Theodoret says, the higher kinds of Divine goodness. Gregory the Great says: "In hoc libro amoris quasi corporei verba ponuntur, ut a corpore suo anima, per sermones consuetos, dicussa, recalescat, et per verba amoris, qui infra est, excitetur ad amorem, qui supra est." Nothing can be more true, or more neatly expressed. "In this book the words of corporeal love are placed, that the soul, shaking off the body, might learn from its accustomed passions to rekindle; and, by using the terms of a meaner passion, rise to a nobler flame." And Theodoret says: "This book teaches τὴν μυστικὴν συνάφειαν, the mystic union of the bride and bridegroom." (See Suicerus, Lex., Vol. I. p. 551.) In a later age, in the letters which Abelard writes to his Eloisa: "De hujus excellentia praerogativae sponsa in Canticis exultans, illa, ut ita dicam, quam Moyses duxit, Aethiopissa dicit, *Nigra sum, sed formosa, filiae Hierusalem. Ideo dilexit me Rex et introduxit me in cubiculum suum.* Et rursum, *Nolite considerare quod fusca sum, quia decoloravit me Sol.* In quibus quidem verbis cum generaliter anima describatur contemplativa, quae specialiter Sponsa Christi dicitur, expressius tamen ad vos hoc pertinere ipse etiam vester exterior habitus loquitur. Ipse quippe cultus exterior nigrorum, aut vilium indumentum, instar lugubris habitus bonarum viduarum mortuos, quos delexerant viros plangentium, vos in hoc mundo, juxta Apostolorum, vere viduas et desolatas ostendit, stipendiis Ecclesiae sustinendas." (Abelard to Eloisa, Epistle III. p. 73.) And Bernard, his enemy and rival, agrees in the same kind of interpretation: "The king hath brought me into his wine-cellar (banqueting-house in our translation),—speaking of this prayer (i. e. the prayer of silence), this sanctuary of the great king, in which he enters with a few whom he hides for that hour from the world; this place of quiet; this vision which does not affright, but cherish; does not weary, but calm; does not bring cravings or distractions, but pacifies and fully satisfies. But, alas! the hour is rare and the duration short,"— *Sed heu! rara hora et parva mora.* (See Sermon XXIII. on Canticles.) And again: "O sweet commerce! but the moment is short and the experience rare. Some one may ask what this is to enjoy the Divine Word. Let him seek one who has experienced it. Or if that happiness were granted me, do you think I can explain what is unspeakable? It is one thing that passes between my soul and God, and another between you and me. That I could feel, but could not utter. If you are desirous to know what it is to enjoy the Word, prepare for Him, not your ear, but your soul. The tongue cannot express this; yet grace teaches it. It is concealed from the prudent and the wise, and is revealed to little ones. Humility is a great and sublime virtue, which obtains what is not taught, which acquires what cannot be learned." (Sermon LXXXV.) I quote from Butler's Lives of the Saints, Vol. II. p. 673. That most popular book, Thomas à Kempis, which has passed through more editions than any other volume except the Bible, and which first saw the light in 1488, adopts the same style: "Para mihi coenaculum grande stratum, et faciam apud te Pascha cum discipulis meis. Exclude totum saeculum, etc. Omnis namque amans suo dilecto amatori optimum et pulcherrimum praeparat locum quia in hoc cognoscitur affectus suscipientis dilectum." (De Imitatione Christi, Lib. XIV. c. 12.) "Make ready for me a large upper-room furnished, and I will make the pash (i. e. Passover) with thee and my disciples. For every lover prepareth the best and fairest room for his dearly-beloved; and hereby is known the affection of him that entertaineth his beloved." Again (Lib. XIV. c. 13): "Hoc oro, hoc desidero, ut tibi totus uniar, et cor meum ab omnibus creatis rebus abstraham, magis per sacram communionem vel frequentem celebrationem, celestia et aeterna sapere discam. Ah, Domine Deus! quando ero tecum totus unitus et absorptus, meique totaliter oblitus? Tu in me et ego in te; sic nos pariter in unum manere concede. Vere tu es dilectus meus, electus ex millibus, in quo conplacuit animae meae habitare omnibus diebus vitae suae." — "Verily, thou art my beloved, the choicest amongst thousands, in whom my soul is well pleased to dwell all the days of her life." It would be easy to multiply quotations from such writers; one more shall suffice. Take the case of M. Magdalen of Pazzi, an Italian saint canonized in 1669.

The spirit of God threw her on the ground in an ecstasy, when her countenance was shining like that of an incarnate seraph. Christ gave her so large a share of his passion, that frequently, under an alienation of her senses, she would throw herself on the ground, exclaiming: " O Jesus, I can endure no longer, — I cannot partake any more of thy pains! " Often in these amorous transports (divinely amorous) she would join herself close to a crucifix, and suck a divine liquor thence, which filled her soul with unspeakable sweetness. Her heart was so inflamed, that she seemed to be dissolved, and about to return to her first nothing. Her private familiar entertainments and communion with God so fired her breast that she would exclaim: " O Love, I can no longer support your flames, — my heart is not able to contain you! " (Enthusiasm of the Methodists and Papists Compared, Vol. I. Part II. p. 7.) I have not the least suspicion there was the least hypocrisy in the ardors of this good sister. Her constitution, indeed, might have increased her devotions, but she uses the inimitable language of feeling and truth. I have not quoted from St. Teresa of Spain, Francis de Sales, Madame de Guyon, Fénélon, Antonette Bourignon, and many others; they all feel the same ardor and fall into the same strain. They talk of the prayer of silence, self-annihilation, self-crucifixion, absorption, the passive prayer, the wordless petition, the mystical union with God, —

and we can hardly conceive of this state of emotion without its clothing itself in the language of Canticles; the affinity is like matter to form, as the old philosophers say,—it is eternal and complete. The old English poets have fallen into a similar strain. Thus Spenser, in his Hymn on Heavenly Beauty: —

> "With all my heart, with all my soul and mind,
> Thou must Him love and His behests embrace;
> All other loves with which the world doth blind
> Weak fancies, and stir up affections base,
> Thou must renounce and utterly displace,
> And give thyself unto Him, full and free,
> That full and freely gave himself for thee.
> . . . .
> Then shall thy ravisht soul inspired be
> With heavenly thoughts, far above human skill,
> And thy bright, radiant eyes shall plainly see
> Th' idea of His pure glory present still
> Before thy face, that all thy spirits shall fill
> With sweet enragement of celestial love,
> Kindled through sight of those fair things above."

So in the poems of Drummond, who died 1649: —

> "Love which is here a care,
> That wit and will doth mar,
> Uncertain truce and a most certain war,
> A shrill, tempestuous wind,
> Which doth disturb the mind,
> And like wild waves all our designs commove.
> Among those powers above
> Which see their Maker's face,
> It a contentment is, a quiet peace,

> A pleasant void of grief, a constant rest,
> Eternal joy, which nothing can molest."

And again, I suppose the following to be written in the same spirit, though the design is not so clearly expressed : —

> "Thrice happy he, who, by some shady grove,
> Far from the clamorous world, doth live his own;
> Though solitary, who is not alone,
> But doth converse with that ETERNAL LOVE:
> O, how more sweet is bird's harmonious moan,
> Or the hoarse sobbings of the widowed dove,
> Than those smooth whisperings near a prince's throne
> Which good make doubtful, do the evil approve:
> O how more sweet is Zephyr's wholesome breath,
> And sighs embalmed which new-born flowers unfold,
> Than that applause vain honor doth bequeath!
> How sweet are streams to poisoned drink in gold!
> The world is full of horrors, troubles, slights;
> Woods, harmless shades, have only true delights."
>
> Flowers of Zion.

So Crashaw : —

> "Dear soul, be strong;
> Mercy will come ere long,
> And bring its bosom full of blessings;
> Flowers of never-fading graces,
> To make immortal dressings
> For worthy souls, whose wise embraces
> Store up themselves for Him, who is alone
> The spouse of virgins, and the virgin's son.
>
> But if the noble Bridegroom, when he come,
> Shall find the loitering heart from home,
> Leaving its chaste abode
> To gad abroad

Among the gay mates of the god of flies;
    To take her pleasure and to play
    And keep the devil's holiday;
To dance i' the sunshine of some smiling,
      But beguiling

Sphere of sweet and sugar'd lies,
    Some slippery pair
    Of false, perhaps, as fair,
Flattering but forswearing eyes;

Doubtless, some other heart
    Will get the start,
    And, stepping in before,
Will take possession of the sacred store."

And again: —

"Rise up, my fair, my spotless one,
The winter's past, the rain is gone:
The spring is come, the flowers appear,
No sweets but thine are wanting here."

"Come away, my love,
Come away, my dove,
    Cast off delay;
The court of Heaven has come
To wait upon thee home, —
    Come, come away."

"The flowers appear,
Or quickly would, wert thou once here."

Mrs. Rowe and Dr. Watts add their suffrage. The former, even when she does not adopt the imagery, has a lusciousness which borders upon it: —

> "Begin the high celestial strain,
>   My ravished soul, and sing
> A solemn hymn of grateful praise
>   To Heaven's Almighty King.
>
> "Ye curling fountains, as ye roll
>   Your silver waves along,
> Whisper to all your verdant shores
>   The subject of my song."

And Dr. Watts: —

> "Sweet Muse, descend and bless the shade
>   And bless the evening grove;
> Business and noise and day are fled,
>   And every care but love.
>
>   .   .   .   .   .
>
> I'll carve our passion on the bark,
>   And every wounded tree
> Shall droop and bear some mystic mark
>   That Jesus died for me."

The thirteen hymns in the first book of Watts are well recollected by all, once admired, though now generally omitted.

Pope, in his Eloisa to Abelard, in describing the blameless vestal's lot, who enjoys the

> "Eternal sunshine of the spotless mind,"

adds: —

> "For her the unfading rose of Eden blooms,
> And wings of seraphs shed divine perfumes;
> For her the Spouse prepares the bridal ring,
> For her white virgins hymeneals sing.
> To sounds of heavenly harps she dies away,
> And melts in visions of eternal day."

This is but a versification of what is supposed to be illustrated in the trances and visions of St. Teresa of Spain, and other mystics. Pope is one of those authors whose appropriations and borrowings increase our admiration of his original genius. In this epistle almost everything is borrowed, either from Eloisa's letters or Abelard's, or the mystic writers, yet with what selective power! with what admirable taste!

Now, the argument is this. What is so general must be natural; certainly the material passion is universal,—"amor idem omnibus." (Georgic III. v. 244.) Certainly Divine love is essential to religion; and certainly the one may be pictured in the other. If, then, all nations have felt this power, and have fallen into this strain; if ardent devotion always verges to mysticism, and if the mystics and semi-mystics have always expressed themselves in this way; if the fervent East began the strain, and the sceptic Greeks and politic Romans have something of the flame; if it has been repeated in every age, and we cannot conceive how glowing piety can find equal figures in any other source,—then we must say, that the man who cannot see the propriety of this union of mortal language with immortal thoughts has not a comprehensive mind; he has neither considered the nature of mind, the nature of language, nor the history of religion. He questions the possibility of that which is almost universal. He stands alone, or associates only with the frozen. The fact is, so far from regarding this book as an objection to the purity of revelation, its fulness would have been crippled without it; and as, when I read that "the Lord God is a sun," I can think of no other object in creation so adequate to image his glory, and believe that later writers, if they had never heard of this comparison, must have found it of their own invention, so I must conclude that the Word of God in adopting this amatory strain only touches a universal chord, and completes its own perfection.

People do not sufficiently consider the amplitude of the Bible. That divine book is written for all tastes in all ages, and is addressed to all the nations of the earth. Its design is simple, but its expedients are endless; and the fancy and the reason are alike made the channels by which it pours its information into the soul. It is like the tree of life, in Revelation, which grew on the banks of the mystic river, which "bare twelve manner of fruits, and yielded her fruit every month; and the leaves of the tree were for the healing of the nations." (Rev. xxii. 2.) Remark the word, — "the nations," not one, but all. Accordingly, the Bible has an astonishing omniformity. It fills every channel of thought; it reaches every soul. We cannot expect the mathematician to have the taste of a poet, or the Greek to resemble the uncultivated barbarian. The Hindoo and the Chinaman are different beings. Even religion enters minds of different conformity and with different degrees of intenseness. The cold sunbeam that plays on the rocks of Hecla hardly seems to be the same thing as the burning ray that falls on the sands of El Arisch. Where, then, is the wonder that God, who knows all hearts, should fill his Word with all the methods of reaching them? "But the word of the Lord was unto them precept upon precept, precept upon precept, line upon line, line upon line, here a little and there a little, that they might go and fall backward, and be broken, and snared, and be taken." (Isaiah xxviii. 13.) The seeming imperfections of the Bible are but varieties of excellence. Truth, like some skilful virgin, increases her charms by varying her dress. The most successful moral writers have been conscious of the same difficulties, and have adopted the same rule. Let us hear Addison: "I may cast my readers under two general divisions, the Mercurial and the Saturnine. The first are the gay part of my disciples, who require speculations of wit and humor; the others are those of a more solemn and sober turn, who find no pleasure but in papers of morality and sound sense. The former call everything that is serious, stupid; the latter look upon everything as impertinent that is ludicrous. Were I always grave, one half my readers would fall off from me; were I always merry, I should lose the other. I make it, therefore, my endeavor to find out entertainments of both kinds, and by that means, perhaps, consult the good of both more than I should do, did I always write to the particular taste of either. As they neither of them know what I proceed upon, the sprightly reader, who takes up my paper in order to be diverted, very often finds himself engaged unawares in a serious and profitable course of thinking; as, on the contrary, the thoughtful man, who perhaps may hope to find something solid and full of deep reflection, is very often insensibly betrayed into a fit of mirth. In a word, the reader sits down to my entertainment, without knowing the bill of fare, and has therefore at least the pleasure of hoping there may be a dish to his palate." (The Spectator, Vol. III. No. 179.)

Now, why may we not suppose the condescension of God has adopted a similar expedient? The best men differ in their tastes. Think of Leighton and Baxter; the first turning away from logic to love, and the other always pausing in his emotions to speculate. I am far from thinking that a man is not a Christian because he does not relish this book. Before I present it to him with the least hope of profit, or even patient attention, I ask, what is the type of his piety, what is his imagination, what is his taste, what is his power of throwing himself into Oriental conceptions? how far has he traced the use of language from its hieroglyphic state in its long progress to Grecian perfection? As Coleridge said of Sir John Mackintosh,

I should despair to build a bridge over the gulf that separates some minds from these beautiful conceptions. But then they are no mean men, and some of them sincere Christians. The Bible, too, has a part and portion for them. But other minds have a different conformation. Augustine, Thomas à Kempis, Luther, Fénélon, Francis de Sales, Madame Guyon, Miss Rowe, Dr. Watts, must have one such book as this; and, I must add, I should deem it a privilege to belong to the coterie; for, given, a mystic turn, a glowing fancy, an ardent piety in a burning heart, and, more than all, a little Oriental training, and such a poem must be eliminated, as certainly as the vernal sun calls forth the flowers.

IV.

DIVINE LOVE

AN INTELLECTUAL AND INFORMING PASSION.

There is a remarkable sentiment in the First Epistle of Paul to the Corinthians, eighth chapter, second and third verses: "And if any man think he knoweth anything, he knoweth nothing yet as he ought to know. But if any man love God, the same is known of him." The Apostle's design seems to be to show the illuminating power of a holy affection. Love in the heart is light in the understanding. If any man think he knoweth anything, — that is, by the exercise of his natural faculties, his ratiocination, — if he supposes he knows anything in religion, — for we must thus qualify his general proposition, — if he supposes this, he errs in the whole subject; he knows nothing as he ought to know it; for the essence of religion in this way is never known. But if any man love God experimentally, if he feel this new passion in his own heart, he is known of God, or, rather, he is made to know by God, — for I should give the *hiphil*-meaning here to the verb, — that is, the very passion is inspiring. Love is light. Love to God in the heart purifies the intellect and spreads light through the mind.

The Apostle adopts the same principle as to knowing our duties to our fellow-men. He tells the Thessalonians (First Epistle, iv. 9) : " But as touching brotherly love, ye need not that I write unto you; for ye yourselves *are taught of God* to love one another." They had only to look into their own breasts, and the powerful impulse, once given, was their best instructor.*

We may lay it down as a principle, that the elementary ideas respecting our whole duty to God and man originate in the affections. Strike off the affections, and all our moral technology would have no meaning. It is here as it is in teaching music; a man may learn the gamut and all the laws of concord and time, the mathematical laws of vibration in producing sound, and yet, if his ear be defective, and cannot distinguish the sweetness and unity of sounds, the lesson comes to an end.

Reasoning presupposes intuition, which gives us something to reason about. Metaphysicians have been per-

---

* One of the most surprising instances of the informing nature of this divine passion is found in 1 Corinth. xiii. 5. It is said of ἡ ἀγάπη that οὐκ ἀσχημονεῖ, it does not behave itself unseemly. Now what a quick perception, what a comprehensive view of all the nicer threads of obligation and life, must that passion have which teaches us to move correctly on these delicate and indefinite lines ! It gives us an instinct neighboring on inspiration.

plexed to know how we can prove the existence of the material world; or, the outer world being given, how we know that our ideas are a representation of it. Some say we assume it, some, that we know it from common sense; and some, that we see all things in God. All confess that our ideas, considered as representations, are very uncertain and inadequate. But there is one idea, or impression, or concept, or whatever you call it, having an outward cause, which must be adequate, and about which there can be no scepticism; and that is PAIN, in all its forms, and, of course, pleasure. I have my pain all to myself, and with it, in all my sufferings and contortions, it brings one consolation, that I think I have one adequate idea; for I cannot conceive where my pain can exist but in my sensation, and I shall be thankful to the man that can give me happiness by giving me ease. Now, with the idea of pain springs up a whole host of concomitant ideas; happiness, its opposite; and the moral ideas, the infliction of pain and the imparting of pleasure, which is justice, or malignity; and the giving of happiness, which is benevolence. I think the old Epicureans were right when they said virtue was an empty and splendid name, when it gave no exponent, — no productive quantity. Without pleasure and pain, benevolence, in God or man, would have nothing to work on, — nothing to express itself by. For let me imagine that yonder busy ants, as they collect the grain (though the supposition is confuted by their activity), were incapable of feeling, how can I do them good or evil? how can I even wish well to their experience? Surround the throne of God with the most exalted intellects, incapable of feeling, — with angels, archangels, and ransomed saints, incapable of feeling, — and I see not how the almighty wisdom of Jehovah could exercise any benevolence towards them. He has nothing to give. Nay, suppose God himself to be pure intellect, how can he be clothed with the Divine perfections? Benevolence must have something to give; indigence and dependence must have something to receive; and it is no paradox to say that hell itself, an eternal hell, is necessary to the highest expression of that infinite Love, which enables some who have deserved it from justice to escape it by grace.

Thus are sensualism and spirituality linked together; thus does one become an exponent of the other, as the water-lily with its sweetness springs from the mud.

We must distinguish, I know, in order to form a conception of the mind, intellect from feeling; but we must not separate them. To view them apart assists our conception, but to tear them asunder destroys them both. The following remarks of a writer of our country, now little known, seem to me to be profound: " The faculties of the mind have been commonly distinguished, by modern divines and philosophers, into the understanding, the will, and the affections. Others comprehend the affections in the will. The object of the understanding is truth; the object of the will and affections is good. The mind by the understanding perceives, judges, reasons, knows, assents; but by the affections loves, rejoices, hates, grieves, &c.; by the will chooses, refuses, exerts, forbears, and the like. These objects and acts of the mind at first sight may seem to be of a different nature; but this may be owing to our viewing the same object, as it were, in a different attitude and light. Thus, good, which is the object of the affections, is knowable; so is an object of the understanding. It may be both known and loved. Yea, to know and to love good seems to be the same thing. What is love but the perception of goodness and loveliness? Perception is referred to the understanding, and affection to the will. But is there any more real difference between perceiving beauty and loving it, than there is between attraction and gravitation? It will be said there is a twofold perception of objects, viz. *sub ratione veri*, and *sub ratione boni;* the former is referred to the intellect, the latter to the heart, or will. But it may well be inquired whether there be any object of perception in nature, or any object in the mind, which does not involve both those respects; and whether perception and taste do not universally, essentially, and necessarily imply each other, their difference being rather nominal than real; whether there be any taste without perception, or any perception without taste; and, consequently, whether the understanding and heart do not really contain each other, and their acts coincide? I have sometimes thought that the promiscuous use of the words mind, understanding, heart, knowledge, love, observable in the inspired books, was very agreeable to this supposition, and gave some countenance to it. And yet the common distinction of the faculties of the mind may conveniently enough be retained for method's sake, provided we take care not to be led into mistake by it." (Dr. Hemmenway's Vindication in Answer to Dr. Hopkins, 1772.)

The intellect and the emotions, then, are one in origin, one in the objective. Love springs from the perception of the lovely, and yet the perception is not from reason only,—i. e. the discursive faculty. It is perceived by the very affection it kindles; that is, the relish for beauty, the love of beauty, are so much one, that we cannot conceive them as existing apart. We must have love to perceive what is lovely, and the perception of what is lovely is necessary to the existence of love. None can tell which is first, which is last,—which is cause, which is effect. Eternal wonder! Enigma which human penetration can never solve! "I went down into the garden of nuts, to see the fruits of the valley, and to see whether the vine flourished and the pomegranates budded. Or ever I was aware, my soul made me like the chariots of Amminadib."

That Divine love is an intellectual and enlightening passion is seen from many considerations.

I. We may begin this inquiry by remarking how much a *worldly* affection can blind the intellect to its permanent and religious duty. We love the world; we are governed by our sensual passions; we pursue the prizes of time; we are solicited by its riches and dazzled by its honors; — and when we come to awake from our dream, and soberly estimate the value of the things we have pursued, all men confess the vanity of life; all men confess the little value of the things which have excited such intense interest. The spark has kindled such a conflagration only by falling on a combustible heart. Every one knows that our duration in this life is but a span, and we plant our fairest flowers only to wither on our graves. Take the candidate for political honor, — how intense his interest, how great his activity, how precarious his success, and how frequent his disappointment! How common it is for us to over-estimate the duration of our mortal life, and all the enjoyment it includes and brings! "What is your life?" says the Apostle. "It is a vapor which appears for a little time, and then vanishes away." That a being of foresight, with the least consciousness of the moral impressions, should purchase affluence by vice, is one of the most astonishing events that can happen. Nothing is more strange, or more common. It can only be accounted for by the intensity of a blinding passion. Suppose the truth of religion, and our eternal interest therein, and a man never cheats another without in a thousand-fold degree cheating himself. If he takes from his neighbor's purse, he takes a richer treasure from his own breast. It is said by divines, and it is implied in Scripture, that if it were not for this blinding power coming from the love of the world, the truth and beauty of the Gospel would beam on us at once, even as the setting sun darts his light through the purified atmosphere, and the cloud is lifted from its descending brightness.

This intense love for an inadequate object is no disputed truth; all own its extravagance, while they feel its power. All government, as Burke tells us, is founded on the maxim, that no man shall be judge in his own cause. No matter what his native sagacity may be, the moment self-interest intervenes he becomes blind to the plainest claims of impartial justice, and the higher the prize, the greater the selfishness. Hence it is often observed that a throne is a prize too great for any human wisdom. The condition of the Roman emperors was a strong instance. It seems astonishing that any mortal should be induced to accept such a dangerous honor. They were every moment liable to assassination and rebellion from their capricious soldiers. Whatever grandeur might adorn their palaces, whatever luxury might attend their feasts, — think of their pillows, attend them to their sleeping chambers, and what a dreadful condition! Every noise must have alarmed them. No wonder many of them were sots. It was drunkenness only that could put them to sleep. How ambition, that fond passion, must have painted its own prizes in order to justify its own choice! And yet there was no want of candidates. Some possessed, and thousands sought, the transient honor, and the almost certain ruin. How irrational! What a mystery! In reading of the French Revolution, the wonder impressed on the reader's mind is, that Louis XVI., when the snares were multiplying around him, did not resign; but the thought seems never to have entered his head. Indeed, the whole of human life seems to be an exhibition of this fallacy, — enormous love for what our experience shows us to be a worthless object. Even in good men a lingering carnality obscures their moral perception. When the scales have left their eyes, it takes time to accustom them to improve the sight. So we must explain some of the striking instances we have in the Bible. Our Lord told his disciples (Mark ix. 31): "The Son of man is delivered into the hands of men, and they shall kill him; and after that he is killed, he shall rise the third day." This declaration seems to us very explicit, and yet we are told of his own disciples, they understood not that saying, and were afraid to ask him. See also Luke ii. 50, and various other instances. Such is the blinding power of a passion which creates its own valuations.

We might instance it in the length we impute to human life, and the distance at which we place eternal things. This fallacy prevents religion from making its appropriate impression. It is the standing delusion, — the great obstacle to the reception of the Gospel. Nothing can be more obvious than that life is short, and that all its rewards partake of its own brevity, and it is very precarious while it lasts. And yet this obvious delusion is everywhere operating. Take any ruling passion and trace its operation on the strongest intellect. It makes the miser poor amidst his riches; it exposed Cæsar to the daggers of his friends; it tears an impenitent world from the cross of Christ, and plunges them into endless ruin.

But there is one remarkable instance in the Bible which shows the blinding influence of an evil affection on the highest capacity. It has often been asked, in the temptation of Christ, — indeed, in his general temptations, — how the Devil could expect to succeed in opposing either the power or the plans of an all-wise and all-powerful God. The character of Satan, it is said, is impossible and inconsistent. But perhaps the objector does not consider the blinding influence of an evil principle when it is infinitely strong and purely evil. It may be a part of his crime and punishment to be hurried on to attempt an absurdity, though his clouded reason may assure him he must always fail. This, perhaps, is the great lesson we are to learn from the character and conduct of the prince of hell. He is a being whose reason is useless to him, because it is a slave to the impetuous depravity of his heart.

Now, the power of Divine Love is, in the first place, that it removes this universal delusion. The *negative* part of its work is vastly important. For until men come to a practical conviction of the perversity of their choice, in prizing things merely because they prize them, they find a very cold and distant meaning in the claims of the Gospel; and if a false passion for an inadequate object has a great influence in blinding the mind to all that is true and beautiful in duty and religion, we may well conclude that a true passion, fixed on Him who is eternal, immortal, and invisible, must raise the mind from its grovellings, and fill it with wisdom and peace. But,

II. There are several considerations which show positively this enlightening influence of a pure affection.

First, its origin; the soul.

Second, from its objective.

Third, from its elements or counters: that is, the very objects it gives to reason to employ itself about, just as quantity is the element of mathematical calculation.

First, then, love is the act or impulse of the soul. It originates in the soul, the centre where the discursive and emotional powers combine. It should be remembered that love, through all the grades of being, from the insect to the archangel, rises from an unreflecting instinct to an intellectual passion. It is exalted by the source from which it proceeds; it is instinct in the birds and beasts, and yet almost inspires *them* with a prophetic foresight. It makes the bird build her nest, and prepare, as if she had prudence, for her future offspring. It drives the brute to sensual gratification, and rises to the most refined and elegant perfection in the human race. Suppose a poet and a clown to be walking together in the field. They see a rose; it is the same object, yet how different the impression, and how much more exalted the feelings of the poet than the clown! They look up to a star, and the poet understands its nature and object better than the clown. He looks with an elevating admiration. Thus the relish lies imbedded in all the powers of the mind, and love never ceases to actuate the thoughts and mental operations with which it was at first combined.

We are told by Aristotle, (as quoted in Cudworth's Intellectual System, Chap. IV. p. 203,) that there is something in man better than reason, λόγου τι κρεῖτων, and which is the principle of reason, λόγου ἀρχή. For, says he, the principle of reason is not reason, but something better. All deductions suppose something already known; — something more sure, more clearly seen than anything to which it leads us. A ray of light is not so clear as the fountain from which it proceeds. A soul cannot exist without the elements of its own existence; and one of these is the all-comprehensive passion of love.

Secondly, but if we consider the *objective* of this passion, we shall find that it is mental and highly informing. In its lowest exercise it must see something, — a child, a landscape, a face, a flower; and the vaster and the more complex the object, the more elevated and refined must be the passion. Some writers, indeed most, and certainly St. Paul, make all virtue to consist in benevolence. "Love is the fulfilling of the law." But consider what an objective they present to produce and guide this noble feeling. President Edwards tells us, true virtue most essentially consists "in benevolence to Being in general. Or perhaps, to speak more accurately, it is that consent, propensity, and union of heart to Being in general, that is immediately exercised in a general good-will." Consider what a vast object the mind is supposed to comprehend; for it must in some degree comprehend it before it can admire, according to the old maxim, *Ignoti nulla cupido.* Hutcheson says: "What reason can a benevolent being give, as exciting him to hazard his life in a just war? This, perhaps,— such conduct tends to the happiness of his country. Ask him why he serves his country, he will say, his country is a very valuable part of mankind. Why does he study the happiness of mankind? If his affections be really disinterested, he can give no exciting reason for it: the happiness of mankind in general, or of any valuable part of it, is an ultimate end to that series of desires." (Illustrations of the Moral Sense, Francis Hutcheson.) What a vast object is here presented to the intellect to awaken its noblest emotions! The happiness of mankind!! Dr. Paley, at first view, seems to differ very much from President Edwards. But their systems are essentially the same. Dr. Paley makes utility the object of virtue; Edwards, benevolence; and they are opposite ends of the same pole. One is subjective, the other objective. Benevolence seeks lasting utility, and lasting utility flows from benevolence; and it is curious to see how the material mind of Paley fastened on the end he saw best, and the spiritual mind of Edwards entered the depths of the soul to find the intention. But after all, the systems are the same; the one is unintelligible without supposing the other. But what a vast objective do they present to the intellect, in order, through its idealizing, to move the heart. Or, if you make God the object, you still present a vast, growing, infinite idea. When the humblest inquirer is exhorted to love Christ, how much is supposed to be understood! Christ is our prophet, priest, and king; he died for our sins; how came we sinners? the fall of man; the law of God; our guilt and condemnation; our redemption and the need of it, — the whole moral history of the world combines and mingles in the object of this glowing passion; and the system must be understood, in some degree at least, before the passion can be felt. We must see the beauty before we can feel the love. *Non est amor, ubi nihil amatur.** And what is the beauty?

It has been objected to Edwards and Hutcheson, that the love they demand is too metaphysical, — that they present only abstractions, the hardest thing for the mind to feel a passion for. Sir James Mackintosh remarks, that to call us to love Being in general is to present to the mind one of the most incomprehensible objects imaginable, — the least likely to touch our emotions. But they have anticipated this objection and provided for it. Edwards says: "When I say that virtue consists in love to Being in general, I shall not be likely to be understood that no one act of the mind or exercise of love is of the nature of virtue, but what has Being in general, or the great system of universal existence, for its direct and immediate object; so that no exercise of love or kind affec-

---

* Augustine, De Trinitate, Lib. IX. 2. From Hagenbach's History of Doctrines, Vol. I. p. 286.

tion to any one particular being, that is but a small part of that whole, has anything of the nature of true virtue. But that the nature of true virtue consists in a disposition to benevolence towards Being in general; though from such a disposition may arise exercises of love to particular beings, as objects are presented and occasions arise." (Nature of True Virtue, Chap. I.) And Hutcheson says: "We may transiently observe a mistake which some fall into. They suppose, because they have formed some conception of an infinite good, the greatest possible aggregate or sum of happiness, under which all particular pleasures may be included, that there is also some one great ultimate end, with a view to which every particular object is desired; whereas, in truth, each particular pleasure is desired without further view as an ultimate end in the selfish desires. It is true the prospect of a greater inconsistent pleasure may surmount or stop this desire; so may the fear of a prepollent evil. But this does not prove that all men have formed ideas of infinite good, or greatest possible aggregate; or that they have any instinct or desire actually operating without an idea of its object. Just so in the benevolent affections, the happiness of any one person is an ultimate end, desired with no further view; and yet the observing its inconsistency with the happiness of another more beloved, or with the happiness of many, though each one of them were but equally beloved, may overcome the former desire. Yet this will not prove that in each kind action men form the abstract conception of all mankind, or the system of rationals. Such conceptions are indeed useful, that so we may gratify either our self-love or kind affections in the fullest manner, as far as our power extends; and may not content ourselves with smaller degrees either of private or public good while greater are in our power: but when we have formed these conceptions, we do not serve the individual only from the love to the species, no more than we desire grapes with an intention of the greatest aggregate of happiness, or from the apprehension that they make a part of the general sum of our happiness. These conceptions only serve to suggest greater ends than would occur to us without reflection; and by the prepollency of one desire toward the greater good, to either private or public, to stop the desire toward the smaller good, when it appears inconsistent with the greater." (Illustrations of the Moral Sense, Sect. I. pp. 222, 223.) No doubt the mitigations of these profound thinkers were intended to meet an objection thus expressed by Lord Shaftesbury (The Moralist, p. 243): "As for a plain natural love of one single person in either sex, I could compass it, I thought, well enough; but this complex universal sort was beyond my reach. I could love the individual, but not the species. This was too mysterious; too metaphysical an object for me. In short, I could love nothing of which I had not some sensible, material image."

No doubt others have felt the difficulty. When we are told that virtue is love to sentient being in general, we can hardly refuse our assent to the proposition, and yet we find a difficulty in forming so vast a conception to awaken our hearts. The Bible shows the amazing wisdom of God in overcoming this obstacle, — in giving us a medium which preserves the force, without distracting us with the vastness of the object. This is done in two ways. First, the law of God says, "Thou shalt love thy neighbor as thyself." Thy neighbor! consider the term. Not thy friend, thy son, thy relative, or thy countryman, but THY NEIGHBOR, — a specimen of humanity whom the providence of God has placed in thy vicinage, and therefore put within the reach of thy loving-kindness or malignity.* Thy neighbor! who may be a good or a bad man, and whose place may be supplied by another bearing the same relation. Thy love to him also may be practical, and therefore he becomes a just representative of the vast idea. Just as one rose expresses the beauty of a class. † The

---

* "The presence of humanity in the person of his neighbor," is the fine expression of Coleridge. (Friend, No. VI.)

† Burke thus describes the sentimentalism of French philosophy, in his letter to a member of the National Assembly (p. 287): "Benevolence to the whole species, and want of feeling for every individual with whom the professors come in contact, form the character of the new philosophy." The Bible reverses this.

other means of approximating the remote and concentrating the vast comes from the incarnation of the Deity in Jesus Christ. Do you love him? Do you embrace the great idea for which Christ came into the world? If you love him, you love God, you love the universe, you embrace the whole. He lays down his life for our redemption, and all that is dreadful in universal misery or cheering in universal purity and bliss combines in his person to make our regard to him an indication of the state of our hearts, and a certain test of our character. "What think ye of Christ?"

In the lowest form of love there is always an objective, and that objective always addresses the heart through the intellect. You admire a landscape; you say with old Burton (Anatomy of Melancholy, Vol. II. Part 3, Sect. 2): "Whiteness in the lily, red in the rose, purple in the violet, a lustre of all things without life, the clear light of the moon, the bright beams of the sun, splendor of gold, purple, sparkling diamond, the excellent features of the horse, the majesty of the lion, the color of birds, peacocks' tails, the silver scales of fish, we behold with singular delight and admiration." The Greek word $\kappa\acute{o}\sigma\mu o\varsigma$ suggests how mental the beauty on which our passion feeds. Why was such a term applied to the world? It was to express their admiration, and to show how many elements of thought and perception combined in producing it. What a view must the astronomer have to kindle his admiration; and if an undevout astronomer is mad, what an impression must he have if he is sane, of the works of God! Even the lover, before he can justify his raving, must impute every perfection to his mistress.

> "O speak again, bright angel, for thou art
> As glorious to this night, being o'er my head,
> As is a winged messenger of heaven
> Unto the white-upturned, wondering eyes
> Of mortals, that fall back to gaze on him,
> When he bestrides the lazy-pacing clouds,
> And sails upon the bosom of the air."

Thirdly, but there is still a greater wonder about the intellectuality of our moral emotions; and that is, they may be said to *create* the conception about which our reason is employed in moral subjects; what I mean to say is, that reason would have nothing to do about duty or sin, religion or virtue, if we could strike out of our minds all that the heart gives to the mind, or all that the mind reflects back to the heart; the heart must teach the mind what virtue is, and the mind must teach the heart the great objects which virtue seeks.* Let us suppose a being born capable

---

* I was never more struck with the truth of this remark, than in a conversation once with my neighbor, Bartimeus. Bartimeus is a freethinker, and some of his notions are so very free as to astonish everybody but himself. He has undoubtedly cultivated a love of paradox, and loves to say startling things. I have no doubt he has a peculiar mind, but whether it is so very peculiar as he often represents it is a question. He is a very ex-

of one sensation, — intense pain. He is born as Lucretius tells us the infant is born: —

> "Tum porro puer, ut saevis projectus ab undis
> Navita, nudus humi jacet, infans, indigus
> Vitai auxilio."   Lib. V. p. 196.

> "Naked he lies and ready to expire,
> Helpless of all that human wants require;
> Straight with foreboding cries he fills the room,
> Too true presages of his future doom."
>   DRYDEN.

It is evident from this single sensation, that the little speculator cannot be a sceptic on the subject of morals; for pain is too real a thing to leave us to doubt cursive man, and has no great reverence for common sense. He loves to startle and perplex, and never more so than when talking on religion. I often converse with him; sometimes out of curiosity to measure a peculiar mind, and sometimes with the faint hope of doing him good. We were conversing the other day, as usual, about religion, and I was endeavoring to enforce the claims of the Gospel from the inadequacy of all our temporal pursuits to our substantial happiness. I was waxing eloquent, when Bartimeus cut me short by saying that he understood nothing that I uttered; he had not the least feeling of this inadequacy; no longings after immortal happiness; he was perfectly satisfied with this life; and as to death, sleep was what he always prized more than conscious existence, or any felicity it could receive; and an everlasting slumber, which he calmly expected, was the greatest blessing he could receive. The only answer I could make him was, Neighbor, if it is really so, and you have given a just description of your inward nature, I must confess you are victor in our discussion. If your feelings are universal, religion falls to the ground. But what shall I say? I must not call you a liar, — it would be unneighborly and impolite; but yet allow me earnestly to hope that the next time we meet you will say something that I find it possible for me to believe: Adversus negantem principia non est disputandum.

our own existence, or an outward cause, and hence an outward world. The sufferer must rejoice in the removal of the pain; and hence a step towards the idea of happiness. Suppose the sensation of pain and relief, and still more positive happiness, then come the ideas of intention in inflicting the one and bestowing the other, and also the ideas of indifference about each; and hence the ideas of will and intention, and law, and benevolence, and selfishness, and conscience, and virtue and vice, — all clustering around the first simple sensation. It appears probable that our longings after immortality and our first ideas of immortal felicity come in this way; for suppose a being thus to suffer and thus to be relieved, as Plato has said, must not such a being have an aversion to misery and a desire of happiness? and on the principle that it desires happiness, must it not desire more happiness, and is not the more the longer? Can we conceive of a being having one moment of felicity, not wishing for two, ten, ten thousand, and so on to an everlasting duration? So when we see a suffering infant, we see the foundation nature has laid for the sublime conception of an everlasting heaven. Even the justice of God himself becomes conceivable from the same experience. The proof is complete; it is both analytic and synthetic. Suppose the capacity of the happiness and the pain, and the whole world of moral ideas rises; take away that capacity, and I see not, though all the world should be intellectual (if intellection is supposable without the capacity of suffering or happiness),— I see not how virtue, merit, conscience, law, justice in God or man, could exist. They would have no material; no relation; no intelligible exponent; no existence. I doubt whether even a theory could be formed of them. Take the very etymology of the word benevolence,— good-will; wishing well. But how can you wish well unless you wish relief from suffering, or the imparting or increase of relief, or happiness? Your moral terms must have an exponent. This is what Dr. Campbell means, I suppose, when he says: "No hypothesis hitherto invented hath shown that, by means of the discursive faculty, without the aid of any other mental power, we could ever obtain a notion of either the beautiful or the good." (Philos. of Rhetoric, Vol. I. p. 204.) And Hutcheson before had said: "Perhaps what has brought the epithet reasonable, or flowing from reason, in opposition to what flows from instinct, affection, or passion, so much into use, is this, that it is often observed that the very best of our particular affections or desires, when they are grown violent and passionate, through the confused sensations and propensities which attend them, make us incapable of considering calmly the whole tendency of our actions, and lead us often into what is absolutely pernicious, under some appearance of relative or particular good. This, indeed, may give some ground for distinguishing between passionate actions and those from calm desire or affection which employs our reason freely; but can never set rational actions in opposition to those from instinct, desire, or affection. And it must be owned that the most perfect virtue consists in the calm unpassionate benevolence, rather than particular affections." (The Moral Sense, p. 283.)

Perhaps Hutcheson goes too far when he calls this passion an instinct. The objective of an instinct is not always seen by the being that feels it. I am laboring to prove that in all intellectual beings it is an exalted affection; it comprehends its own end. Hutcheson always adds, "or affection,"—instinct, or affection. President Edwards has beautifully corrected this defect in Hutcheson in his Essay on Virtue, chapter eighth, which is the profoundest part of that profound Essay.

We come, then, to the conclusion, that our lowest sensation is the latent foundation of our highest knowledge. Love is the original, all-pervading idea in religion; and the nature of love is known by what it seeks. It is the character of God himself that he "shall wipe away all tears from their eyes." (Rev. xxi. 4.) That tells the whole secret. Without the previous conception of happiness and misery, morality and religion have no existence. These open the sphere for all the virtues, human or divine; and this is perhaps what Bishop Tayler meant when he said:

"Every man understands more of religion by his affections than by his reason. It is not the wit of the man, but the spirit of the man; not so much his head as his heart that learns the divine philosophy." (Via Intelligentiae.)

The writers who, like Cudworth, More, etc., have traced virtue and vice to our reason, have always been obliged (consciously or unconsciously) to enlarge the meaning. Reason with them is not the power of reasoning; it is the comprehensive source of all our moral knowledge.

Perhaps it may be too nice a speculation, but I cannot help thinking that the reason why the fearful threatening of an eternal hell is so clearly revealed in the Bible, is not always clearly understood. The thought steals on me when I read some of Lord Shaftesbury's speculations concerning the mercenary nature of a religion founded on rewards and punishments. Is it the design of the doctrine of eternal punishment to address our fears only? Is the opposition solely between a crouching and a disinterested spirit? Do we not gain his Lordship's avowed object better in the teaching of Christ than his own? God is love; the magnitude of his love is seen in its exponents. He delivers us from a great ruin. The Gospel is a great salvation; great, because it pardons and removes great sin. But sin, likewise, is seen in its exponents. Eternal punishment is the fact, the measure in which we see the extent of our sin and the justice of God. O when such a load is felt to be merited, and when Divine compassion takes it off,—then we see how great His mercy to the children of men! In a word, the man that believes his sins to be so great as justly to plunge him in all this ruin, and sees the compassion of Christ in taking away this penalty by his own substituted suffering, has the conception of a favor which no one can conceive in any other way. The purpose of hell, then, is not to work on our fears solely, or mainly, but to show the infinite magnitude of the love of God. Again, Divine love must be a disinterested passion. But what possible opportunity is there for an heroic self-sacrifice where there is no danger? Paul shows the highest flight of this spirit when he says: "I could wish myself accursed from Christ for my brethren, my kinsmen according to the flesh." Lastly, if we love God, it must be for his perfections. Justice is one; now the dreadful penalty takes us from our finite conceptions to the great idea which cannot exist unless verified by facts. This is the great fact, which presents us at once with a mirror and a test; a mirror to see what Divine justice is, and a test to see whether we bow to its manifestation.

In fine, run through the whole vocabulary of religion,—ruin, redemption, a Saviour, a sacrifice, mercy, justice, repentance, faith, a conscience, a law, sin, holiness,—we shall find that they all derive their meaning from the sentient nature of man, and from the concepts which, if reason uses, the passions and feelings alone can create, or make intelligible.

I need not, therefore, avail myself of the common remark that the passions are useful to stir up the sluggish intellect, to concentrate the attention, and to put the powers of the soul in motion, —

> "The rising tempest puts in act the soul,
> Parts it may ravage, but preserves the whole," —

since they CREATE their own vision, and give coloring to the picture which justifies their existence.

This subject may explain how it is that in religion such sudden revolutions happen in the mind. To-day a man cannot see the proofs of revelation; it is all a dream to him; to-morrow it becomes a dread reality, — all his views are changed. Are such sudden impressions enthusiasm? Are they miraculous? No, neither; but the foundation impression is made on his heart. The elements of a new reasoning enter his soul. He has found out that pain may come from sin; and as pain is a reality, so sin is a reality, and from these dread realities relief is desirable. The Gospel now has a meaning, because it has an object. The feelings are inspiring, — they really give the ideas. It is true that all know what pain is; but when sin and danger are positive conceptions because deeply felt, then all the truths of the Gospel have an end and a reality never seen before. They have a foundation in experience.

Another mystery may be explained by the view which we have taken. All anthropology leads us to recognize the ignorance of man. Whether you trace knowledge to reason, or experience, the one is feeble, and the other is of yesterday, and knows comparatively nothing. In matter, for example, no analysis is final, — no chemist has as yet found the elements of things, or can conceive or imagine how they can be found; that is, you cannot imagine yourself to find a substance so simple as to give you certain proof that it is not susceptible of a new analysis. Nature keeps retiring as with new implements we pursue her, and no one can say that a simple substance has yet been found. Every discovery reveals new questions and new ignorance; and even the known leads to the unknown. So in metaphysics, who can say that the permanent terminology has yet been found. Every analysis has been analyzed upon, and the absolute idea eludes our grasp. It is not sceptics alone, like Hume, that enforce this confession of ignorance in order to perplex our faith, but the most earnest writers, the most sincere, have been the first to allow it. Nay, even the Bible itself says, "We see through a glass darkly." (1 Cor. xiii. 12.) Let any one read the thirty-eighth, thirty-ninth, and fortieth chapters of Job, and reflect on the testimony of God himself to a position which, by denying all *human* wisdom, leads to the truest wisdom. Pascal owns it. Bishop Butler, the acutest of all moral writers, and the most earnest, lays the foundation of his whole system in the ignorance of man. "Our own nature, and the objects we are surrounded with, serve to raise our curiosity; but we are quite out of a condition of satisfying it. Every secret which is disclosed, every discovery which is made, every new effect which is brought to view, serves to convince us of numberless more which remain concealed, and which we had before no suspicion of. And what if we were acquainted with the whole creation, in the same way and as thoroughly as we are with any single object of it. What would all this natural knowledge amount to? It must be a low curiosity indeed which such superficial knowledge could satisfy. On the contrary, would it not serve to convince us of our ignorance still, and to raise our desire of knowing the nature of things themselves, the author, the cause, and the end of them?" (Sermons, Ser. XV.) And in his Analogy he says: "To us probability is the guide of life."

Indeed, every self-knowing man must assent to the proofs offered by philosophers, repeated by saints, and confirmed by the solemn testimony of inspiration itself. We seldom find an intelligent believer in revelation who is not something of a distrustful sceptic in philosophy.

But now comes the difficulty. How shall we reconcile the testimony to the weakness of our powers with the claims of revelation? Our Saviour requires faith, — strong faith, — strong enough to conquer our sins and throw us even on martyrdom. We must take up our cross; we must have a strength of principle which pleasure cannot soften nor danger subdue. In short, we must be enthusiasts in his cause. But did enthusiasm ever arise in a speculating, questioning, objecting, balancing, doubtful mind? Does it not spring from deep conviction? Must not the mind be sure before the heart can burn? Could Bayle, Gibbon, Hume, be religious enthusiasts? And does not even the reverential Butler, — though he answers objections wonderfully, and satisfies our intellectual nature, — does he not in his Sermons and Analogy leave the reader's heart as cold as his own? This objection to such rational but weak convictions is an old one. It was made by Lucullus in Cicero to the old Academics, whose views of human ignorance were very similar to those of Butler: "Maxime vero virtutum cognitio confirmat, percipi et comprehendi multa posse. In quibus solis inesse scientiam dicimus; quam nos non comprehensionem modo rerum, sed eam stabilem quoque atque immutabilem esse censemus: itemque sapientiam, artem vivendi, quae ipsa ex sese habeat constantiam. Ea autem constantia si nihil habeat percepti et cogniti, quaero, unde nata sit et quammodo? Quaero etiam, ille vir bonus, qui statuit omnem cruciatum perferre, intolerabili dolore lacerari, potius quam aut officium prodat, aut fidem, cur has sibi tam graves leges imposuerit, cum, quamobrem ita oporteret, nihil haberet comprehensi, percepti, cogniti, constituti? Nullo igitur modo fieri potest, ut quisquam tanti aestimet aequitatem et fidem, ut ejus conservandae causa nullum supplicium recuset, nisi iis rebus assensus sit, quae falsae esse non possunt." (Cicero's Lucullus, Sect. 8.) And we all feel that ardor leads to strong conviction, and strong conviction increases our ardor. Hence our Saviour inculcates strong faith on his disciples, and they pray to him, " Lord, increase our faith."

Now how are these opposite claims of our nature to be met? How are we to avoid at once the blind confidence of a deluded mind, and the cold indifference of a doubting heart?

The answer, it seems to me, is suggested in this wonderful Song of Solomon, and in the view of our nature and of religion to which it leads us. The bride is full of ardor to her celestial bridegroom, and has no doubt of the beauty she perceives. He is to her the chief among ten thousand, and altogether lovely. She is at least sure of *that*. Her confidence does not come from a doubtful solution of doubtful doubts, but from a vivid perception of unspeakable excellence. "My beloved is like a roe or a young hart: behold, he standeth behind our wall, he looketh forth at the windows, showing himself through the lattice." (Solomon's Song, ii. 9.) Religion has a region of its own. Divine beauty warrants its own reality; and then it stands on the basis of one of our most certain conceptions.

Take the Platonic way of proving, first supposing the existence of a principle, then its non-existence; place it, take it away, and see the consequences of each hypothesis. First, let us deny that an individual has any perception or any belief that his susceptibility of pleasure or pain have anything to do, as exponents or effects, with justice or benevolence in God or man; or suppose the perception to be feeble or doubtful; of course the world of religious ideas is lost to him, — he can no more be susceptible to religious impressions than iron can have the malleability of lead. Tell him the story of the good Samaritan, or of Christ dying on the cross; it is lost to him, — he cannot believe in a world that he cannot see. Place the perception before him, with all its circling host of beauties and glories, and a new scene opens. The ideal is at least beautiful. Give him the relish for benevolence, — the aim, the design, the pleasure, — and his ardor is kindled, and he knows how to found a strong faith on a system that has every evidence but that of a mathematical demonstration. His metaphysical proof, perhaps, has not increased, but his heart burns.

I lately looked out of my window, and saw the fragment of a rainbow painted on the fragment of a cloud. Whatever a rainbow may be as a series of causes, it is, it was, supremely beautiful; and its beauty is nine tenths of its existence. My admiration was fixed on its greatest reality.

This, then, is the nature of strong faith. It is strong relative to the powers of man, because it is felt under the condition of feeble powers, moral proofs, natural doubts, sinful blindness, and a perception vivid enough to overcome them all. It is strong, as the earthquake is strong when it shakes the mountain, because it overcomes the strong power of gravitation. It is strong, because it can conquer the natural apathy and scepticism of the human heart. It is strong as a lighthouse beam is strong in a stormy night when it shines over a dark sea.

Our Saviour seems to sanction our view of the origin of all the benevolent affections, and, of course, all virtue in our susceptibilities of pain and happiness, when he says: "All things whatsoever ye would that men should do to you, do ye even so to them; for this is the law and the prophets." (Matt. vii. 12.) This passage is an appeal to our experience, — our Lord makes our selfishness our instructor. The meaning seems to be, You have suffered from your fellow-men; you know the bitterness of an injury. Have you been neglected, scorned, slandered, imprisoned? Let your sufferings instruct you, and beware how you inflict what you shudder to feel. On the other hand, have you been relieved? Have you heard the sweet voice of consolation? Were you hungry, and did some one feed you? Were you in prison, and did he come unto you? It is at once a lesson and a motive to scatter the bliss which your own experience has taught you to prize. Now, in all this, is not the assumption that all our moral conceptions spring up from one centre, our sentient nature, our susceptibility of pain and pleasure, the exponent of a good or bad intention in him that imparts them?

There is yet another application of this subject. Our Saviour says: "Wisdom is justified of all her children" (Luke vii. 35); implying, no doubt, that she is not justified by those who are not her children. And it is curious to see how, in all the forms in which the wisdom of God is manifested, men judge as their moral taste directs their attention. Everything has two handles, and we may take hold of it by the best or the worst. We can scarcely admit a moral or political hypothesis, but we can collect a train of facts to support it. If there be a God, no doubt the material creation is a manifestation of his wisdom; but then, as Burke says, "a mind that has no restraint from its own weakness, would not find it difficult to criticise creation itself. Indeed, it has been done. That beautiful order which Cicero's Lucullus sees in the creation — "Terra vestita floribus," &c.,

in the Second Book *De Natura Deorum* — is reversed completely by Lucretius in his Fifth Book. The one says the earth is so beautiful that it must have been made by God; the other says it is so abominably bad that it cannot be the work of a good being.

> "Nequaquam nobis divinitus esse paratam
> Naturam rerum, tanta stat praedita culpa."
> *De Rerum Natura*, Lib. V.

Where Dr. Paley finds such proofs of wise design, the Epicurean sees nothing but disorder and confusion; and the way they prove their point is, — the theist selects all the good things in creation he can find, and the infidel all that he fancies to be bad; the one fastens on the rose, and the other the thorn; so, in surveying the course of providence, how different the selection! The pious man can tell you how often his prayers have been answered, and the sceptic can show how often they have been frustrated. Bayle and St. Bernard would each have their long catalogue, not one item of which would be the same. Claudian differed from himself; and, in Diogenes's view, Harpalus bears witness against the very existence of the gods. The question whether the good old times were better than the present, always sets different men to selecting different series of facts. In order to prove that mankind have degenerated, all you have to do is, hunt up the heroes, collect their good deeds leave out all their faults and imperfections, throw into shade common life, present the worst side of modern life, — in short, instead of two full pictures, get two profiles of faults concealed and beauties selected, and *vice versa*, and you can prove your point to your own complete satisfaction. But there is no place where our Saviour's remark is more applicable than to the Bible. If the Bible is the *Word*, it is, of course, the wisdom of God; here wisdom is justified of *all* her children, and of none others. I have often admired, in reading the criticisms of Eichhorn, Rosenmüller, Strauss, &c., how ingenious they are in finding all that makes against supernaturalism, and nothing in its favor. It is really marvellous. Difficulties which I never thought of — which occurred not to the Calvins and Pooles, and even the Grotiuses of the Reformation — spring up in their minds like weeds among the flowers. Thus the story of the garden of Eden and the Fall, illustrating the purpose and design of God, is a myth; the flood, instead of being a surprising miracle, is an impossibility; the awful darkness on Sinai is a thunder-storm, and, some say, a brushwood fire kindled by Moses; while the wonderful law engraved on tables of stone (certainly wonderful for the charlatan that kindled the brushwood fire) attracts no attention. The sublime unity which runs through the Old Testament and the New, such as is shown by Edwards in his History of Redemption, they never see nor suspect. The Bible to them is a book of fragments. Its supernaturalism is not needed, and has, therefore, no end or aim. They expatiate on the trifling laws in Leviticus, but not a word about the remarkable book, Deuteronomy. The ritual of Moses they gloat on; the pure devotion of the Psalms they cannot see;— in short, there reigns in all their works this sophism: with a perverse ingenuity to select all the archaisms of the Bible, exaggerate them and turn them into myths, ignore all that is sublime and spiritual, totally to overlook its unity, and thus prove that the Bible cannot receive our veneration as the word of God. O what blindness! O what penetration! Penetration to see all that has the shadow of an objection, and blindness to all the truth by which the objection might be removed. If Psyche, when she was ordered to select the seeds, had taken the poppy and vetches to herself, and left wheat and barley to the goddess of beauty, she would have left us an expressive myth of modern learning.

Now the question comes, How is it that men, professing to be scholars, — and some of them Christians, — can see the word of God in such a wonderful light? We can only quote the Saviour's maxim, — "Wisdom is justified of all her children." The reason why men select in this way must be that they have no perception of the glory that gilds the sacred page. If the wisdom of God is there, they certainly do not see it.

I allow, indeed, that there are difficulties in the sacred history; but I utterly deny that a man is prepared to encounter them until he has seen the wisdom with which they are combined. No man is fit even to weed a garden, until he is taught, both by taste and experience, to distinguish the weeds from the flowers. I will only add, that I suppose all the apparent weeds in the garden of God (i. e. the apparent myths in this ancient record) to arise from the Divine condescension to the wants of mankind. If the Bible comes from the sublimest of Beings, we must equally remember it is addressed to the meanest.

V.

THE DRAMATIC ELEMENT IN INTERPRETING THE BIBLE.

The first and most important principle in the Christian religion is to believe in the existence and authority of a Divine revelation. Our religion is founded on faith, and our faith rests on a Divine testimony. God has spoken, and "the voice of the Lord is powerful; the voice of the Lord is full of majesty." It is implied in a revelation, that we have more power to see and prove that the Bible is a Divine revelation, than we have to foretell what its components should be, — that is, we have a *recognizing*, but not an *inventing* power.

The authority of Scripture depends on inspiration. "All Scripture is given by inspiration of God." (2 Timothy iii. 16.)

I am in favor of adopting the highest ideas of inspiration. The teachings of God cannot be too complete. He has exhausted the power of language. It is a marvellous instrument used by an omniscient tongue. So that we may say, with Hilarius: "De intelligentia haeresis, non de scriptura; et sensus, non sermo, fit crimen;" — "Heresy arises from misunderstanding the Scripture; not from any defect in the Scripture itself. The fault is in the interpretation."

But though I believe in the highest inspiration, for that very reason I do not believe in a verbal inspiration.

The reasons for not believing in a verbal inspiration are: —

First, it is not necessary to the highest accuracy; a single word is not the best way to fix an important meaning. Secondly, if the inspiration were verbal, it would cease with the first translation, and no one pretends that translators were inspired. Thirdly, the Apostles are very careless about verbal accuracy. They have a holy indifference to a minute and literal exactness. They quote from the Septuagint, and sometimes apparently from memory. Fourthly, God has not preserved the copies verbally perfect, which seems necessary to place us on a level with the first receivers of the Word. He is no respecter of persons. Fifthly, each writer shows his own spontaneous genius. Sixthly, the Greek language makes a distinction between λόγοι and ῥήματα, — the mental and the spoken word, — and it seems to confine inspiration to the former. Seventhly, in the parallel places (as the inscription of the cross, &c.) there is a verbal variety. How is this, if the Scriptures aimed to teach us a verbal inspiration?* Eighthly, if verbal accuracy had been necessary, God would hardly have chosen so primitive a language as the Hebrew as a vehicle of the greater part of inspiration. And, lastly, none of the passages claimed as teaching verbal inspiration necessitate that meaning, as 1 Cor. ii. 13; *not in the words of mortal wisdom, but* λόγοι *which the Holy Ghost teacheth, interpreting spiritual thoughts in spiritual terminology.* And further, the most important words in revelation depend upon something behind themselves. A long history is sometimes given to prepare the way for the conception of a word. Thus the word GOD would not be understood by a pagan mind. The history of what God has done shows who God is. CREATOR is a word that poorly imparts its own meaning. Providence, soul, sacrifice, expiation, the Holy Spirit, Divine influence, faith, justification, an apostle, — all are terms which are explained by their collocation in the great system. We must travel beyond the word to find its

---

* The two recensions of the eighteenth Psalm are sufficient to show that the sacred writers did not embark their meaning in a bottom of frail verbalisms. Let the reader compare the readings in 2 Samuel xxii. and those in the eighteenth Psalm, and mark the significance. Two things are noticeable; — first, the verbal variety, precluding all possibility of contingency, and secondly, the non-importance of the difference. Not one of the changes in the later copy (whichever it be) has more than a shade of change in the meaning. The lesson of comparing the two seems to be, — Be not a pedant; be not a word-catcher, that lives on syllables; rise to the grandeur of a Divine conception, and place the strength of Scripture where God, by his own example, has placed it.

meaning. If you insist on a verbal inspiration, you inevitably narrow your mind down to a partial conception, and, of course, a weaker one; to say nothing of the host of difficulties which you raise against your system, which will inject doubts into other minds, if not your own. The Bible is as perfect as it can be. It has the perfection of God.

The aim of the verbalists is good, but is not reached. The sacred writers seem to feel very much as a lawyer does in making out his declaration or rejoinder in a cause; he dare not trust *one* word,—he varies his expressions; and I have been told that Judge Parsons was accustomed to say, "Better use twenty words too many, than one too few." The Hebrew language is always correcting itself,—repeating the idea. You see the relics of picture-writing. The parallelisms in Psalms, Proverbs, Job, the Prophets, are remarkable, and they use poetry and comparison endlessly,—just like men who did not embark their meaning in a single delegated word. Indeed, the question becomes useless when we remember the omniscience and general perfection of God. Contingencies are nothing to him. His will shines through them. The Syro-Chaldaic was spoken in Palestine in the time of Christ, and Dr. Davidson thinks Matthew was written in this dialect. So the most important teacher eludes our verbal grasp. The original verbal inspiration of Christ's discourses is not preserved to us.

One of the difficulties respecting inspiration arises from not understanding its nature and design, — in whose mind it originates, and to what purpose it is directed. It originates in the Divine mind, and is a perfection of God, and its object is to set before man an infallible standard of religious instruction. It is a perfection of God, or rather emanates from his perfection, and therefore transcends the artificial and postulated perfection of man. When men hear of perfection, they immediately think of a minute, pedantic perfection of their own. God's perfection is not our perfection, as "his ways are not our ways, nor his thoughts our thoughts." I grant that Divine inspiration implies an infallible rule; but that rule lies deeper than some suppose. The rule is infallible when we find it; just as the healing root is powerful when we dig it from the earth. The material world, I have no doubt, for the Divine design is perfect. It was built and shaped by an unerring hand. But how many random contingencies are revealed beneath its surface! The central heat, the sea, the frost, the rain, the warring elements, in all their apparent discord, have combined to build up the beautiful surface of our inhabited earth, — a wise result from the most chaotic operations. Nature tumbles her elements into a divine order. Wisdom is there with a veil over her face.

So with regard to inspiration; it conforms to no rules of postulated perfection. I object to a literal, verbal inspiration, because it does not place the authority of the Bible high enough. It transcends all such narrow rules. The dispute whether God gave the very words to Isaiah or Ezekiel, and whether the affirmative is necessary to the highest authority of Scripture, forgets one manifest perfection in the Author of inspiration; and that is, his foresight of all contingencies, and the impossibility that Isaiah or Ezekiel, if they were selected by his wisdom, should cross his intentions. Paul was a *chosen vessel.* Did not God know his genius, his character, his turn of thought, his favorite expressions, all he had done and all he would do, and, when he was writing his Epistles, did he for a single moment evade the eye of Omniscience? Let us illustrate. We read (2 Samuel viii. 16, 17) that, when David was king, " Joab the son of Zeruiah was over the host; and Jehoshaphat the son of Ahilud was recorder; and Zadok the son of Ahitub, and Ahimelech the son of Abiathar, were the priests; and Seraiah was scribe." We will suppose that the king wishes Seraiah to make out some written despatch to convey his royal will to some remote part of the kingdom. He knows very well his capacity, his style, — often the very words he will use. He chose him on the grounds of this knowledge. The order is made out, is read to the king; he approves or suggests some correction. The order is sealed and sent. Now, I ask, can anything be conceived, as far as language can go, more adequately to convey the mind of the king? He is sagacious; he selected the man; he knows his style, and he has reviewed his composition;—and yet the writing has all the peculiarities of style and expression belonging to Seraiah, and not to David. But when we ascend to an infallible God, and consider his omniscient foresight and perfection, how much stronger becomes the case! It is utterly superfluous to ask for words, the dress of thought, when we have the thing itself beaming into the soul. If the inspiration were merely verbal, the infallibility would cease with the first translation. But now it stands on higher ground. It transcends all language,—it is above the imperfection of the instrument that conveys it. It is "holy light, the bright effluence of bright essence increate."

I pass by many other imperfections, which, as a darkling veil, seem to cloud this recondite perfection of God,—such as the errors in the copies, the imperfections of an early language in which the older part of the Bible is written; the unexact chronology; the discrepancies of the books that relate the same things and cover the same period; the harshness of some commands, and the vindictive piety which appears in the prayer and praises of the early saints,—all these are explained, or greatly mitigated, by our imperfect judgments, formed at a distance from the scene. There is one mode of instruction adopted by the sacred writers which has perplexed the doctrine of inspiration more than any other; I allude to the DRAMATIC ELEMENT, which the sacred writers have often chosen to impress their sentiments, and which has failed of its purpose because in interpreting it we apply a rule demanded only by our artificial exactions.

When you depart from the didactic school, all the other methods of instructing become necessary and important, such as rhetoric, poetry, painting, tautology, figures, soliloquies, and dialogues. These are eminently the implements of thought in an early age. They are used by the sacred writers, and inspiration itself has chosen them to clothe its instructions in. But one form most frequently used has been least understood, and that is *the dramatic*, — and even learned critics have hardly comprehended its laws when applied to the Bible. The reason is, they hardly have been conscious of its existence. They have hardly recognized this important element in its infant form, in an early age. They have not felt that we should interpret the Bible as we do Æschylus or Shakespeare, making, indeed, due allowance for the degree of development. It is well known that all the families of languages cognate to the Hebrew were spoken by a people as remote from the drama as possible, — the Ethiopians, the Arabs, the Jews; they never had the drama in the Greek form. They had no stage. Even the Caliphs of Bagdad and the Arabs in Spain had no proper drama; and the Jewish literature throughout seems very remote from it. But because a people have no *formal* drama, it does not follow that they have no budding elements, no embryos of it, from which its manhood first grew. I have sometimes thought that the want of a developed drama only necessitated the use of a greater portion of these incipient modules. The dramatic is essential to man. Our whole intercourse of life is a conversation. We never go into company without a scene and a dialogue. We may say the scene is a wood, a meadow, a parlor, or a car; and the dialogue was so and so, witty or pathetic, interesting or otherwise. Now this peculiar form in which the Biblical drama meets us has deceived the critics. It is never formal, it is often transient, and it is always infantine. It is sometimes a single soliloquy; it is often a mental dialogue; the dialogists are never announced; the changes in the persons are sudden; there is never a regular plot. It is a fragment of a drama; it is the picturing of passion, hope, fear, resentment, grief, repentance, temptation, agony, despair, — things which demand a dramatic interpretation without warning you of a dramatic form. Thus the Book of Ecclesiastes is a continued record of personal disappointment, in which the future is taught under the paulo-post present. "It is a certain fact," says Professor Richardson, "confirmed by universal experience, and it may be laid down as an important axiom in the study of human nature, that our notions and opinions are ever influenced by our present temper. Happy is the man that is often calm and dispassionate; who, impelled by no eager appetite, nor urged by any restless affection, sees every object by the unerring light of reason, and is not imposed upon by the fallacious medium of his desires." (A Philosophical Analysis and Illustration of some of Shakespeare's Remarkable Characters.) Now, this profound remark, which Richardson applies to explain the difficult character of Hamlet, is the very key to explain the Book of Ecclesiastes. Every sentiment of the book is the coloring of the moment, and as the author recovers the healthful tone of the heart through his own experience, he comes to a more correct view of life and of God. This whole result, this grand effect, this total impression, is the infallible instruction of inspiration. The Fifty-first Psalm is a soliloquy of one under the sorrows of repentance. It is a picture of its progress. You might say,—Scene, a closet; David alone, leaning his head on his hand; his neglected harp unstrung; tears falling from his eyes; and in a tremulous voice he speaks, חָנֵּנִי, Mercy, have mercy! In one verb, he puts words into our mouth, thoughts into the mind, emotions into the heart. Something far more powerful than didactics can reach. So the Hundred and Third Psalm is the language of prosperity. In the Prophets, the germs of a dialogue appear and vanish so suddenly, that our Occidental slowness can hardly follow them; and yet the drama is there, — the primitive drama, intelligible only to him whose exercised taste grasps the design.

Perhaps it will be objected, that, if this principle be admitted, it throws the meaning so far back that the book intended for the common reader becomes unintelligible to him. No, — the unintelligibility belongs to a mind in the transition state, — the half-learned, not the primitive. Common life, even now, is full of such dramas, so uttered and so understood. When a man cries out "Murder!" or "Fire!" he is not laying down a proposition, but he is expressing a passion. If a watchman in Boston were to say, There is a murder now being committed in State Street, opposite to number thirty-seven, at this very hour, half past one, of this foggy night, — no one would believe him. The difficulty is, we approach the Bible in the anti-original state. It was eminently popular and perfectly intelligible in its day; and even now many of its passages would be better understood by a pious old woman with good taste, than by a half-learned professor whose taste had been manufactured for him. Three things deceive us, and prevent our applying the simple rule; — first, the great antiquity of the book; secondly, the informal and primitive character of the dramatic element; and thirdly, the solemnity of its instruction; or, in other words, inspiration at first view seems to necessitate a perfection which would supersede and destroy all the human modes of teaching. Hence the modern reader approaches the Bible in a frame of mind the very excellence of which deceives him. It is important for us to have veneration; but let us remember an uninstructed veneration may sometimes mislead us.

Every scholar knows that Plato's Dialogues, as to their diction, are written with all the airy lightness of conversational life. But they are on great subjects; they are written in Greek; the dialogue is sustained by Socrates, the great philosopher; and the airy conversational tone is the very difficulty which impedes the early learner in finding the meaning or relishing the beauty. There is an expression in the Phædo of Plato which the beginner is very apt to misconstrue, ἀλλά μοι πάλαι πράγματα παρέχει (E. 63), through the lightness of tone, which escapes the elaborate state of mind with which we must acquire the Greek language. The same may be said of the latent irony found in the Dialogue De Oratoribus, sometimes attributed to Tacitus (Sect. 40, 41).

It has been supposed by some that a dramatic writer in painting a passion obscures his direct sentiment. It is not so when it is his intention to reveal it. It is just as clear under this form as any other. Can any one suppose that, when Shakespeare put all the epicurean ribaldry that a London tavern could afford into the mouth of Falstaff, he intended it as his own sentiments, or the sentiments of a moral teacher? or when the Friar talks to Romeo in the passion and despair of his pupil, that he did *not* mean it as the words of true wisdom? or when Mrs. More, in her drama of "Moses in the Bulrushes," puts these words into the mouth of Miriam, —

> "Know this ark is charmed
> With incantations Pharaoh ne'er employed,
> With spells that impious Egypt never knew;
> With invocations to the living God
> I twisted every slender reed together,
> And with a prayer did every osier weave," —

she is not teaching her own piety in the personage she has formed? A good character generally utters good sentiments; and even a bad character may be the vehicle of direct instruction, as in the following speech of the King in Hamlet: —

> "'T is sweet and commendable in your nature, Hamlet,
> To give these mourning duties to your father;
> But you must know, your father lost a father;
> That father lost, lost his; and the survivor bound
> In filial obligation, for some term,
> To do obsequious sorrow; but to persever
> In obstinate condolement is a course
> Of impious stubbornness; 't is unmanly grief;
> It shows a will most incorrect to heaven," &c.
> *Hamlet*, Act I. Scene 2.

PARTICULAR APPLICATION OF THE DRAMATIC PRINCIPLE OF INTERPRETATION.

OUR first business is to state to ourselves the difficulties. First, we must remember it is the infant and primitive drama, in its Jewish conception, undeveloped, — where the object is not delight, but instruction. No regular plot, no fixed characters; but the object is cursory illustration. Secondly, it is important to know who are the speakers; for, in consequence of the vivacity of the early mind, the transitions are very quick and sudden, and the speaker's name is not always announced. Thirdly, a great difficulty is to fill up a natural ellipsis (natural to that age), and this, indeed, is one chief difficulty in all Hebrew poetry. And, lastly, as in all the drama, to see through the veil of character, to reach the didactic intentions of the author; and this, I must contend, is not more difficult in the dramatic than in any other mode of instruction. The great rule of distinguishing the mere painting of character from the direct lesson is — THE INTENTION OF THE AUTHOR.

But let us specify. Take the Book of Job as an example. Let us ask the question, Where are the teachings of inspiration found? We dismiss the question of the antiquity of this book, as, for our purpose, a point of no importance. It is obvious that much that is said by the speakers cannot be true as maxims of direct instruction; for God himself says, "They have not spoken of me the thing that is right, as my servant Job hath." They are suspicious, jealous; they accuse him of false sentiments, and pervert right sentiments by a false application to him; and even Job himself can scarcely be defended in some of his complaints: " Let the day perish wherein I was born, and the night in which it was said, There is a man-child conceived. Let that day be darkness; let not God regard it from above, neither let the light shine upon it." These feelings are not to be approved,— these sentiments are not to be copied. But surely the intention of the author is obvious. In the case of Job's jealous friends, we are taught that men should not judge of established piety by superficial appearances, and that true maxims become dangerous by being falsely applied. We may often utter the truth on a wrong occasion; our motives may be defective, when our tongues are wise; and as to Job himself, we may see how real piety may be clouded by impatience; how a good man may be an imperfect man; how deep affliction tries the soul and produces indulgence from God; and how, more than all, an undeveloped faith (for such was Job's condition,— he did not live under the last revelations of immortality) plunges the soul into perplexity, and sharpens the pang which it cannot remove. In Job's perplexity we see what he wanted by what he felt. He wanted the Gospel,— its certainty, its support, its triumph, its consolation. Compare his speech with that of Paul: " We rejoice in the hope of the glory of God; and not only so, we glory in tribulations also; knowing that tribulation worketh patience, and patience experience, and experience hope, and hope maketh not ashamed."

When the design is double, that is, when a character is pictured, and in picturing it a true sentiment is uttered, the design of the author is equally clear Take the speech of Eliphaz the Temanite, in the fourth chapter: "Now a thing was secretly brought me, and mine ear received a little thereof. In thoughts from the visions of the night, when deep sleep falleth on men, fear came upon me, and trembling, which made all my bones to shake. Then a spirit passed before my face; the hair of my flesh stood up. It stood still, but I could not discern the form thereof; an image was before mine eyes; there was silence, and I heard a voice, saying, Shall mortal man be more just than God? shall a man be more pure than his Maker? Behold he put no trust in his servants, and his angels he charged with folly. How much less in them that dwell in houses of clay, whose foundation is in the dust, which are crushed before the moth?" Who does not see the correctness of these sentiments, and the falseness of the application? The character of the speaker is most beautifully seen in both these circumstances. He was too good a man to utter a falsehood; he was too wise a man to reason from false premises; and he was too much blinded by suspicion and prejudice to make a right application. The didactic truth of the sentiment does not destroy the painting of character, but rather heightens it.

Let us adduce one example more, — the famous passage, Job xix. 25, 26 : "For I know that my Redeemer liveth, and that he shall stand at the latter day upon the earth; and though, after my skin, worms shall destroy this body, yet in my flesh shall I see God: whom I shall see for myself, and mine eyes shall behold, and not another, though my reins be consumed within me." Dr. Noyes translates it thus: "Yet I know that my Vindicator liveth, and will stand up at length on the earth; and though with my skin this body be wasted away, yet in my flesh I shall see God. Yea, I shall see him my friend; my eyes shall behold him no longer an adversary, for this my soul panteth within me." Dathè has it thus: "Enim vero novi vindicem meum vivere, tandemque pulverem oppugnaturum esse. Deponam cutem meam, quam ista arrodunt. Atque e carne mea Deum videbo. Hunc ego mihi videbo. Hunc ego mihi videbo propitium, oculi mei eum videbunt, non amplius inimicum. Vehementer desidero hanc causae meae decisionem." — "I know that my Vindicator liveth, and that at length he will defend my dust; I shall lay aside my skin, which these sores and worms deform; and in my flesh I shall see my God. I shall see him for myself; I shall see him propitious to me. My eyes shall see him, no more an enemy. This is the decision of my cause which I desire."

Take either of these translations, and the best way of arriving at the true meaning is, to interpret it on the dramatic principle. Indeed, there is no other rational. Job, in his sorrow and perplexity, looks round for some hope. He is a good man; he has a heart-born faith, that rests upon a most imperfect revelation. He has a disposition to trust, with an insight into the promises. In his agony, from the exigencies of his case, and from his infantine piety, he grasps the idea of the future state and its rectifications. "I know that my Redeemer" (or Vindicator, translate it as you will) "liveth," &c. Just as Addison makes Cato say:

> "'T is Heaven itself that points out an hereafter,
> And intimates Eternity to man."

How clear and how forcible the meaning! How suitable to the speaker and the place! It is one of those kinds of prophecy, when, not the individual, but human nature itself, speaks from the force of its sorrows and the pressure of its wants,—when the obliquity of the channel gives power and pureness to the stream it conveys.

I must contend that there is no obscurity in the dramatic mode of teaching when one has once grasped the principle. It is instinctively understood in the early ages of society, and in its last state of improvement; it is only in the transition state, from accidental causes, it becomes obscure. Perhaps there never was a people less prepared to apply it than our Puritan fathers. They had departed from the early state; they approached the Bible with an awful veneration; they postulated for it a didactic perfection, and their very respect for its substance sometimes led them not to regard its dress. They had little taste for any poetry, and still less for the dramatic; indeed, all the commentators of the older schools, Grotius himself, did not fully grasp this principle. Hence it now appears at first view a critical refinement, when it is only a return to the simplicity of nature.

It has been better understood in all other literature. Mr. Addison, with his usual taste, points out one of its rules. Speaking of a tragedy of Euripides, from the performance of which Socrates is said to have retired to show his disapprobation of a particular passage, he says: "This was no sooner spoken but Socrates rose from his seat, and, without any regard to his affection for his friend, or to the success of the play, showed himself displeased at what was said, and walked out of the assembly. I question not but the reader will be curious to know what the line was that gave this divine heathen so much offence. If my memory fails me not, it was in the part of Hippolytus, who, when he is pressed by an oath, which he had taken, to keep silence, returned for answer, that he had taken the oath with his tongue, but not with his heart. Had a person of a vicious character made such a speech, it might have been allowed as a proper representation of the baseness of his thoughts; but such an expression out of the mouth of the virtuous Hippolytus was giving a sanction to falsehood, and establishing perjury by a maxim." (Tatler, No. 122.) Let us add, that had the writer been painting the frailty of a good man, it would have been no proof that he was sanctioning a bad sentiment.

I strongly suspected, when reading this account of Socrates, that the poet was right, and the philosopher was wrong. I have since examined the play, and I find my suspicions verified. Hippolytus says nothing inconsistent with his virtuous character. The case was this. Phædra was his mother-in-law, married to his father, Theseus. She falls in love with her step-son, not from any unchaste desire in herself, but through the anger of Venus. Phædra is wretched and miserable, and the nurse, pitying her case, goes to Hippolytus and tells him her passion. Before she tells him, however, we are led to infer that the nurse had exacted a promise from Hippolytus that he would not tell his father the terrible secret,—his mother-in-law's passion for him. But when Hippolytus comes to hear the enormous crime, he hesitates about keeping his promise, and he then utters the sentiment which moved the indignation of Socrates: "I swore with my tongue; but my mind is not held to the oath;"—which only means this: I did not know the nature of the oath I took; I feel as if, under such horrible circumstances, it is my duty to break the promise. If Herod, when he made his promise to Herodias, had reasoned as Hippolytus did, he would have been a better man. At any rate, the sentiment is perfectly natural in his condition, and as he did not tell his father, it is probable he was perplexed and delayed until he was anticipated in the letter which was found in his mother's hand after she hung herself. However, if the wise Socrates was deceived in the dramatic lesson, we should be on our guard, and look through the poetic dress to the lesson taught. Euripides was right, though so competent an auditor misunderstood him.

Perhaps there is no writer more hard to turn into a direct teacher than Shakespeare. He appears by nature to have been very little of a moralist; he belonged to no sect in religion, and he had that indifference to opinion which was engendered alike by his Protean genius and his Epicurean heart. He was intent on his pictures; and if he could only please, he was not careful to instruct. "He seems to write," says Dr. Johnson, "without a moral purpose." Yet it is not difficult in this Proteus of the moral school to see his sentiment through his coloring. His first object is, no doubt, to put suitable sentiments into the mouths of his characters; but that does not hide, it rather reveals, his secondary lesson; that is, he is always conscious of the moral truth his audience will recognize. And the one purpose never disturbs the other. Thus when Iago says: —

> "Good name in man and woman, dear my lord,
>   Is the immediate jewel of their souls;
>   Who steals my purse steals trash; 'tis something, nothing;
>   'T was mine, 'tis his, and has been slave to thousands;
>   But he that filches from me my good name
>   Robs me of that which not enriches him,
>   And makes me poor indeed."

Now it is evident that Iago is a bad character; there is no truth in him; and his object in this scene is not to utter moral sentiments, but to poison the mind of Othello with jealousy; and yet no one can doubt that he here means to utter a true maxim of morality; and the reason is, this exactly suits his purpose. A true maxim, in this place, covers his design, increases his insinuations, and makes the false impression more fatal by the very truth it presents. On the contrary, when Emilia, in the same play, says of husbands generally, —

> "They are all but stomachs and we all but food;
>   They eat us hungerly, and when they are full
>   They belch us;" —

or when Mrs. Page says, in the Merry Wives of Windsor, after receiving Falstaff's letter, "Well, I will find you twenty lascivious turtles ere one chaste man;" — or when Ariadne says, in Catullus, after Theseus had forsaken her, —

> "Jam, jam nulla viro juranti femina credat
>   Qui, dum aliquid cupiens animus praegestit apisci,

> Nil metuunt jurare, nihil promittere parcunt;
> Sed simul ac cupidae mentis satiata libido est,
> Dicta nihil metuere, nihil perjuria curant;" —

> "Let not a woman trust the vows of men;
> They promise while they seek our love, but when
> Their purpose is obtained, we sadly find
> Their solemn vows are scattered to the wind;" —

every one sees that this is not the sentiment of the poet. It is the natural exaggeration of the moment. The falsehood of the sentiment is essential to the truth of the feeling. In a word, just as certainly as we penetrate the design of the poet, just so clear we see his secondary purpose. In the School for Scandal, Joseph Surface is intended to be a consummate hypocrite; he never for a moment ceases to wear his mask; and yet all the maxims he utters — and he is full of maxims — are important and true. How do we know this? We see the design of the author; it suits his purpose to put these fine sentiments into the mouth of Joseph Surface, in order to deceive Sir Peter Teazle, who is constantly admiring him. It is impossible to see the design of the writer, and not see at once the blackness of his character and the beauty of his maxims.

We might extend this rule over all the dramatic writings of ancient and modern authors. In the ancient tragedies, there is the Chorus, expressly contrived to give the moral sentiment; and whenever any obscurity occurs, it is because the reader is as much perplexed as to the truth of the picture as he is in the propriety of the sentiment.

The design of the chorus is thus described by Horace: "Let the chorus defend the actor, and speak the voice of humanity. Let it chant nothing between the acts, which does not conduce to the main design. Let it approve the virtuous and smile on the friendly; let it rebuke the angry and approve the conscientious. Let it applaud the frugal table, salutary justice, laws, and peace with her open gates. Let it not reveal the plot; and let it pray and beseech the celestial powers that prosperity may depart from the proud and return to the depressed." It is impossible to preserve the meaning of the first sentiment — *Actoris partes chorus officiumque virile defendat* — by a mere translation. I imagine the thought to be this. It was not uncommon for a bad character in the old tragedies to utter a shocking sentiment, which was yet perfectly characteristic; as when the tyrant of old said, "I swore with my tongue and not my mind," &c. The people expressed their disapprobation; for it is a mistake which a careless listener is tempted to make. Even the polished Athenians, brought up in theatres, were not always mercurial enough to preserve themselves from such an illusion. Now in such cases, says Horace, let the chorus defend (*Actoris partes*) the part of the actor, by showing in his immorality the author's design. We have in the Bible implicitly such a chorus;

for very often, in the parallelism or in the course of the dialogue, we have the reply or the rebuke. We are often tempted to wonder, and the wonder ends in making a new and beautiful impression. Take the book of Ecclesiastes as an example. What strange sentiments in single paragraphs, and yet how clear the whole design!

So true is it that the moral sentiment shines through the painting of character, and is generally seen when the painting is understood (that is, they go together), that in the Greek fragments preserved by Cumberland, though the drama itself is lost, and we are under the disadvantage of not knowing the plot, yet, I think, I can see the direct sentiment. Who does not recognize the utterance of a brazen-faced female in the following lines?

> "No animal in nature can compare
> In impudence with woman; I myself
> Am one, and from my own experience speak."

Here is a monstrous hyperbole, intended, no doubt, to paint an unusual character. It was probably one of those clap-traps so frequent in the ancient and modern drama, and no doubt it answered its purpose; it brought down the house. On the contrary, the following sentiment the author meant for an unvarying and eternal truth, and it is the same whether found in a sermon or a play:—

> "Hence, vile adulterer! I scorn to gain
> Pleasures extorted from another's pain."

So true is it that the didactic always appears, not only in *strong* irony, *strong* hyperbole, and *strong* painting, but even middle sentiments are seen, when the abstract truth is more shaded. As in the following:—

> "If love be folly, as the schools would prove,
> The man must lose his wits who falls in love;
> Deny him love, you doom the wretch to death,
> And then it follows he must lose his breath.
> Good sooth! there is a young and dainty maid
> I dearly love, a minstrel she by trade;
> What then? Must I defer to pedant rule,
> And own that love transforms me to a fool?
> Not I, so help me! By the gods I swear,
> The nymph I love is fairest of the fair.
> Must I not love her then? Let the dull sot
> Who made the law obey it,—I will not."

No doubt the author here had the natural excess of love in his mind, and yet he does not totally disapprove; he has only a half-smile of censure on his brow at a sentiment which he regards as half wrong.

In a word, I would be willing to pledge myself to go through the books of Job, Ecclesiastes, and Solomon's Song,—the most dramatic books in the Bible,—and to say, I AM AS ABLE TO PICK OUT THE SENTIMENT AS I AM TO UNDERSTAND THE CHARACTER. They both shine with an interlocked and common light.

As in painting, so in dramatic poetry, there are some

things difficult, almost impossible, to be done. Thus, in painting, you are confined to the instant; motion and succession must be dispensed with; you cannot paint a depression in a landscape lower than the front ground of your picture; it is very hard to distinguish between the rising and setting sun; and he that selects the rainbow as his pattern must be content to follow at an awful distance the perfection of nature. In dramatic writing, one of the standing difficulties is, to paint a good character. Virtue is seen in *action*, not in *profession;* and the difficulty is, to make a perfect man manifest himself, without being a man of buckram, — not sounding a trumpet in his own praise. In this department the best writers have often failed. I must confess, I have never been much charmed with Xenophon's Cyrus; I have not always gone along with Plato's Socrates; I have never wept, as Cicero did, at the pathos of the Phædo; Socrates and Cato are too stern for my pity. The Edinburgh Review calls Sir Charles Grandison the prince of coxcombs; and Blackwood's Magazine wishes that Miss Hannah More's characters had a little sin in them, to set human nature on its legs again. This lady has often been ridiculed for her precise and buckram characters. The critics have been very unjust to her. " In every work, regard the writer's end." She has always an object in view, precisely the reverse of that of Shakespeare. Shakespeare is always giving you specimens of human nature; he paints man as he is; but Miss More is always giving you patterns and examples; and the only reason why she seems to be ridiculous is, the intrinsic difficulty of painting a good character, and because we are always trying her by rules she did not adopt and could not be expected to follow. Her characters are stiff, no doubt, and not very natural; but let us remember virtue is not natural to man; it is a triumph over his nature.

It has often been remarked that Shakespeare has no heroes; he never paints the self-sacrificing martyr or the disinterested man; he always dashes his best personages with mingled imperfections. He has none of Plutarch's patriots, nor the Bollandists' saints; and one reason is, perhaps, he instinctively saw that such characters were too perfect for the interest he wished to excite. When he does approach this ground his success is far from being complete. Isabella, in Measure for Measure, has a somewhat stiff religion; she is what Mr. Addison would call outrageously virtuous. Cordelia, in King Lear, is ostentatious of her own parental affection, and not at all conciliatory towards her sisters; at least we may say such talk in real life would not be regarded as laying the ground of confidence. Other writers have not been able to conquer the same difficulty. Thus Sallust, in the speech which he puts into the mouth of Cato, in the Roman Senate, at the time of Catiline's conspiracy, — " that as he never was indulgent to any one fault in himself, he could not excuse those of others," — is exceedingly unfortunate; and Bishop Butler says: "This speech with decency could scarce come out of the mouth of any human creature.' But no doubt Sallust mistook what he would say of Cato for what Cato might say of himself. There is a very remarkable example of this utter frustration of a writer's purpose in Cornelia's address to Paulus, in the Eleventh Elegy of Propertius, Lib. IV. It is the solemn address of the departed spirit of a wife to her husband, and therefore is intended as a most perfect expression of her virtue, and yet it is one continued piece of arrogance and boasting. It concludes with these lines: —

"Moribus et coelum patuit; sim digna merendo
Cujus honeratis ossa vehantur avis."

"Heaven opens to the good; let me be found
Worthy of names like ours so much renowned."

"Nor did time change me; pure was all from blame
Between the nuptial torch and funeral flame.
Me nature governed through ingenuous blood,
Nor was it fear or law that made me good."
The Shade of Cornelia to Paulus, Frothingham's Translation.

She says of her life, "Sine crimine tota vita est." One is reminded here of Job's words: "If I justify myself, my own mouth shall condemn me; if I say I am perfect, it shall also prove me perverse." (Job ix. 20.)

It is a proof, I think, of the superior wisdom of the Bible, that this difficulty is conquered in the speeches of that pattern of perfection, Jesus Christ. We have his discourses; and think for a moment what a character he had to sustain! not abstract perfection, but perfection under his claims, — perfection as Redeemer of a lost world. He was always to make the future state a positive idea, and sustain the personage he was sent to assume. And yet how completely has he accomplished his object! He never boasts; he is never arrogant; he is always easy. He conquers one of the most remarkable difficulties that ever perplexed the genius of man. *Somebody* drew the character, and surely that character could not be a fiction.

Some objections have indeed been made by learned critics against the abuse of this principle. Thus Michaelis observes in one of his notes on Lowth's Lectures: "It is certain that many of the Psalms are dramatic, which some commentators observing, delighted with their own discoveries, whenever they meet with a passage more difficult than usual, or are able to catch any new and visionary explanation, more agreeable to their theological notions, they have eagerly resorted to the change of the persons or characters, though no such change existed. Such are those commentators who have fancied, in accommodation to the quotation of Paul (Hebrews i. 10), the spirit and purpose of which they did not understand, that the former part of the Hundred and Second Psalm, to the twenty-fourth verse,—"Take me not away in the midst of my age,"—consisted entirely of a speech of Christ, and that the remainder—"As for thy years, they endure throughout all generations," &c.—was the reply of God the Father. Whoever indulges himself in this mode of explication, may easily find out anything he pleases in the Psalms, and, with little or no philological knowledge, without the smallest assistance from criticism, can give a meaning to the most difficult or corrupt texts of Scripture,—any meaning but the right one."

But surely it could not be the object of the critic to deny or depreciate the legitimate application of this principle to the interpretation of a book which so frequently uses it. For not to insist that one hardly sees the importance of the specimen of alleged abuse he quotes, we may ask him, whether the Bible really adopts this mode of instruction in all its poetic parts, and, if it does, whether it can be understood without a recognition of the fact. For my part, I must say I could form no meaning of the Twentieth Psalm, without asking who the speaker is, and who the second person spoken to is,—"The Lord hear thee in the day of trouble," &c.; and both these questions must be answered; i. e. I must adopt the dramatic principle in interpreting the Psalm. I will only add, I know no principle of exegesis which has been less abused, or is less liable to abuse. It seems to me that the Professor is singularly unfortunate when he insinuates that it has been obscure, or a frequent source of bad interpretation. Where are the proofs? Whoever is conscious of the existence of this principle in the Bible, and understands its nature, is almost sure to apply it right.

In the foregoing remarks, I suppose myself to have established the following principles: — First, that the Bible has adopted the dramatic element; secondly, that it is Oriental, fragmentary, and peculiar in its character; thirdly, that the adoption of this element does not darken, but rather enforces, the light of revelation; that whenever we can discover the picturing of the characters, we equally discover the sentiment or doctrine they teach; and, finally, that the key to this sentiment is the *intention of the author*, which is just as discoverable in this mode of writing as any other, when our attention is drawn to the fact, and we become accustomed to see it as it is applied to the solemnities of revelation. This discussion will not be without its use, if it only leads the expounders of Scripture, whenever they take a text from the Book of Job, the Psalms, Ecclesiastes, and many parts of the prophets, to have this principle constantly before them. Sure I am, that without it the best commentators have made the most dangerous mistakes.

In conclusion, when we remember that the dramatic

form in Scripture was expressly adopted to make the truth more clear and impressive, — that it was prompted by simple nature, and was eminently suited to an early age; when we reflect that all which could make it obscure in Shakespeare would make it clear in the Bible, the purposes in each being so different; and, finally, that it is not peculiarly obscure in Shakespeare, — we may safely conclude that we need only to fall back on the simplicity of antiquity, and what was suited to instruct them will be found to instruct us. We shall find the fruit among the flowers. The imagination was given us by God. It is not a vain function; it is as sacred and as useful as reason itself, and the Bible is the only book that always puts it to its right use. Here, in the sacred page, it turns our passions from their dangerous strength to the path of pious instruction. It approximates God; it paints truth; it brings eternal objects near; it shows us a dying Saviour on the cross; and it helps us to realize the scene "when the heavens shall pass away with a great noise, and the elements shall melt with a fervent heat;" we see the burning world; the Judge enthroned; the final sentence, and the solemn reward. We have a power given us by which the objects of faith are almost turned to sight. It works a perpetual miracle. While a polluted mind paints voluptuous scenes, bowers of love and streams of pleasure, revelation turns this dangerous faculty into an instrument of salvation. It is certainly an instrument of instruction. It assists our conceptions; it wakes our attention; it impresses our hearts. Let us study its laws, and we shall find we never knew its value until we found its skilful use in the pages of God.

THE USE OF THE IMAGINATION.

The Bible teaches the right use of the imagination. Bishop Butler, who was a severe reasoner, speaks depreciatingly of the imagination. "However," says he, "as one cannot but be greatly sensible how difficult it is to silence the imagination enough to make the voice of reason distinctly heard in this case; as we are accustomed from our youth up to indulge that forward delusive faculty, ever obtruding beyond its sphere, of some assistance, indeed, to apprehension, but the author of all error," &c. (Analogy, Chap. I. Part I.) He hardly seems to be aware how much he was indebted to the faculty he decries. His imagination was all but miraculous. What I mean to say is, that, in communicating thoughts where an illustration seemed almost impossible, he is never wanting, but brings the most remote similitudes together; and thus makes his severe imagination an handmaid to his severe reason. To be sure, it is not the imagination of Milton. See an instance (Analogy, Part I. Chap. III. Sect. 3). President Edwards had a similar power. An imagination that seldom beautified, but always stood ready to illustrate, and delighted in conquering difficulties. I hardly know of a more startling instance, in which an insuperable difficulty seems to be overcome, than the supposition in *God's Last End in Creation*, Chap. I. Sect. 1, p. 15, where he introduces a second God as an arbiter to judge between the first God and his creatures, and then shows the necessity of such an arbiter is superseded by the perfections of God himself. Mr. Addison has a surprising example in the Spectator, No. 575, where he finds an intermediate thought to illustrate the duration of eternity, — the globe of sand as big as our earth, and one grain abstracted every thousand years. The Hebrew Scriptures can hardly be said to afford such intricate examples, and yet it is remarkable, the difference between the sacred use of the imagination and its use in all the heathen writers. It is remarkable of the Bible through all its pages, that it turns the imagination into its own religious channel, TO ILLUSTRATE SACRED TRUTH. To our taste, it may sometimes seem to be negligent, and not always use the most delicate coloring. It was written in times of great simplicity, but it has always one object in view. A fertile imagination may be said to work a natural miracle, — it calls new powers into being; it embodies sentiment and animates matter; it brings the unseen world into sight; and it is one proof of the wisdom of revelation, that so dangerous a power is always employed to so good an end.

Objections have been made to this Song, as being too luscious in its imagery, and leaning to the sensual side, but surely by critics who never put their antique shoes on. The fact is, considering the age in which it was written, and the stand-point of the author and the first readers, it is remarkably delicate; so much ardor was never expressed in such refined language; that is, primitive refinement. If the communion of love is expressed, it is always by the purest figures. No doubt the author then was thought superfluously scrupulous. Take the sixth verse of the fourth chapter as an example: "Until the day break and the shadows flee away I will get me to the mountain of myrrh and to the hill of frankincense." So the first verse of the eighth chapter: "O that thou wert as my brother, that sucked the breasts of my mother! when I should find thee without, I would kiss thee; yea, I should not be despised." Can purer love be pictured than a sister's kiss? Not a sensual thought is hinted at through the whole poem. Even the description in the seventh chapter, verses 2–4, from an Oriental point of view, has nothing in the least degree indelicate in its articulate enumeration. Consider the object. With the Orientals, fulness of figure as well as fulness of dress is considered as a great beauty, and this passage is merely a full description of such a figure.

If the reader wishes to see the purity of revelation compared with the pollution of earthly poetry, let him compare a Greek song with a Hebrew psalm. Both are ardent; both use the boldest personification, and both impute their own raptures to the silent motions of the surrounding creation! Anacreon and David have both lighted the torch of the imagination at the fireplace of the heart, and have illuminated the creation with the blaze they had kindled. But how different!

First, Anacreon : —

> "The thirsty earth soaks up the rain,
> That drinks and gapes for drink again;
> The plants suck up the earth, and are
> By constant drinking fresh and fair;
> The sea itself (which one would think
> Should have but little need of drink)
> Drinks ten thousand rivers up,
> So filled that they o'erflow the cup;
> The busy sun (and one would guess
> By 's drunken, fiery face no less)
> Drinks up the sea; and when he's done,
> The moon and stars drink up the sun;
> They drink and dance by their own light,
> They drink and revel all the night.
> Nothing on earth is sober found,
> But an eternal health goes round;
> Fill up the bowl, there, — fill it high,
> Fill all the glasses, then; for why
> Should every creature drink but I?
> Ye temperance-people, tell me why?"
>
> Cowley's *Translation.*

The Psalmist hears a different voice from nature: "Praise the Lord from the earth, ye dragons and all deeps, snow and vapor, stormy wind, fulfilling his word; mountains and all hills, fruitful trees, and all cedars. Beasts and cattle, creeping things and flying fowl. Kings of the earth and all people; princes and judges of the earth. Both young men and maidens, old men and children. Let them praise the name of the Lord; for his name alone is excellent; his glory is above the heavens."

Such are the different revelations of nature to different minds, and such are the contrary ways in which the most fertile imagination may be employed. Where the Greek poet sees nothing but a drunken creation dancing around him, the Psalmist beholds a chorus of worshippers praising his God.

VI.

THE DOUBLE SENSE.

As I shall consider this book as a continued allegory, it becomes very important to trace that fact to a general principle. This Song is not a single example. The practice of using allegories reigns among all the sacred writers of the Old Testament, and this practice generates the double sense. Let us, then, endeavor to state the reality and naturalness of this peculiar mode of pleasing and teaching a primitive people.

By the double sense we mean generally historical symbols, — that is, one event in history may bear such an analogy to another, that it may be a figure and a sign of what is yet to come.* Thus, the return from the Babylonish captivity may be a sign of the general redemption of mankind, and all those passages in Isaiah and the other prophets, of passing through the wilderness, of opening rivers in high places, of levelling every mound and filling up every valley, may be ap-

---

* It must be allowed that other symbols beside historic events generate the double sense.

plied to the spreading of the Gospel and the recovery of our world.

When we consider that, in the order of things, no individual exists which does not belong to a class and have a reference to its own individuality and to the class to which it belongs, we may say that something of the double sense pervades all nature. We know of nothing whose whole signification is confined to itself. Cicero saw this; for he makes Antony (in his dialogue, De Oratore) censure the pedants who divided all causes into the individual and general; for he says: "Ignari omnes controversias ad universi generis vim et naturam referri" (Lib. II. § 31), — "They are ignorant that all controversies belong in force and nature to general questions." We cannot imagine an object in existence — except God and the universe — which does not indicate the species or genus to which it belongs; and surely the fall of Babylon, or the deliverance from Egypt, must bear *some* similitude, and of course give some indication of all the other inflictions and deliverances by which God manifests his protection of his people and the progress of his kingdom.

It is a general law, that the double sense should indicate itself not only by its magnificence and oneness, but also by other unmistakable signals. There is a general form which it adopts as certain as any other law of language. As in the imagery which Homer or

Milton applies to Heaven, so in the expressions which look beyond the passing event, their pregnancy shows their design. When Apollo comes down from heaven, his quiver rattles on his shoulders, his arrows fly; but they are invisible, and they produce malignant disease and death; and from the circumstances of the Grecian army, exposed on the marshes around Troy and under an Oriental sun, and from the mythological character of Apollo, these celestial arrows must be sunbeams. No mistake here. So in the Seventy-second Psalm, when it is said: "And great shall be his prosperity as long as the moon endureth." (Noyes's translation.) And again:—

"He shall prosper, and to him shall be given the gold of Sheba:
Prayer, also, shall be made for him continually,
And daily shall he be praised.
There shall be abundance of corn in the land;
Even on the tops of the mountains the fruit shall shake like Lebanon;
And they of the cities shall flourish like grass of the earth.
His name shall endure forever;
His name shall be continued as long as the sun;
By him shall men bless themselves;
All nations shall call him blessed."

Surely it is as plain that this is not solely said of Solomon, as that Apollo's arrows are not literal ones, for we are reduced to this alternative,—either that the sacred writer has used enormous hyperboles, violating taste as much as truth, and ancient taste as much as modern, or we must conclude he has something analogous, but something deeper than the surface-meaning; and as to what has been said, and so idly repeated,—" Quae interpretandi ratio, qua una eademque oratione, dispari sensu accepta, plures simul eventus disjunctos tempore, natura dissimiles designari statuatur, ab omnibus rectae interpretandi artis praeceptis ita aliena est, ut qui in Graeco aut Romano aliquo scriptore adhibere illam velit, is in communem prudentiorum reprehensionem incurreret,"—can there be anything in this objection? In the first place, as to the fact that the Greek and Roman writers have no specimens of this under-meaning. Whenever they approach the field of double authorship and imaginary inspiration, they give plain indications that they *are* forced upon similar exigencies; they conform as much as their barren religion allowed them to conform to similar language. The very wolf that suckled Romulus was a double being,—partly literal and partly a symbol of what Rome was to be. But, secondly, if the Greeks and Romans never had used similar modes, it would be nothing to the purpose. All language is colored by its subject. The Hebrew writers stood on peculiar ground. Their object was peculiar; and, as Paul tells us, they were πνευματικοῖς πνευματικὰ συγκρίνοντες, explaining spiritual ideas in a spiritual terminology. It is not true, moreover, that the events brought together, though *disjunctos tempore*, are *natura dissimiles*,—dissimilar in nature. The Jewish economy was one great preparation; the culminating point was always before them. Every king was a Messiah or an anointed one; they stood in a long line of succession, the great Messiah closing the procession. Every king not only resembled him, but actually prepared the way. The prophets supposed themselves inspired by an all-foreseeing Mind. They did not pretend to understand all they said. Their brightest visions were partial revelations; and they had before them an illustrious history, very illustrious, but very indefinite as to time and extent. Now, in such cases, was it unnatural — was it not almost necessary — that they should fall into that line of revelation which the best interpreters (such as Lowth, for example) have imputed to them? Instead of finding any difficulty in one great under-meaning, I should have been very much astonished had it not been so.

When a writer or speaker in any time or language has some dark communication to make, it is a good rule of interpretation to find his end or terminating point. We interpret his ῥήματα by his ὁ λόγος. Thus when Tiresias comes upon the stage, in the Œdipus Tyrannus, or Clytemnestra in the Agamemnon of Æschylus, their language is very obscure, — designedly so; and in the case of Œdipus, for example, we always forerun him in understanding the prophet's language. We almost wonder at his dulness. We forget that ὁ λόγος is always before us. *We* see the end. It is just so in reading the sacred prophets. It is expected, it is the design, it is the wisdom, it is the beauty of prophecy, that *we* should understand it better than those to whom it was first uttered, or at least that we should have a key which they had not. Surely the development reflects back on the antecedent indications. The enigma which the great Author himself has explained is solved forever.

However, there is abundance of indication that this mode was common to all nations. It violates no law of language, because it violates no custom. It introduces no obscurity, except an intentional and temporary one. It is founded on this great principle, that A FACT MAY BE A SYMBOL; and when a nation or the taste of the age abounds in symbols, and has a taste for them, why should they not sometimes, *often*, take facts? A myth is a fact exaggerated and shaped so as to be a symbol. But if fiction can answer this purpose, why not truth? If the story of the fall of Adam, considered as a myth, shows the propensity to and prevalence of sin, how much more does it impress that idea considered as a fact! The story of Christ is an idea, to impress a useful lesson, says Strauss. Very well; the idea becames doubly impressive when it is supported by the fact.

Two considerations are important: —

I. In the first place, we may say the double sense arises from the general law of development in human language. Language — written language — begins by picture-writing, as we see in the rude specimens left by our Iroquois; then it proceeds to symbolic pictures, and finally to an alphabet, or phonic sounds. During all the time when symbol-signs prevail previously to the invention of letters, the whole art of writing depends on a sort of double sense. The art of reading is the art of interpreting these latent symbols. A dove may signify love, or meekness; a lion, a hero; a dog, fidelity; one man leading another by a string (as is actually seen in the relics of the Iroquois preserved in the Documentary History of New York, Vol. I. p. 13) may signify a victory in which captives were taken. Thus springs up from necessity a symbolic meaning joined to the literal, or, in other words, the double sense. But, as Dr. Warburton observes (Divine Legation, Vol. II. p. 143), "that which had its origin from necessity came in time to be employed for secrecy and improved for ornament." It long lingered in the primitive languages which had escaped from the narrow limits of picture-writing. Their taste had been formed on it; it was regarded as a great beauty, and it was even still necessary to convey the great impressions which the Hebrew writers aimed to produce. When they wished, therefore, to produce by anticipation the conception of John the Baptist, they call him Elias, or, as we should say, an Elias. To picture the kingdom of Christ, they portray the expanded reign of Solomon. This was all

L

natural, and almost necessary, in the line of linguistic improvement in which they then stood. Instead of its being true, as Michaelis has said, and others have ingeminated, that such a mode is "peculiar to the sacred poetry of the Hebrews, that the sacred writing must be interpreted by rules in every respect different from other writings," (see Note on Lowth's Ninth Lecture,) I should say nothing can be more natural; it is all but a necessary law; it marks the dawn of literature; it is just as natural as some of Homer's infantine expressions; so impossible to be used now, and therefore such exquisite proofs of the genius of the man and the age.

We say, then, that double sense arises from the form of language and the grade of its progress in that early age. But again,

II. It arises from the double authorship of the Bible and the double object of most of the prophecies. Most of the Psalms and the prophecies had some occasional subject, — some incident in a greater chain. The first meaning arrests the attention of the contemporary speaker; but the inspiring spirit is supposed to have a deeper intent; of course God sees farther than man, and this recondite meaning is one of the signals of inspiration. It is an exquisite proof and characteristic of the presence and wisdom of the wiser mind. All this is exemplified in the unwilling prophecy of Caiaphas (John xi. 47-52): "Then gathered the chief priests and the Pharisees a council, and said, What shall we do? for this man doth many miracles. If we let him alone, all men will believe on him, and the Romans will come and take away both our place and nation. And one of them, named Caiaphas, being the high-priest that same year, said unto them, Ye know nothing at all; nor consider that it is expedient for us that one man should die for the people, and that the whole nation perish not. And this he spake not of himself; but, being high-priest that year, he prophesied that Jesus should die for that nation; and not for that nation only, but that also he should gather together in one the children of God that were scattered abroad." Who does not see the deeper purpose of the Power that overruled his speech beyond his meaning? All the high-priest intended was to teach the doctrine of expediency. It is true, he concedes Christ may not be guilty according to any positive law, — certainly not the Roman law; but it is necessary for our safety that he should die. The high-priest looked no further, — he meant no more. But God overruled his words to a higher purpose, and this unwilling testimony was very striking. Such prophecies have always been considered as an example of God's speaking through the voice of man. Shakespeare has used this proof of double authorship in the scene between Margaret and Richard (Richard III., Act I. Scene 3):—

Gloster. Have done thy charm, thou hateful, withered hag.

Q. Margaret. And leave out thee? Stay, dog, for thou shalt hear me!
If Heaven have any grievous plague in store
Exceeding those that I can wish upon thee,
O let them keep it till thy sins be ripe,
And then hurl down their indignation
On thee, the troubler of the poor world's peace!
The worm of conscience still begnaw thy soul!
Thy friends suspect for traitors while thou livest,
And take deep traitors for thy dearest friends!
No sleep close up that deadly eye of thine,
Unless it be while some tormenting dream
Affrights thee with a hell of ugly devils;
Thou elvish-marked, abortive, rooting hog!
Thou that wast sealed in thy nativity
The slave of nature and the son of hell!
Thou slander of thy mother's heavy womb!
Thou loathed issue of thy father's loins!
Thou rag of honor! thou detested——

Glos. Margaret.

Q. Mar.   Richard!

Glos.   Ha?

Q. Mar.   I call thee not.

Glos. I cry thee mercy, then; for I did think
That thou didst call me all these bitter names.

Q. Mar. Why so I did; but looked for no reply.
O let me make the period to my curse.

Glos. 'T is done by me; and ends in — Margaret.

Q. Eliz. Thus have you breathed your curse against yourself.

Every one, I think, must see the poet's design in this dialogue. It is to make Queen Margaret the unconscious instrument in the hand of Providence of pronouncing a curse against herself; just as, when Samuel turned from Saul, and he caught hold of the garment and it rent (1 Samuel xv. 48), the prophet seizes the occasion to say to the king: "The Lord hath rent the kingdom of Israel from thee this day, and hath given it to a neighbor of thine which is better than thou." A wise Providence can use the simplest incident as a sign. Such seems to be the spirit of the narrative. When Paulus Æmilius was appointed to conduct the war against Macedon, he returned home to meet his little daughter at the door, who told her father that Perses (the name of her lapdog) was dead. It was the name also of the Macedonian king. He embraced the child with rapture, and received the words as a prediction of the fall of his regal foe. Here we have the double sense. The girl meant her little dog was dead. The father supposed he saw a deeper signification, and what gave a charm to the incident was, that the gods were believed to overrule such a trifle to signify their high, celestial will. As Xenophon has told us of Socrates, those that use auguries, and voices, and symbols, &c., do not imagine that the birds, and the speakers, and the portents themselves, know what conduces to our future prosperity, but that the gods by THESE THINGS signify our welfare; — so at least thought Socrates. Now, it would have been very strange if the Hebrews had not imbibed such an opinion, for the whole theocracy was inwoven with significations of the Divine will. The waters of jealousy implied a perpetual presence of a miraculous providence. The Urim and Thummim, the seer, the ephod, &c., postulated the idea that God to them was always present; and nothing was more natural, not to say necessary, than that they should seek these Divine intimations in one great under-meaning. It arose from the magnificent ultimate design of their great economy.

It is often asked, why the Bible should be subject to laws applicable to no other book. The answer is obvious. Properly speaking, the Bible is subjected to no unusual laws. When it is said the Bible must be interpreted like any other book, a great fallacy is often suggested. We interpret the Bible like any other book, supposing it possible to place any other book in similar circumstances. The very heathen themselves, when they supposed the writing inspired, imputed a double sense to it. It is an everlasting law, — it is perfectly natural. The Deity has a deeper meaning than mortals.

One of the clearest examples is found in Acts ii. 25. The occasion was important, the speaker was inspired, and the audience versed in the Old Testament. It was Peter's first discourse to prove the divine origin of the Gospel he was called upon to proclaim. He was to set the key-note and to build his conclusions on a strong foundation. Prophecy is his foundation, and he quotes the Sixteenth Psalm, verses 8 – 10: "I have set the Lord always before me; because he is on my right hand, I shall not be moved. Therefore my heart is glad and my glory rejoiceth; my flesh also shall rest in hope; for thou wilt not leave my soul in hell; neither wilt thou suffer thine Holy One to see corruption." Peter does not quote the Hebrew, but the Septuagint, and hence the variation in the words between the Old Testament and the Apostle's quotation. The sense, however, is the same. When we turn to the Psalm, we find not the least hint that David was speaking of any other except himself. The Psalm seems to be simple and clear; the inscription gives it to David; he is speaking of himself through the whole course of it, and in these verses it is "my right hand," "my heart," "my glory;" and yet the Apostle tells us, both negatively and positively, that it does *not* in his own application of it apply to David, and it *does* apply to Christ. "Men and brethren, Let me freely speak" (μετὰ παρρησίας, a phrase which the Apostles often use when they are deducing the Gospel from some latent passage in the Old Testament, and it may be rendered, Let me burst away from the old, narrow application) "unto you of the patriarch David, that he is both dead and buried, and his sepulchre is with us unto this day. Therefore, being a prophet, and knowing that God had sworn with an oath to him, that of the fruit of his loins, according to the flesh, he would raise up Christ to sit on his throne; he, seeing this before, speaks of the resurrection of Christ, that his soul was not left in hell, neither his flesh did see corruption." So in the thirty-fourth verse he says: "For David is not ascended into heaven," &c. Now it seems to me impossible for language to be more explicit. We have a double affirmation,—what is and what is not; and I see no way in which we can meet the Apostle's expression but by allowing that he finds an under-meaning in David's words. Their whole force was not exhausted in him; and if any one should ask, How is it then a prediction, if no one so understood it before the fulfilment, and no such meaning is necessitated by the laws of language,— we answer: First, that prophecy occupies all the varieties of prediction, the latent hint and the clear expression, and it may be the design of God in this case to give us one of the forms which to the Jew was very impressive. Besides, it is obvious that David is feeling after some deeper thought,—some vast idea which he does not fully comprehend and hardly knows how to manage. The conception of immortality through a resurrection seems to be before him, and the author of that resurrection was to be Christ. Peter unfolded the idea, the germ of which was in the patriarch's mind.

We have here, then, a clear example of an inspired Apostle arguing the proof of the Gospel from a passage applicable only through a double sense.

We should hardly look to Archbishop Leighton for acute criticism on Scripture; he had no taste for philology and little confidence in learned speculation; but he sometimes sees by intuition what others must find by long research, and he has in one of his discourses this profound remark, which I would recommend to all such as overlook the truth because it lies so near them: "That which some call divers senses of the same Scripture, is indeed but divers parts of one full sense." (Select Works, Edinburgh ed., 1744, Sect. IV. p. 47.) It seems to me this is an important truth uttered without the least parade.

The great art of interpreting this ancient volume — the Bible — seems to be to modernize it; that is, to make its instructions bear with equal force on modern times as on ancient institutions. The forms of the old world have perished; but the sacred lesson is permanent. Now there are two ways of modernizing these old instructions. One is to see the precedents, — involving in temporary events eternal principles; the other is a legitimate use of the under-meaning; such a use as does not lead to the old extravagance. Now I contend there is a use justified by eternal truth and confirmed by eternal laws. The very fact, too, that this mode of interpreting harmonizes the Old Testament and the New, gives it importance. If you do not adopt it, you are in danger of falling into a barren neology, or the old Jewish contradiction. The golden thread is broken.

The Frenchman who saw Othello performed, and, not well understanding the language, supposed the hero was raving about the loss of a handkerchief, was in the exact condition of a philologer reading his Bible without the under-meaning. He loses the spirit of antiquity, the fulness of meaning, the force of prophecy, the comprehensive sublimity of the design, the authority of inspiration, and he stands on a slippery grade, where he is in danger of sliding down to the lowest and most barren views of revelation, if he is not partially saved by a happy inconsistency.

It is therefore no violation of a Hebrew custom to suppose this divine Song to be an allegory. Indeed, the latent and allegorical mutually imply each other.*

* Perhaps it is not considered that logic implies a double sense in every object we see, — the individual and the generic, — a house, a field, a tree. Nothing meets the mind without its classifying appendage. We never suppose ourselves to know a thing until we can assign it its rank, or class. In a similar way the double sense of Scripture arises. For example, deliverance from the Babylonish captivity, a sample of all gracious deliverances, with our great Christian redemption prominent at the head of them. It is but an emphatic specimen of the double sense that pervades all creation. Every object in existence has two significations, — itself and the genus to which it belongs; and it is by this double signification that we know how to give it a name.

VII.

METAPHYSICS.

Perhaps it may raise a wonder that a book giving important instruction on such topics as the Bible should employ as its chosen instruments the indefinites of fancy, the coloring of poetry, that it should veil its doctrines in figures of speech, and that it should seem so often to sacrifce the understanding to the heart. In later times men choose for religion a more accurate method; they choose a system, a definition, a syllogism, a demonstration; whereas the Spirit of God, in its enlightening and inspiring influences, chooses a song, an allegory, a figure of speech, a painted cloud, bright as the morning sun, but far less certain in its glory or its light. This is a method which our second thoughts only pronounce to be wise. Our first objections to it lead to the last discovery.

Now the solution is, that this method, with reference to the peculiar subject of religion, is not only more impressive, but even more clear, than one more didactic and more metaphysical. Men are always forming systems, — drawing nice lines, in morals as well as mathematics; they are fond of points without magnitude and lines without breadth and thickness; and from these fixed ideas they hope to draw certain demonstrations. But it is not so in the kingdom of Nature. Look round the world. Who can tell us where the sea commences and the dry land ends? How high must the swelling mound be to pass from a hill into a mountain? When does a shrub rise into a tree, and what is the difference between an elegant house and a palace? Is New Holland an island or a continent, or are the Bermuda Islands in the West Indies or not? Nature delights to make her works perfectly obvious without nice lines, and she seems to say to man, You must understand me on these conditions. Strictly speaking, there is no such thing as metaphysics, and still less have the metaphysical sciences shed light on religion. As I consider this as one of the greatest discoveries of modern times, allow me to illustrate and prove this important conclusion.

For the sake of method, we will first state what we mean by metaphysics; secondly, show that it is an endless pursuit without a finding,— an eternal hunt without the captured prey; thirdly, the reason why it ever has been and ever must be so; and, lastly, this fact foreseen threw the inspired teachers on a very different method.

First, then, let us not contend about an airy cloud. Let us state what we mean by metaphysics as a science.

It is one of those words which we seem to understand before we attempt to define it. Its meaning must be learned from its prevailing use. Now the metaphysicians uniformly complain of the language of the forum; it is not accurate enough for them; they quit the common use of language for something *more accurate*, and as the *more accurate* necessitates the *most accurate*, they never can cease their pursuit until they reach an accuracy that never can be altered. The subject usually, to be sure, is the human mind; and yet metaphysics is not, strictly speaking, synonymous with mental philosophy. But when a man in mental philosophy departs from the language of common life in pursuit of the precisest precision, when he seeks fixed ideas for fixed words, he becomes a metaphysician; and the more he approaches the words and meaning of them so perfect as to be fixed, the better metaphysician he is. As Democritus, and Epicurus, his imitator, in considering the material world, chose to resolve it into atoms (that is, particles that had undergone their last dissection) so fine that they could not be finer, so the metaphysician, in considering mind, wishes to analyze it into its last elements. The moment he dissects beyond common life, he stands pledged never to quit his pursuit until he has landed himself and his readers on the coast of absolute perfection. He is a man in pursuit of language and ideas permanent from their perfection.

Hence Locke invented a terminology of his own; and Kant is said to be a still stronger instance. The latter claimed to have put the very cap-stone on the edifice of mental analysis.*

This, then, is the science of metaphysics; a science which leaves the foggy sea of probability and common life, to land us on the cape where the sun shines with undeviating and unsetting beams. A metaphysician is in pursuit, not of omniscience, to be sure, but a human perfection.

But, secondly, we remark that this is an endless pursuit without a finding, an eternal hunt without the captured prey. Every one the least tinctured in literature knows the everlasting mutations which have existed in the several systems which have chased each other down like the clouds of a summer day. Ever since Aristotle and Plato have established their antagonist schools, the metaphysical writers have had a very transient reputation for truth; they have erected their systems only to find them overthrown. They have had a great influence over each other, but a curious influence. One generates another,—it is constant action and reaction. One is a servile follower of another, or a determined opponent; and when an opponent, he sees nothing but absurdities in the system he opposes. The influence of a predecessor over

* Certainly his admirers claimed it for him; I do not know whether he claimed it for himself. His cumbrous terminology seems to imply it.

a follower is immense. He either enlarges his system or overthrows it. Hobbs produces Malebranche; Malebranche, Locke; Locke, Berkeley and Hume; then come Reid and Stewart; then the German school; and the most subtile cannot agree. The most renowned of them are destructives. It is a curious fact that the most subtile speculations in this indefinite science produce almost universal conviction in the uninitiated, and awaken objections in the mind of the collateral few; a system is built up to be overthrown, — built up to the admiration of the world, and overthrown to its astonishment. The history of metaphysics represents the course of the Neponset River in our vicinity; a dike is built up to accumulate a great pond of black water, full of mud-turtles and bloodsuckers, and which seems to be deep because no man can see to the bottom, and whose force is employed in turning a paper-mill. The engineering lasts for a time. Some one comes and breaks the dike; the water is dissipated, the stream becomes shallow, and the dike with its black water is removed to a new place, and a world of paper of similar texture is made in several spots. There have been metaphysicians of great ingenuity, of the greatest subtilty; but on what was their fame founded? The greatest of them have been destructives. Locke begins his work with a destructive introduction, — no such thing as innate ideas. Hume, by far the acutest metaphysician that England (perhaps I may say the world) ever produced, is a self-conscious and intentional destructive. He means to reduce all that has gone before him to a *reductio ad absurdum*. He aims to destroy all the paper fortresses which were deceiving mankind by their seeming strength. Berkeley, a little earlier, was a destructive without knowing it. He stood one grade lower than Hume, because he had the acuteness to build the system which he had not the acuteness to see must be destroyed. Kant is said to be a destructive. His fame rests on what he overthrew; and Sir William Hamilton, the wonder of our age, whose miraculous learning guided his almost miraculous sagacity, reposes at last in what he calls a learned ignorance. Such a history may show the Divine wisdom in choosing other channels by which to pour out the effusions of revealed truth.

There is another consideration. Revelation is for the people, not for the few. When we consider that mankind at large have neither patience or ability to understand these nice distinctions, we may well rejoice in the Mercy that, in pitying our hearts, has pitied our intellects, and has condescended to clothe the words of salvation in a vesture of light. The Lord God is a sun as well as a shield.

In the works of God and in the ways of man we find one remarkable contrast. Mankind are forced by both their strength and weakness on a logical view of the works of God. They must view creation, not as a huddle of unarranged atoms, but under the form of genus and species; and what we call understanding a thing is, not knowing its metaphysical essence, but arranging it in its proper class, according to its similitude and the formal laws of thought. This art of arranging begins very early in children. They know what a dog or cat is, because they know how to arrange them according to the technics of a future logic. The first impression gives the distinction. But in this arranging the source of all future knowledge, there springs up one false impression which becomes very deceptive. We impute to Nature the lines drawn by our own thoughts. Nature always makes a comparatively wide margin at the border. The species fade into each other in confused lines. Man is always distinguishing, Nature is always confounding; man tries to grasp an ideal perfection, Nature only approximates. Hence the Platonists always view ideas from the centre, while the metaphysician demands the boundary and the border. But this is a knowledge which God perhaps has denied to all beings except himself.

Thus the history of metaphysics shows that it is a vain pursuit of unattainable perfection; that is, the perfection of a permanent resting-place. True, some one may say that it is fallacy to suppose that the past is a measure of the future; that what man never has found, he never can find; since before the period of any modern discovery this would have been found false, or might have generated a despair which would have prevented it. I allow the force of the objection, and will proceed to show why the science of metaphysics is so unstable and floating, and in this *why* we may find a sufficient answer to the above plausible objection.

Thirdly, then, we maintain that we can see the reason of this everlasting uncertainty that overhangs all the systems which have been offered to the world. It never can have a fixed terminology, because it never can support it by fixed ideas. The last analysis of thought can never be found. The mathematics is supposed to be the most certain of the sciences, because it sets out with the most fixed definitions. But how does it secure them? The answer is instructive. It secures them not by a real entity, but by an abstraction. A point is defined position without magnitude. Did such a point ever exist? No,—nobody supposes it. We only attempt to consider position without magnitude; that is, for all the purposes of demonstration, we consider the place and leave out the magnitude, knowing all the time that a point as a metaphysical existence never can be found. The thing is an utter impossibility for every purpose but a mathematical demonstration. So of a line, so of a surface. But, *a fortiori*, when we pass out of the mathematical region, the elementary idea becomes an impossibility.

Time is the condition of all existence. But what is time? Is it the motion of the sun? the succession of thought? the channel of thought? or what is it? Ask the question, and the answer vanishes. We can form no idea of time as an absolute whole which may not immediately become an integral part. No portion of time so small that it may not suffer division and be yet smaller. What is present time? I see no reason why time should not be as indefinitely divisible as matter; that is, we may suppose a second to be divided into a billion of parts, and only one of these parts present *at once.* How easy would it be to show that the sharpest pain may be easily borne, for it can only endure the billionth part of a second. But who cannot endure the sharpest pain for so short a duration? It is absolutely zero, and many zeros amount to nothing. *Ergo,* the sharpest pain is no pain whatever, — it being always remembered we speak metaphysically. Moreover, with regard to time, contradictions must be true. If time is not eternity, it must have had a beginning, an absolute beginning; but this is impossible, since we can imagine no era so high that we cannot go higher. Here, then, is a necessary contradiction. We postulate an absolute beginning which we immediately pronounce impossible. Sir Wiliam Hamilton has demonstrated that the absolute, which we are always seeking, and to which we are always tending, is inconceivable. So our ideas of cause and effect, absolute unity, personal identity, the one and the many in the mind, how its unity is to be contemplated and how many it is to be divided into, — all these things admit of no solution. But these are the counters with which Metaphysics professes to perform her operations. But if her counters are uncertain, so must be her conclusions. She is ever pursuing the absolute. Now if the absolute does not exist, her search must ever be in vain. She has never found an entity which does not admit of a new section, — a *one* which may now become many. Just as an integer in arithmetic may be turned into an infinite fraction by increasing the denominator.

This question was distinctly before the old Greek philosophers; it is discussed by Plato, in his Parmenides. The one and the many, — the ontological one and the ontological many. This is the sum of all philosophy. This constitutes the archetypal world, — the world of ideas. Science demands that these ideas should be rigid, fixed, immovable, because they are the elements of certain knowledge. But how can we postulate that they should be fixed or not fixed? If they are not fixed, there is no science; and if they are fixed, how shall we compare them, and how shall we know that they may not demand a new fixing? Before Plato, the schools had started this question, and in his Parmenides he attempts an answer. But how dark and unsatisfactory! The difficulties of that dialogue, and the various hypotheses as to its design and meaning, are a proof, not of the voluntary obscurity of the author, but the darkness of the subject. In a word, to form an idea, known to be complete, of anything (except our pleasures and pains, and these are never so high but they may be higher), — a tree, a rock, a mountain, a drop of water, a gas, or any chemical substance, — or so simple that it cannot be simpler, — is beyond the abilities of the human mind. But this is what the metaphysician professes and designs. If then his materials fail him, no wonder his edifice is never finished. His successor always comes with a nicer analysis; he professes to get nearer the absolute to which his predecessor has aimed. He questions his analysis, and says his elements are not elements, and if these elements exist out of the circle of human comprehension, — and this is demonstrable, not from history only, but from the very nature of the mind and the object it pursues, — why then it is manifest that the pursuit is vain.

The language of the forum is confessedly approximatory. You not only know that you fall short of ideal accuracy, but you have in your mind the comparative standard by which you speak. You aim to be in harmony with your fellow-men. Your rule is a conventional one. You talk of envy, love, hope, fear, government, liberty, the Church, or the State, and you are under a tacit obligation, and, if you are a man of common honesty, it is your earnest aim to mean what your fellow-men mean. You catch your note from société; you sing the tune of the times. You know very well that these words are capable of a nicer analysis; and if you use one of them in such a way you give notice of your intention. But this is not the stand-point of the metaphysician; he departs from the language of the forum, and in his first step professes and obliges himself not to rest until he has found the absolute element of thought. He must analyze until no one can analyze on him. For where is the advantage of calling a compound a simple? and where is the benefit of a journey that lands you among the ambiguities from which you started, and which it was the sole object of your migration forever to escape?

What are the recent metaphysicians constantly saying of Locke? It is, that his language is ambiguous, vacillating, and uncertain. So say Reid, Stewart, Cousin, and Sir William Hamilton. They complain of his terminology and wonder at his vagueness. Even the word *idea*, the hinge of his whole system, is not used in the Platonic sense, and is used with the least precision.

Such is the universal complaint. I suspect, however, that the vagueness of Locke is only comparative, and is owing chiefly to the finer analysis which his speculations have enabled his disciples and antagonists to make. Continued investigations always lead to new discriminations. Kant is said to have been so dissatisfied with the result of the past as to have given himself an unbounded license in introducing a new terminology. Well,—did he reach the end? Did he render superfluous all future analysis? Did he put the capstone on the mental arch? Nothing like it; he set all the initiated to examining his systems, and he now "sways a doubtful sceptre amidst a host of opponents." Finally come Fitch and Cousin, finding, as they claim, the absolute, that is, the world of ideas radiating from one all-inclusive One (such as Plato said could only exist in the Divine Mind), ideas absolved from all the grossness of matter and all the imperfections of a finite mind. And Sir William Hamilton steps in and shows the absolute; the unconditional has been inconceivable in past ages, and must be so in all ages to come. The only metaphysician in the universe is God on his eternal throne.

It might seem strange to borrow an illustration from a material science. But I have often thought that the history of chemistry for a century past might illustrate our difficulties in the department of metaphysics. It is evident that the chemists in the days of Chapital and Lavoisier contemplated a perfection in the science and an adequacy in the terminology which the recent experimenters have long since abandoned in despair. It is pretty clear that the analyzer never can know or prove that he has found a simple substance. Those now regarded as such may turn out, in the nicety of our future experiments, to be endless compounds; and Nature retires to a more secret cell as we pursue her in her hidden recesses. She draws before her naked form a thicker veil, and refuses to be known. So far as accuracy is concerned, the four elements of the ancients, with their sublime quintessence, may be as good a division of matter as any we yet have discovered. The zero of the thermometer is a remarkable witness of our efforts, our presumption, our defeat. Zero was first considered, with some hesitation and doubt, as the highest degree of cold that nature allowed; and now all chemists confess there is no zero, or if there is, it never can be known. We never can find the highest degree of heat or cold. Now, if this material science thus presents us its insoluble problems, how can we expect to reach the last, the fixed, the eternal analysis of the human mind? If the crucible and the voltaic battery fail, how shall a man succeed when his implements are the same as his objects? Almost the only thing that a chemist is sure of is, that his finest analysis may be yet finer. And though a psychologist may know the usefulness and certainty of his relative knowledge, yet the true metaphysician must sit down in despair when he contemplates the blunders of his predecessors, and even his own acuteness in detecting them. The same sagacity that tells him he has surpassed them on the troubled sea, must show him more clearly that he has not reached the shore.

To this illustrious modern (i. e. Locke) we may add the example of Plato; his testimony is strong against the possible existence of any practical system of metaphysics. No one saw more clearly, or divined more accurately, what an absolute idea or simple concept should be. Science was the harmony of ideas, and before there was harmony the note itself must be fixed. The simple idea did not, according to Plato, exist in anything else, οὐδέ που ὂν ἐν ἑτέρῳ τινί, but ἀλλὰ αὐτὸ καθ' αὑτὸ μεθ' αὑτοῦ μονοειδὲς ἀεὶ ὄν, itself according to itself, always the same. Such were the necessary elements of absolute science. But where do they exist in their necessary perfection? In the archetypal world; that is, the objective contemplations of the Supreme Mind. Plato saw the necessity of such simple concepts; he believed in their existence, and he found them only in the Supreme Being. To understand one of his ideas (since its intrinsic nature is modified by its relative standing), he postulates omniscience. *Ergo*, this kind of science is impossible to man.

We may illustrate this impossibility of fixed ideas to our wavering minds in many instances. We use the words "present consciousness" and "memory" in common parlance without suspecting there is any difficulty in distinguishing them. We are conscious of the joys or sorrows of the passing hour, we remember the events of yesterday; but suppose we were required to draw the accurate line between present consciousness and memory, how difficult! how perplexing! how impossible! The moment is gone before we can contemplate it; consciousness becomes memory before we can ask what either of them is. Our very existence is a sliding stream, and the drop before us slides by while we are fixing its place. We are trying to fix an idea whose very nature is to be unfixed. So in the moral world; we love the lovely object. Call it beauty, if you please. The love of it is produced by the perception, and yet the perception implies a previous love; for no man loves by his intellectual powers. Now, which goes first? which is parent? which is child? which is cause? which is effect? Answer, O analyst, if you can.

Such being the negative point in which all these researches culminate, we come, lastly, to say, that this fact foreseen threw the inspired writers on a very different method. We may first remark the certainty of the fact.

With respect to the Old Testament the case is obvious. No one will deny that it is delivered to us in a language as far from the abstract as possible. Its abstract terms are of the most primitive character. It teaches by history, by biography, by example, by poetry, by allegory, by the embryo-drama, by moral painting, by the sighs of sorrow and the gratulations of joy;— through all its pages, from its simple history to the strains of the prophets, there reigns the evidence of the most primitive simplicity. It has not even risen up to the language of the forum, and the wonder is that so much truth can be communicated by such simple materials. There is the most of system there with the least of form, of any book in the world; and it comes from this fact, that higher wisdom never spoke to greater ignorance. But when we come to the New Testament, though a nicer language is chosen and we see the marks of a more cultivated age, yet we see no traces of metaphysics; that is, no one of the speakers or writers attempts to depart from the terminology of the forum. Not even St. Paul, educated as he was in the highest schools of his nation. I defy a man to point out a single word in all his writings that has the least tincture of a scholastic use. His dictionary is always a conventional one. He was perfectly understood in every synagogue he addressed. It is true, he often departs from the popular Greek, and he once gives us notice of it, I think (1 Cor. i. 13), in the words which our translators have rendered " comparing spiritual things with spiritual," which may be translated, " explaining spiritual thoughts by a spiritual terminology." But this terminology did not come from a metaphysical school. It came from two sources, — the magnitude of his subject, and the hue which Hebrew usage had cast over his Greek dialect. It is remarkable of his mental terms, that they are all from the forum; that, so far from nice distinctions, many of them are synonymous; and so far is he from showing any dependence on closet-distinctions, that he seems rather ambitious to show how completely he can convey his meaning without them. The passage (1 Thessalonians v. 23), "The very God of peace sanctify you wholly (ὁλοτελεῖς), and I pray God your whole spirit, and soul, and body, be preserved blameless unto the coming of our Lord Jesus Christ." How misleading it would be to do as some Platonic Christians have done, — to make an intentional distinction between soul and spirit! even the distinction between soul and body fades away in this passage, — ὁλοτελεῖς is the explanatory word, — the Apostle's intention being to say, I wish you to be entire Christians.

See, then, the wisdom of abjuring a science progressive in its nature, and when it reaches its goal vanishing into the inconceivable. I am aware no theological seminary has or can exist without teaching the science of mental philosophy and all the metaphysics involved in it. It is a science whose history is useful; it sharpens the intellect, develops our nature, and even its negative discovery is very important; as, when we come to a river where one place is not fordable and another is, knowing the danger of one spot may urge us to another, so the discovery in this case is not a vain one. We have had the hunt, and if we have taken nothing, we have enjoyed the chase and go to a field of equal pleasure and greater profit.

The sacred writers, therefore, renouncing this source of teaching, are directed to use every other. They call the imagination, the heart, the picturing hymn, the painted emotion, the related fact, the sublime illustration, to their service. In using the abstract as a minimum, they resort to other sources as a maximum, and it is one preparation for receiving Solomon's Song as a sublime allegory, to remember that it is found in a book which, foreseeing the imbecility of man, lisped to him in the language which his childhood needed, and to which his age, after all its specious improvements, must be compelled to return.

EXEMPLIFICATION.

It has been peculiarly disastrous to religion to apply an impossible mental analysis to explain any system of its doctrines. Predestination, the foreknowledge of the Deity, his immutable purposes, how prayer can obtain aught of a perfect and unchangeable nature,— all these and similar difficulties are enhanced by postulating a precision of knowledge beyond our faculties. We should remember that God's ways are not our ways, nor his thoughts our thoughts. The doctrine of the Trinity loses its objections when it reminds us of our ignorance. The whole rationale of the day of judgment, the great trumpet that is to wake the dead, — how a personal Saviour is to judge the millions that have lived, — all this admits of no accurate analysis. The first solemn impression is the best we can ever receive. Whenever we begin to analyze, we plunge into difficulties; and why should the subtile reason undertake to mend what was mainly addressed to the yielding heart?

But there is one doctrine of our holy religion which I think has suffered wofully by being presented to us with a background of metaphysics to increase its precision and diminish its effect. I allude to the doctrine of the ATONEMENT, or the moral import of the death of Christ. It is called in Scripture a sacrifice, and we are said to be "reconciled to God by the death of his Son." Now the whole narrative is a simple and affecting display of his mercy and our guilt. They go together; and if *one died for all, then were all dead.* The first impression of the narrative (after we are told of the Godhead and incarnation of Christ) is the most affecting. It was a great effort, for which there must have previously existed a great reason. But the theological metaphysician thinks he must explain it by an analysis, — by an application of the rigid metaphysical art. He first assumes an abstract Justice which is itself independent of all consequences, all the practical evils of transgression, and this abstract Justice must be satisfied. This has been the assumption since the days of Anselm; and has prevailed over the minds of those that seemed to modify or deny. This Justice must be illustrated by earthly analogies; not one of them being adequate or fully reaching the case. Thus a king is said to give up his son, to honor the law, while he pardons the criminal. Thus one soldier is whipped in the place of another.* It is remarkable, however, that, when these cases occur apart from any theological illustration, the very men who use them for illustrations should regard them as proofs of barbarous ignorance. We have an example. Cotton Mather apologizes for and even denies the fact, that an old bedrid weaver was hung in the place of a strong and vigorous warrior of the Puritans, to satisfy the Indians. Gutzlaff mentions it as a proof of the obtuseness of the Chinese, that such substitutions prevail among them. When the Arabs, or some barbarous tribe on our American coast, in their wild ideas of justice, — by a double mistake confounding the idea of the deed and the identity of the people who do it, — murder the crew of one American ship because another has robbed them, all see the cause of the deed. The fact is, there is no finite example on earth that can illustrate the justice of God in substituting Christ as an expiation for us as penal sufferers. Every analysis, accompanied as they usually are with a human illustration, only weakens the impression which the great mystery makes. Christ died for us for reasons infinitely deeper than time can reveal. I doubt

---

* See the third Sermon on the Atonement, by the younger Edwards.

myself whether there is any such thing as an abstract Justice, or, in other words, a justice which is conceivable independent of the consequences of our good and evil deeds. Justice *is* justice, because conformity to it promotes social happiness and a disregard of it involves the community in misery and ruin. Tear the ideas asunder, and both of them are lost.

These popular illustrations are more deceiving because they *do* illustrate a part of the subject. For example, you say that a king finds a province in rebellion; he wishes to pardon them, but fears that sin followed by no suffering will seem a light thing, and weaken justice. He gives up his only son, &c., &c.; — and thus you hope to illustrate the justice of God and the love of Christ. Now the fact illustrates the love, but not the justice. If the king's son were to consent to die in such a cause, it would be a wonderful act of love, provided always that he saw the necessity and the wisdom of the deed. But I cannot see how it illustrates the Divine justice; for such an example on earth could never be viewed with approbation.

The old divines most fond of similar illustrations have been obliged to save their theory by saying, that Christ stood in a peculiar position; he had his own rights; his submission was voluntary; he was a Divine Being, and was not a common subject to the law; he had a right to be a substitute, because other rights did not hold him. How destructive is this concession to their whole purpose! Where there is no resemblance, there can be no illustration.

Christ was wounded for our transgressions; he died, the just for the unjust; his death has a vicarious import, but surely not in the strict sense which the absolute idea of a substitute demands. No party pretends this; those that carry their ideas of a substitute or an imputation highest do not claim that Christ was punished for us in the strictest sense. The strictest justice would demand the offending victim; and the moment you depart from this, you take your stand on the comparative ground.

THE EXAMPLE OF THE SACRED WRITERS.

But the grand proof of the uselessness of metaphysics in religion is the example of Christ and the sacred writers. They have all thrown themselves on the popular terminology. They make nothing depend on a nicer analysis. They seem ambitious to show us that religion, with all its sublime conceptions, may be communicated in those broad terms which are every day used in the intercourse of common men. As John Bunyan has shown us that his allegory could be related with scarcely a help from the Latinized terms of our own language, so the inspired writers seem to be determined to show us that they need no technics of the mind, — no distinctions or names beyond the usages of the plainest men. High thoughts can be imparted in simple terms. There is a remarkable passage in one of Christ's discourses (John viii. 43): Διατί τὴν λαλιὰν τὴν ἐμὴν οὐ γινώσκετε; Ὅτι οὐ δύνασθε ἀκούειν τὸν λόγον τὸν ἐμόν,— "You cannot understand my diction because you have not grasped the spirit of my system." There is a distinction here between ὁ λόγος and ἡ λαλιά; the one the all-comprehensive word, such as Gospel grace, &c., and the other the articulate parts. When you grasp the one, the inclusive mental word, you understand the other. I have been curious to pass over the New Testament and select all the words that express the operation of mind and its faculties, and not one of them is such as a metaphysician would think necessary to his simplest discussions. The broad faculties are named, the broad lines are distinguished; but the Divine language would be a golden fetter to Locke, Berkeley, or Kant. In 1 Thessalonians v. 23, we have a seeming philosophical distinction. The Apostle speaks of τὸ σῶμα, the body; ἡ ψυχή, the soul; τὸ πνεῦμα, the spirit; but certainly not, as some Platonists have dreamed, with the least approach to the Platonic distinction. The exponent of these words is found in the first clause of the verse, "May the God of peace sanctify you wholly," ὁλοτελεῖς. The specific mention of these powers is to give emphasis to that idea. The other mental words used are all of the forum. The following are the chief:

συνείδησις, καρδία, πάθος, πάθημα, σύνεσις, γνῶσις, θέλημα, the will, θέλησις, φρήν, *intelligentia, mens,* φρόνησις, reflection, wisdom, prudence; ἐνθύμησις, imagination, thought, vain desire; αἴσθησις is opposed to ἐπίγνωσις,— the first the sensual perception, the last the intellectual knowledge; αἰσθητήριον, the seat of the senses; νοέω, *mente intelligo* (this perhaps is the most philosophic word in the Bible); νόημα, the counsel of the mind; ἐπίσταμαι, to know well, to know supersensually. The affections of the mind are all obvious and popular; ἀγανακτέω, *indignor;* ἀγαπάω, the best love; ἀγάπη, ἀγνοέω, αἰδώς, ἀθυμέω, ἀνάμνησις, βουλή, βούλημα, rational will, deliberate conclusion; γνώμη, purpose, decision; γνῶσις, knowledge, discernment in religion; δέος, διαγνώσκω, accurate inquiry; διακρίνω, to judge, to hesitate. Εἶδος, not its Platonic meaning, from the Hebrew מַרְאָה; εἴδω, to see, to discern; ἔκστασις, *alienatio mentis,* the ecstatic state; ἑκών, *volens;* ἐνέργημα, *effectum;* ἐνέργεια, inner power; ἐνθυμέομαι, *animo volvo;* ἐνθύμησις, *cogitatio;* ἔννοια, the same; ἐπιθυμέω, to desire,— the noun; ἐπίγνωσις, accurate knowledge; ἐπίνοια, *praepositum;* ἐπιποθέω, *desidero abreptus;* θυμός, the mind, the seat of aversion and desire, *ira, furor,* &c.; ἰδέα, not Platonic, explained Matt. xxviii. 3; καταλαμβάνω,— a remarkable word, applied to the mind and yet popular in its origin,— I understand, I take your meaning. Λογίζομαι, not emphatic, λόγος,— both these words noticeable; they have a tinge of Platonism, because Platonism cast its coloring on the language of common life. They are colored by that philosophy, just as the word *idea* in the English language has been colored by the philosophy of Locke, not directly, but through its influence on the popular dialect. These words, and the τοῖς ποιήμασι νοούμενα (Romans i. 20) and τὸ θεῖον (Acts xvii. 29), are the words which come the nearest to being shaded by philosophy; I have no doubt the word νοούμενα is emphatic, and is meant to express the action of reason in its supersensual operations. The word λόγος too has its philosophic double meaning,—the inward and the spoken word, the thought and the sign. Ὄρεξις, *appetitus*. The two words ὅσιος and δίκαιος have the usual distinction which pervades all languages,—holiness and justice. Παρατήρησις, accurate observation; πεισμονή, *persuasio*; πεποίθησις, confidence. The cardinal word *faith*, πίστις, *persuasio cum fiducia*, has an entirely different hue in the sacred writers from what it has in philosophy; it comes from the Hebrew; its meaning and its bearing are to be sought for wholly in the Hebrew Scriptures; it corresponds to אֱמוּנָה; the Hebrew meaning prevails,—subjective truth,—the influence of revealed truth on the heart. Πρόθεσις, purpose, design; συμβιβάζω,—a word remarkable for its intellectual meaning, and for its remote origin,—to glue one thing to another, to prove by a chain of arguments; συνίημι, to understand; ψυχικός, opposed to πνευματικός. These are some of the most important specimens of sacred terminology; they are all remote from analytic nicety; they are taken from common life, and they show that religion can be taught without the mental philosophy with which it has been too often confounded.

To this catalogue we may add those words which are purposely comprehensive. Discrimination in language advances with the progress of thought. We are constantly dividing generic words, and making them more specific. But our Saviour and his disciples in their choice of terms are hardly up to the age in which they lived. Religion in our Saviour's discourses is Life, Ζωή, which may mean spiritual power, spiritual influence, holiness, activity, joy. It is purposely comprehensive.

I have said that metaphysics differs from psychology. Let me explain what I conceive the distinction to be. Metaphysics aims to find the fixed, invariable, certain, incontestable, elementary idea. It professes to stop only at the last solution. The psychologist, or writer on mental analysis, abandons such a hopeless design. He wishes only to give us an analysis of the mind which shall be practical because it is relative to the improved conception of others. If he departs from the language of the forum, it is only because he expects the forum at some time to follow him. He has not the least thought but what acuteness may make new distinctions and divide his elements into new component parts. He is doing what the chemist does,— not proving to a certainty he has found the last element, but only relatively the last; that is, relative to the present state of knowledge. The chemist knows well that he has not found, and never can be *sure* that he has found, a simple which may not in the process of experiment turn out to be a compound. We may illustrate it by the atoms of Epicurus. An atom, according to the system of Democritus, is a section which cannot be bisected. Epicurus allows it to be invisible. Now suppose two men: one of them is pulverizing some friable matter in order to find the finest powder that he can use, or its partial identity; the other is pursuing or laboring to find the strict philosophic atom. Which of them is engaged in the most hopeless task? The one resembles the mental philosopher, the other the metaphysician.

Bishop Berkeley has clearly recognized this distinction, though himself the victim to the error he so clearly saw. "Time, place, and motion," says he, "taken in particular or concrete, are what everybody knows; but having passed through the hands of a metaphysician, they become too abstract and fine to be apprehended by men of ordinary sense. Bid your servant meet you at such a time and such a place, and he shall never stay to deliberate on the meaning of the words. In conceiving that particular time and place, or the motion by which he is to get thither, he finds not the least difficulty. But if time be taken, exclusive of all those particular actions and ideas that diversify the day, merely for the continuation of existence, or duration in abstract, then it will perhaps gravel even a philosopher to comprehend it." (Principles of Human Knowledge, Part I. Sect. 97.)

Let me, however, be understood. I by no means intend to say that the psychologist as well as the metaphysician does not mean to depart from the looseness of popular language, and both of them may have the same terminus in their minds. But herein they differ; the psychologist allows the end of his analysis to be at an infinite distance from perfection; his object is never to lose sight of the relative; his object is always practical, and he attempts to analyze no further than he can take the thinking world with him. When he departs from the forum he expects to stop, not only short, but infinitely short, of the metaphysician's goal; whereas the metaphysician (perhaps half unconsciously to himself) expects to reach the goal. He will untwist the thread to the last filament, and present it to our admiring eyes. He is essentially analytic, and he means that his analysis shall be final.

There is another point in which I conceive they differ. The psychologist regards his analysis as found, to be sure, on lines drawn by nature, but not the only lines. He chooses those which he conceives to be the most useful. He pays great attention to the distinctions handed down to him from past generations. In a word, he regards his departments of mind and the consequent terminology very much as we regard the division of counties in Massachusetts, sometimes arbitrary, sometimes natural; sometimes the boundary lines following a river or a range of hills, but by no means excluding the possibility of another division, and made principally on the grounds of political utility. But the metaphysician regards his lines of analysis as fundamental, essential, eternal. They are foredrawn by nature, — he has only discovered them. Blot them out, or question them, you disturb his whole system. His terminology is the voice of Nature; his discoveries are drawn from her deepest recess.

There is another difference. The metaphysician does not allow that an idea or mental impression should be regarded as an image, or proof of a corresponding object in the outward world. Hence he feels himself obliged elaborately to account for his ideal system and its correspondence with outward causes. The objective and the subjective with him are at everlasting war; and while he is ambitious to prove all things, failing in his attempt, he falls into universal scepticism; or, if he does not reach this point, he is inconsistent, — he mixes proofs and assumptions together; just as Locke often passes over the point you wish him to prove, and proves that of which you never thought of doubting. Now the psychologist ignores or passes by all these difficulties; he is contented with a probable assumption. He knows that his terminology may be floating and his discoveries relative. To him probability is the foundation of his system as well as " the guide of life." *

It must be allowed that the psychologist is very apt to degenerate (perhaps I should say soar) into the metaphysician. He would hardly write his book if he did not in some degree depart from the diction of the forum. The question is, Where shall he stop? In his anxiety to be as subtle and as perfect as the case demands, he is tempted to grasp at intangible objects and pursue unintelligible distinctions. Thus the moral philosopher is sometimes lost in the fogs of the metaphysician. We can best make our distinction clear by examples. The writers who have best seen their own boundaries, and pursued accuracy without plunging into useless subtilties, are Augustine, Pascal, Baxter, Hutcheson, and, above all, Bishop Butler.

The impossibility of any finished system of metaphysics is indicated many ways. First, by the very nature of the subject, it seeks the ideal perfect, — the fixed, the absolute. Wherever it begins, it is driven to this line. Secondly, it demands an account of, and a demonstration of the correspondence between, the ideal and outward world, which is found impossible;

* Introduction to Butler's Analogy.

Thirdly, it forgets the weakness of the human faculties. Fourthly, it postulates a whole system, the one in the many, the many from the one, which can be known only by omniscience. Fifthly, the history of its speculations shows the impossibility of its aims. No system ever lasts, it exists only to be overthrown; and necessary truth to one man is an absurdity to another. The comments that the acutest minds make on the acutest are severe, contradictory, and astonishing. Sixthly, a system is often proved by the most irrefragable arguments, which every rational man sees to be false. As Hume says of Berkeley's speculations, "They admit of no answer and produce no conviction." Berkeley's Essay on the Principles of Human Knowledge is an astonishing example. The writer is honest, the premises are strong, the argument is safe, and the conclusion is irresistible; and yet who can believe what he sees irrefutably proved. The book is a wonderful example of an IMPOSSIBILITY DEMONSTRATED; and, finally, the science existing for more than two thousand years, employing the minds of the most ingenious artists, shows not the smallest tendency to a result. Nothing is settled; its negative power is strong, its affirmative nothing; it still continues to roll the same turbid stream to a sea as turbid as itself. Indeed, it seems to me that the most matchless metaphysician of our age has put the only termination possible to these investigations, when he says: "We are wholly ignorant of existence in itself; the mind knows nothing except in parts, by quality and difference and relations; consciousness supposes the subject distinguished from the object of thought; the abstraction of this contrast is the negation of consciousness; and the negation of consciousness is the annihilation of thought itself. The alternative, therefore, is unavoidable; either, finding the absolute, we lose ourselves; or, retaining self and individual consciousness, we do not reach the absolute." (Review of Cousin, Edinburgh Review, Oct. 1828.)

It is a fact, which perhaps we do not sufficiently notice, that logic is destructive of metaphysics,— the two arts cannot subsist together. The establishment of logic is the destruction of metaphysics. How is it so? Logic deals with genus and species. The syllogism is founded on this arrangement of the articles and operations of nature. But how do we make this arrangement, and on what principle? It is done very early, and before we are aware fully of the principle on which it is done. The generic or specific resemblance by which we arrange our conceptions is founded on central ideas,— central kinds, when the borders are very dark and indefinite. Taking the centre for our original division, the difference is very clear between a dwarf and a man, a shrub and a tree, a hill and a mountain, a gulf and a sea, a solid and a fluid, an animal and a plant; but when we come to the border, the difference fades away; we are perplexed and confounded. Who can tell or trace the insensible line which separates the infusoria from the vegetables among which they swim?

Now metaphysics delights to trace these borders; she is not satisfied with the popular logic. She tells you at once that your classification is a bad one; she does not understand one of your terms, nor accept one of your deductions. Tell me, she says, how large must your dwarf be before he becomes a man? which is the sea, and which is the gulf? Draw your immutable line, and give me the *absolute idea.* Yes, give me one fixed notion, with which all others must harmonize, and I will confess the possibility of science. But I disdain your confused approximations; I will not consent to wander with you in the dark, where you are alike ignorant of your starting-point and your goal. Logical *deduction* supposes a previous *induction*, and when was that induction made? When you only knew enough to see that a sheep differed from a horse, and that all horses and sheep were alike.

The common people suppose themselves to know a thing when they can classify it; that is, assign its place among genus and species. Present any individual object to them, and if they cannot classify it, they say it is unknown; but if it resemble what they have seen, they can always find its place. But genus and species themselves are wholly relative. They depend on external resemblances, and relate to our former ideas. Absolute ideas in this department have no place. The two sciences of logic and metaphysics are destructive of each other; if the one is established, the other is overthrown.

It is far from being the object of these remarks to depreciate the study of metaphysics. It not only sharpens the mind, but perhaps there are no writers to whom, on the ground of collateral utility, the world owes so much as to metaphysicians. When we ask directly what they have discovered, we answer, never what they sought. They uniformly travel a road that leads to nothing. But it does not follow that their speculations have been useless. In the first place, the negative discovery is vastly important. Such is the fascination which this science presents to the youthful aspirant, so much light does it promise to shed on his own being, and especially on religion, that nothing but experience — investigation, and close investigation — can convince him of the fallacy of his first impressions; and then, moreover, the ignorance to which his closest investigations lead him is not the ignorance from which he started. The ignorance of experience is not the ignorance of inexperience. The precise ideas which he has been seeking serve by contrast to show the nature of that proximate and probable ground on which, after all his excursions, his soul must rest. We know all things by contrast and comparison. Of those absolute ideas which the metaphysician seeks, we know two things,— we know they must exist, and, secondly, we know we never can find them. This teaches us the amplitude of knowledge, and gives us a lesson of humility. Indeed, when we consider what a fascination metaphysical speculation has held over the theologian, metaphysics must be taught in order to cure him of the charm. It is not a mere negative discovery. He is taught the difference between a perfect intellect and his own; and human knowledge has a perfection in its own sphere, when it has found those dread limits which separate the eternal light from our clearest mental vision. Mr. Locke has said:—

"It is of great use to the sailor to know the length of his line, though he cannot with it fathom all the depths of the ocean. It is well to know that it is long enough to reach the bottom at such places as are necessary to direct his voyage, and caution him against running on shoals which may ruin him. Our business here is not to know all things, but those which concern our conduct."*

* Locke's Essay, Introduction, Sect. 6.

PART II.

THE VERSION.

THE VERSION.

In the following translation I shall impose on myself these rules: — First, to be as literal as possible, but not so literal as not to aim to give the parallel meaning; for the meaning of the Bible is the Bible. I shall endeavor to give not only the meaning, but to preserve the poetic and moral shading, so that a word or a metaphor may give the same impression now as to the primitive readers. This is my *aim*, though I am conscious that the attainment is scarcely possible. I shall not shun the old translation where I find nothing to alter, — and some parts of it, I confess, are matchless and inimitable, — as the description of spring, chap. ii. 8–13, and of the lost interview, chap. v. 2–6. These have always appeared to me, like Shakespeare's piece of prose in Hamlet (Act II. Scene 2), — "This goodly frame, the earth, seems to me a sterile promontory, this most excellent canopy, the air," &c. — to be magical outbursts of felicity, both in thought and language, which all must admire, and none can hope to mend. I shall abandon the method adopted since the days of

Lowth, of giving broken lines, because it offers a show of poetry which the performance does not justify, and therefore lays a trap for the reader's dissatisfaction. These broken lines are like the forms in Egyptian coffins, ghastly forms of a life that does not exist; they indicate neither measure nor rhyme, and they lure the reader to expect either the one or the other. Only think of these words passing for measured poetry!—

"The Burden of Dumah.

"He calleth to me out of Seir, —
Watchman, what of the night,
Watchman, what of the night?
The watchman said,
The morning cometh, and also the night;
If ye will inquire, inquire ye:
Return, come."

Surely such poetry reminds one of Dr. Johnson's burlesque line, —

"Lay your knife and your fork across your plate."

If the reader will count his fingers, he will find that all his fingers and his thumbs on both hands exactly correspond to the number of syllables in this beautiful line, and in this respect it is as good as any line found in Pope's Iliad or Milton's Paradise Lost; nay, it is better, for many a line in these great poets must be saved from false quantity by an ecthlipsis, or synæresis, or some other grammatical device; and in this way I have no doubt that President Buchanan's last message can be turned into surprising poetry. But surely the prophet intended no such device. The Hebrews had the elements of poetry in them, but not ripened in its modes, nor polished into its subsequent perfection. Let us leave them in their native simplicity, and not make them answerable for promises which they never will fulfil, because in fact they never made them.

As to the notes, I am anxious to show that this Song of Songs has a constant practical lesson, a lesson which could be taught in its force and beauty in no other way. I wish to show that a pious reader with a congenial taste may find matter of improvement, not only from the whole, but from the compact parts. In showing this, I impose upon myself these restrictions: not to be wire-drawing; not to force out a latent meaning, — not to torture language, or violate common sense; not to fall into the track of the Jewish or Christian mystics on the one hand, and on the other to shun, as I would a syrtis, the sensualism or the literalism of such writers as Grotius, and Dr. Noyes of our own country. I blame not these men; they are scholars, and faithful perhaps to their own light. But they could not understand such a book as this. There was not a responsive fibre in them.* The great difficulty is in the first step. Is

---

* There was a man in a neighboring town, some sixty years ago, a very worthy citizen, who was very indifferent to appropriating any money for the improvement of sacred music. He was not more avaricious than the rest of his neighbors. Everybody wondered at his reluctance. He at

the book a spiritual allegory? If it is, the higher interpretation follows of course. Now I do not pledge myself to find an articulate meaning, in every part, to the reader's satisfaction. But such is my aim. I am more clear as to the general design of this song, than I am as to its particular application; but I am not without hope, that, without borrowing the robe of Philo or Origen, I may find, under the luxurious dress, an obvious — at least a probable — application for every period. These last, like branches of a noble tree, grow out of the original design.

THE GOLDEN SONG OF SOLOMON.

Solomitis.

Let HIM greet me with a kiss from his sacred mouth, WHOSE love is sweeter than wine.

Let us pause a little on this important verse. It opens the whole subject, it strikes the key-note, and demands our attention. We must not stumble at the threshold. It is to be understood by the help of the emphasis, and under the shadow of that emphasis I

last told the secret. "I never yet," said he, "could see any use in cultivated music. All we want is a little joyful noise. For my part," added he, "the falling of a shovel on the hearth, provided it rings well, or the rattling of a pair of tongs in a brass kettle, is as good music as I ever desire to hear."

have ventured to insert the word *sacred*, as indicating the person and the nature of the salutation. I suppose the words to be spoken by the espoused one in the very spirit with which Mary Magdalene addressed her risen Saviour: "But Mary stood without at the sepulchre weeping; and as she wept, she stooped down and looked into the sepulchre, and seeth two angels in white, sitting, the one at the head and the other at the feet, where the body of Jesus had lain. And they say unto her, Woman, why weepest thou? She saith unto them, Because they have taken away my Lord, and I know not where they have laid him. And when she had thus said, she turned herself back, and saw Jesus standing, and knew not that it was Jesus. Jesus saith unto her, Woman, why weepest thou? Whom seekest thou? She, supposing him to be the gardener, saith unto him, Sir, if thou have borne him hence, tell me where thou hast laid him, and I will take him away." (John xx. 11–15.) Now the latter part of this speech has been greatly admired. Three times the pronoun is used without a consciousness of the absence of the antecedent. Her heart is so full that she supposes every one must know who she means by HIM. So, in the abrupt beginning of this book, there is but one antecedent to which the pious mind can recur. The sacred kiss can come from none but the Heavenly Bridegroom. The ellipsis is impressive and significant.

But wine and tokens of love fill the first strain of the poem! If we may suppose these words first to be put into the mouth of some rustic beauty, espoused to King Solomon, the ellipsis is natural and impressive. To be taken from her native vale, and from an idolatrous nation, and to be preferred by such a wise and holy king, must have given an interest to any salutation she might receive, and Solomon must have filled her heart. Going up to the holy city must have given a religious interest to her unusual nuptials. But this was only a stepping-stone. God had a deeper design; the fact was significant; and the same God who could make a dream or a name a symbol of prophecy could make this union a foreshadowing of the union of the Gentile church with its Redeemer.

But then the sensuality of wine and love! Why use these as images of the purest passion that can actuate the heart? Why dress piety in such wanton robes? Because in that age, and in all ages, certain minds have sought such images to express the breakings of the heart. It has been delightful to some nations, and to all ardent minds, to picture devotional feeling in erotic poetry. If a colder criticism should oppose it, it would be like quenching the conflagration of a burning city with a few flakes of falling snow. It is not difficult to see whence this proclivity arises.

First, the glowing mind, intense in its feeling, looks

round for adequate expressions, and finds them here. Nature is too strong for art. We are told that, when Madame Guyon wrote her ardent poetry, it was in vain that the celebrated Bishop of Meaux exposed her doctrines with all the powers of his wit, aided by all the splendor of his eloquence. He only increased the flame. His criticism probably never abated the lusciousness of a single expression.

Secondly, the mystic feels a secret satisfaction in triumphing over the tainting influence of the figures. The unconsciousness (of which it is half conscious at least) is pleasing. The rapid application of the figure to the higher subject is a testimony to the mind of its own purity.

Thirdly, the satisfaction of finding the resemblance in the remote. The contrast is great. The rich treasure is deeply hid.

Lastly, such similitudes take our whole nature with them. They familiarize the mystic and ennoble the familiar. They elevate the natural propensity into a divine one. As the incarnation of Christ unites the definiteness of a mortal conception with the sublimity of a divine one, so this union takes the whole strength of our minds and our hearts, and gives double ardor to the compound passion. All the fire of a mortal love joins with the purity of the divine to increase the outflow of the soul. No wonder that such representations should be so fascinating.

Perhaps the mortal passion itself has a deeper signification than at first appears. Perhaps the rant and raptures of love were designed to show us how false and fair our first idols, and how true the beauty to which our disappointment turns us. Perhaps Otway may teach us divinity : —

> "O woman, lovely woman, nature made you
> To temper man : we had been brutes without you;
> Angels are painted fair to look like you;
> There's in you all that we believe of heaven,
> Amazing brightness, purity, and truth,
> Eternal joy, and everlasting love."

It teaches us, at least, that the passions justify themselves by borrowing and imputing perfection. So Virgil : —

> "Quis novus hic nostris successit sedibus hospes!
> Quem sese ore ferens! quam forti pectore, et armis!
> Credo equidem, nec vana fides, genus esse deorum."

No one can read Rousseau's New Eloise without thinking of the strength of the passion and the frailty of its earthly foundation. A novelist always substitutes the indefinite for the eternal. He conducts his afflicted pair to social happiness *not terminated*, and there leaves them ; just as a painter, not able to picture an infinite road, makes it wind round a hill, and leaves the spectator's fancy to finish what the power of his limited pencil could only begin.

The spirit of this paragraph is clear. It supposes a

mind so full of Christ that an elliptical pronoun suggests him. It turns away from all earthly attractions to seek some token of his love. Let him own me as his, and fill my soul with his love, and it is all I ask. My obedience is secured when I find my chief happiness in his service; when his love is sweeter than wine, i. e. all sensual good. Under another figure the same sentiment is expressed, chap. viii. 6: "Set me as a seal upon thine heart, as a seal upon thy arm; for love is strong as death."

We may give a specimen how these sentiments might appear in a modern dress: —

"From all the enchantments of time,
  Where bitterness waits on desire,
Where pleasure is blended with crime,
  And love is a vanishing fire,
I turn to the Bridegroom above,
  Whose looks can such sweetness impart,
Whose kiss can our passions improve,
  Because it encounters the heart.*

"I am weary with phantoms that fade, —
  They cause me to weep and repine;
I would be in *His* garments arrayed
  Whose love is much better than wine.
When the heart from its idols is loosed,
  And the soul for its tenant makes room,
Then his name is like ointment effused,
  Affording the richest perfume."

---

* "The hearts of princes kiss obedience." — *King Henry* VIII., Act 3, Scene 1.

SOLOMITIS still speaks. (Verses 3, 4, 5, 6.)

Thy ointments have a delicate flavor; thy name is like ointment effused. Therefore the virgins love thee. Draw me; we will gladly follow. The king has brought me into his conclave; and there we will heartily rejoice. We will praise his love more than wine. The good love thee. I am dark, but fair; dark like the tents of Kedar; fair like the curtains of Solomon. O daughter of Jerusalem, — do not scorn me because I am dark; 't is my native sun. My native people were angry with me; they appointed me to keep the vineyards; but while I kept their vineyards, I lost my own, — i. e. my heart.

In the first place, let us regard the historical meaning. It is the address of a rustic girl to a refined king. She is a fair brunette, — just what we should expect from an Arab tribe. She has ointments preparatory to her exaltation; just as Esther was purified to go in to the king; "for so were the days of their purification accomplished, to wit, six months with oil of myrrh, and six months with sweet odors and with other things for the purification of the women." (Esther ii. 12.) Let us suppose, then, King Solomon to have had a mingled motive in espousing this Sheik's daughter, — partly the extension of true religion, partly empire, and partly personal glory; she has native charms and a wild cultivation. Suppose he affords her the sweet-scented unguents, and prepares her for his own seraglio. What a perfect fact to shadow out a higher union in the admission of the Gentile Church, the gratitude and love which would glow in her heart, and the purer piety which would at once pave the way and follow that event. It was not merely a figure; it was partly a specimen.

And then the wisdom behind the mortal council, and overruling the fact to its own designs! This was charming to a Hebrew mind. It is no more than what the poet has said: —

> "There's a Divinity that shapes our ends
> Rough-hew them how we will."

This, then, is the unforced lesson, certainly unforced when you have got over the difficulty of admitting the allegory. I merely hint.

"O let me have conscious communion with God;" or, to translate it into a proposition: "It is a privilege to feel in my heart that he loves me, for then I shall love him;" or, to reverse the proposition: "When I feel that I love him, I know that he loves me."

And for this, Divine attraction is necessary (see fourth verse); we should pray for it. This simple passage tells the great secret; how to get a will for virtue, — a question which has always perplexed the sensual man. It is by prevenient grace. "Draw me; we will run after thee." "No man can come to me, except the Father which hath sent me draw him." (John vi. 44.)

Now, I ask, admitting the allegory running through

the poem (and unless you do admit it you plunge from the sublime mountain into the muddy ditch that stagnates at its base), is this meaning arbitrary? Is it unnatural? Is it forced? Is it not all but necessary?

CHAP. I. 7–17.

SOLOMITIS.

Tell me, O beloved one, where thou feedest thy flocks; where is thy noontide shade. Why should I wander among other folds?

SOLOMON.

If you know not, O thou most beautiful of women, trace the footsteps; feed thy kids near the shepherds' tents. I compare you, O my loved one, to the horses of Pharaoh's chariots. How graceful are thy cheeks among thy chains, thy neck with its necklace! We have prepared for you golden collars with silver stars.

SOLOMITIS.

While the king sits in his circle, my nard diffuses its odor. A bundle of myrrh is my beloved to me; he shall rest in my inmost heart. A cluster of copher is my beloved to me in the gardens of Engedi.

SOLOMON.

O thou art fair, my love, thou art very fair, with eyes looking the dove. Yes, thou art beautiful, divinely beautiful; while our nuptial couch is the rural grove. The cedar-trees are the only beams to *our* house, — our only rafters are the branches over us.

Here, I think, we have indications of the historico-literal and the mystico-spiritual. It is impossible to be sure as to the meaning of such imperfect hints; for the whole poem is a succession of hints with a chasm of ellipsis between. The first speech, — " Tell me, O thou loved One! where thou feedest thy flock," &c., — may be a natural mistake of the rural lass on her first union with the king, or it may be the king went into her country to rusticate, or it may be an allegorical expression by which she signifies that the king is a shepherd and his kingdom is a flock. Whatever it be, it is a wish for love and communion; and the next verses are the language of encouragement from a superior: " You say you are black, and yet you hope you are fair. I compare you to the most polished and precious objects, — to Pharaoh's chariot. I will load you with every ornament," &c., &c.

But what is the higher meaning? Sure, it is obvious. Christ has selected human nature from its state of degradation and corruption, and he sees every beauty in it through the comeliness he puts upon it. As there is something remarkably beautiful in supposing a refined king, like Solomon, dwelling in such a house as described in 1 Kings vii., going into the country, dwelling in a tent, with the cedar-trees murmuring over him; so when the greater than Solomon condescends to adopt the Gentile sinners, beautify their hearts, and seeing the beauty that he has imparted, the parallel is complete. Then, too, the humblest scenes are beautiful with the presence of Christ.

CHAP. II. 1-7.

SOLOMITIS.

I am but a wild flower of the field, a lily of the valley.

SOLOMON.

Yes, but as the lily among the briers, so is my beloved among other women.

SOLOMITIS.

As the apple-tree among the woodland shades, so is my beloved among the youth; under his shade I sat and still desire to sit, and his fruit was sweet to my taste. He led me to the nuptial room; his banner over me was — Love. I faint — I languish in love. Restore me with grape-cakes; recover me with apples. His left hand is under my head; his right enfolds me. O daughters of Jerusalem, I adjure you by the roes and gazelles of the country, that you disturb not my loved One, nor recall him to the city until he chooses.

This whole speech belongs to the bride, as we have given it. She is showing that she knows how to appreciate her lover-king as well as her rivals of the city. It is impossible to translate the fourth verse by a mere translation. I think the *house of wine* was the nuptial-room, and the banner was the flag intended for the caravan which was to carry her up to Jerusalem. So that the sentiment in the historical part is: " He has already adopted me. I see the scene; the nuptial banquet is prepared; the banner waves; love floats in its folds, and we are just ready to depart. He will own me in Jerusalem, as well as in my native groves. But amid such delightful scenes, I have no haste to go. I adjure you, daughters of Jerusalem, by the roes and hinds of my native fields," &c., &c. How beautiful the objects by which she swears! the semi-paganism of the oath, too, is extremely natural. She sheds one tear over her native animals, though she triumphs in going. Longinus has praised the oath of Demosthenes, when he swore by those that fell at Marathon; but this adjuration is more beautiful. It is exactly suitable to the rustic nymph in her condition, who shows her love for what she chooses by her regrets for what she leaves.

Such is the historical part. But what could you do with it applied to the higher purpose? And remember you are not to copy Origen, nor to be a reckless mystic. It seems to me, if it is really an allegory, if the book has a latent application, the word is nigh thee, in thy heart and in thy mouth. The design is very much the same as that of the parable of the prodigal son and his envious brother. Then the mingled joy and humility of the bride, — how parallel to a lost soul returning to God! The genius of the Gospel, that salvation is by grace, was never better illustrated than when salvation was sent to the pagan nations. They were sunk in corruption; the Jews called them dogs, exiles, wretches, babes, and things *which were not*, that is, nonentities in religion, and yet the purest manifestation of religion was sent to them. The murmuring of the oldest son, in the parable before alluded to (Luke xvii.), shows how long the self-righteous objection lingered even in a sober mind.

If I were discoursing on the gracious spirit, on humility, on a humble trust, on the hope of a soul sealed to its Saviour, I should not hesitate to quote the speech of the bride: "I am but a wild flower of the field." I am sorry in this translation to lose the specific definiteness of the original; but I know not any plant which would produce the instantaneous recognition in the English reader's mind necessary to the beauty and effect of the original. I might have said, I am a wild rose, — I am a harebell, — I am a sprig of whiteweed; but these would be false translations, and would not produce the intended effect. I am forced to lose much in being general. Let the reader imagine any late, unusual, modestly beautiful, or rustic flower of a native land, like the shamrock to the Irish or the native thistle to the Scotch, and use it for the emblem.

CHAP. II. 8-17.

SOLOMITIS.

Hark, — it is the voice of my beloved; it is he; he comes; he comes leaping on the mountains, — bounding over the hills.

My beloved is like a hart or a wild-goat. Lo! he is there; standing behind *our* wall, showing himself through our windows, peeping through the wicker-work. My beloved spake and said unto me, Rise up, my love, my fair one, and come away. For lo! the winter is past, the rain is over and gone. The flowers appear on the earth; the time of the singing of the birds is come, and the voice of the turtle is heard in our land. The fig-tree putteth forth her green figs, and the vines and the tender grape give a good smell. Arise, my love, my fair one, and come away.

We may suppose some time to have elapsed between the utterance of the last paragraph and the occasion of this. The bride had gone up to Jerusalem, and after a stay there had gone back to the country, and was to remain there until the season came of her husband's rustication, which would naturally be in the spring. In that cool season, when the weather would neither be too hot nor too cold, he hears her distant voice in the listening ear of affection: "Rise up, my love, &c. For lo! the winter is past," &c. Something like this might be its first application.

But seasons of desertion come to the Christian, seasons of decline to the Church, — a wintry state, when iniquity abounds, and the love of many waxes cold. A pious instinct almost would lead them to adopt this language while watching and finding the first symptoms of returning life: "Rise up, my love, my fair one," &c.

CHAP. II. 14-17.

Solomitis.

O my Dove, let me hear thy voice, though in the recesses of the rock, — though thou art up the deepest ledges; let me see thy form; let me hear thy voice, for sweet is thy voice, and thy form is beautiful. Come, my love, let us go and take the foxes; the little foxes that spoil the vineyard, for our vineyard is yet in bloom. My beloved is mine and I am his, while he feeds among the lilies, — i. e. stays in the country, acting the shepherd in its beautiful scenes. From the cool of the morning until the shadows are stretched upon the plain, stay, my love, stay, and be like a hart or a roe on our secluded hills.

Perhaps the most difficult passage in this chapter is the 15th verse. What does it mean historically, and what does it mean spiritually? The knowing of the one is needful to the knowing of the other. I understand it historically as a beautiful picture of the sports and employments of the care-worn king, when he retired for relaxation to the rural world. The wisest men in such hours are ever most like children. It is said of Webster that he was a perfect boy in his hours of relaxation. I suppose it was so with Solomon. Cicero tells us of the Roman heroes who loved to retire to Cuma and gather shells on the shore. These words, then, are an expression of these rural employments, by which the bride allures her husband to the mountains and the vineyards. Its covered meaning is seen on the veil. It signifies, first, that the spirit of the higher type of religion is a free spirit; love consecrates as well as lightens everything. Secondly, that it is as devout in its recreations as its duties. "Whether therefore ye eat or drink, or whatever ye do, do all to the glory of God." (1 Cor. x. 31.) Thirdly, that every condition of life offers it a sphere, a scope for cultivation, — the rural retirement as well as the populous mart. As a flower bears its fragrance to whatever vase the owner may remove it, so the perfected soul bears its influence to every scene it occupies. And lastly, that even its bounding recreations look towards utility, either to fit the person for future toil, or to make amusement itself conducive to some profitable end. "Take us the foxes, the little foxes *that spoil the vines*." The end is useful, though the employment is recreation.

If any one smiles, and says this last inference is wire-drawn, let him consider the historical application of the words and the analogy.

CHAP. III. 1 - 11.

SOLOMITIS.

On my bed by night I sought him whom my soul loves; I sought him, but I found him not. I will arise, I will go round the city; I will seek him whom I love in the squares and in the streets. I sought him, but I did not find him. The keepers of the city met me. Have you seen, said I, the One whom my soul loveth? I scarce passed them, when I found him whom my soul loveth. I grasped him, I would not let him go, until I brought him to my mother's house, into her chamber who bore me; and I charge you, O daughters of Jesusalem, by the roes and gazelles of the field, that you disturb not his repose, nor call him back until he chooses.

* * * * *

Who is this that ascends from the wilderness like a column of smoke, like the incense of myrrh and Lebanon, with all the aromatics of the caravans. Behold the palanquin of Solomon; surrounded by sixty guardsmen, brave men of Israel, all grasping the sword, all expert in war; each one with his sword on his thigh, on account of terrors of the night. King Solomon made himself a palanquin; wood of Lebanon, columns of silver, a golden seat, a purple cushion, paved by a Love better than that of the daughters of Jerusalem. Go, ye nymphs of Sion, go and see your king, wearing the wreath which his [new rural] mother wove for him, in the day of his espousals [to her daughter]; in the day of his gladness of heart.

Several things are here to be noticed. First, the rapid transitions; the Song, like the bridegroom which is its subject, goes so rapidly, leaping from hill to hill, that it is almost impossible to preserve the train of thought in a mere translation. We are to suppose the espoused one to project herself into the city, into the country, according to the varying tenor of her passion. By night in the country she thinks of her absent one. "When away from you," she seems to say, "on my bed my thoughts were fixed upon you." She then imagines herself in the city, and relates the incidents in verses third and fourth. There is no need of supposing it a dream, — it may be accounted for by the vivacity of Eastern thought. The striking exclamation in the sixth verse has been attributed to a chorus. There is no need of introducing a chorus; it hardly comports with Eastern simplicity. The exclamation may be accounted for by the amazing power of an excited mind to project itself into any pleasing or painful situation. She is suddenly rapt into a condition to behold the spectacle, and asks the question, "Who is this coming from the wilderness?" &c. Secondly, we must consider the opposition between the rustic bride and the polished daughters of Jerusalem; the rivalry is everywhere kept up, and the jealousy between them is obvious, and an important item in interpreting the book. Thirdly, I would remark that no chorus is necessary; all those passages may be accounted for by the amazing activity of the Eastern mind. Their very thoughts were dramatic. The questions which have been put into the mouth of a chorus, I consider as the suppositions of an excited passion, — as the questions which an inflamed heart may easily ask itself. "The mother of Sisera looked out at a window and cried through the lattice, Why is his chariot so long in coming? Why tarry the wheels of his chariots? Her wise ladies answered her, yea, she returned answer to herself." (Judges v. 28, 29.) Formal critics often go too far. Paul has something of the dialogue in his didactic epistles, and Horace, also, in his odes and satires; but it has always appeared to me better to regard these dialogues as mental rather than real. In the famous one in Horace between the poet and Lydia (Ode IX. Lib. III.), it was an imaginary Lydia that spoke to him. Passion flies on fiery wings, and scorns the formalities of place or person. Then the Hebrews had hardly recovered from the hieroglyphic state, and to a primitive people with an infant language rapid transitions are almost necessary. Fourthly, it is remarkable that the bride, though earnestly seeking, does not find her mate BY SEEKING; it is always good luck. This I consider as an important element in the higher application. Fifthly, let the reader remark the great difficulty in supplying the interstitial ideas. This is the Gordian knot in explaining allegorical, and indeed all prophetic poetry. I am not so sure I am right in each instance, as I am of the rectitude of the general principle. And, lastly, remark that Solomon was a peaceful king; he uses soldiers on account of the terrors of the night (i. e. to keep safe from the Arabs of the wilderness). "Then he said unto them, When I sent you with purse, and scrip, and shoes, lacked ye anything? And they said, Nothing. Then said he unto them, But now he that hath a purse let him take it, and likewise his scrip;

and he that hath no sword, let him sell his garment and buy one." (Luke xxii. 35, 36.)

Now the historical analogy will conduct us to the spiritual meaning. First, that we all begin religion as a duty in the way of conflict and self-denial. Every young Christian has a host of unconquered lusts which war against the soul. The conflict is a severe one, and often discouraging; he makes great efforts, and sometimes these efforts are unsuccessful, because ill-directed. But let him remember the better state. The bride found her spouse not directly by seeking, though the seeking was by no means in vain. She sought him, but she found him not. She went round the city; she asked the watchmen, but she found him not. "But I scarce passed them, — or, I had passed but a little way from them, — when I found him. I grasped him; I would not let him go." Every Christian during the period of conflict should be reminded of the second period, the period of spontaneity. It comes rushing upon us in an hour when we think not, just as, in a contrary way, Satan entered into Judas Iscariot, when he had long paltered with the evil principle. It is ours to toil and pray and struggle, and prepare the heart for the entrance of the celestial guest. Sooner or later this period of spontaneity will come to most Christians. We cannot bring it on directly; it must come to us; we cannot go to it. But bearing the cross is our preparatory discipline. Let us use an illustration. Suppose a man to be watching for the morning; he must wake before daybreak; he must unclose his shutters and lift his curtains; and though he can do nothing to hasten the sunrise, yet he must prepare his house to receive the glorious beams when they come rushing into his chamber. The free state, the victory, is the happy goal to which all exertion tends.

There are other significations in this passage. But we give only specimens.

CHAP. IV. Totum.

SOLOMON.

Behold, thou art fair, my love, behold, thou art very fair; thine eyes, as they peep behind thy veil, look the dove. Thine hair is like that of the goats which hang over the clefts of Mount Gilead. Thy teeth are white as the flock of newly-sheared sheep, which go up from the washing; each having twins, — none of them barren. Thy lips are threads of scarlet, thine accents beautiful; thy cheek, half seen through thy veil, is like a fragment of citron. Like the tower of David, built for a magazine with a thousand shields suspended, — the bucklers of heroes, — such is thy neck. Thy two breasts are like two hinds feeding in a field of lilies. When the day declines, and the shadows are extended, I will go to these hills of myrrh, — to those protuberances of frankincense. Thou art all beautiful, my love, — there is not a spot in thee.

Up, up from Lebanon; with me, with me, come from the head of Amana, my spouse, from the head of Shinar and Hermon, from the cottages of Araoth, from the hills of Nemairim.

O my sister, my spouse, — thou hast subdued my soul with one glance of thine eye, — with one look at thy beaded neck. How beautiful thy bosom, my sister, my spouse! thy bosom is better than wine, and thy savor sweeter than all other spices. Thy lips ever distil, — honey and milk are under thy tongue, and the smell of thy garments is like a breeze from Lebanon. — Yet, with all her attractions, my spouse is chaste; she is a garden enclosed, a spring shut up, a fountain sealed.

Thy fair form is a Paradise of citrons, with other celestial fruit, the cypress, the frankincense, the nard, the crocus, the reed, the cinnamon, with all the groves of Lebanon; the myrrh, the aloes, with all the best spices. Thou art a fountain enclosed; a spring of living water flowing from Lebanon. — Wake, north wind; come, thou south; blow upon my garden, that the spices may spring; that my beloved may come into his garden and enjoy his nobler fruits.

CHAP. V., 1st verse.

SOLOMON.

I come into my garden, my sister, my spouse; I crop the myrrh with spices. I eat the comb with the honey; I drink the wine with my milk. I call my friends to share the banquet. Eat, O friends! drink to satiety, O my companions in love!

The first thing noticeable here is, how the spiritual meaning peeps through the allegorical veil; and this seems to me a sufficient answer to Dr. Noyes and others, who say there is no indication of an under-meaning through the whole poem. But one of the constant indications of the sublimer purpose is a train of comparisons and hyperboles too strong for the lower purpose to which they are first applied. Thus Solomon, in the seventy-second Psalm, is said " to have dominion from sea to sea, and his kingdom shall last as long as the moon endureth." Now this is so false as to Solomon, and so true as applied to Christ, that the conclusion is inevitable; we must so apply it, and vindicate the truth of the Divine declaration. It is the very way in which Peter reasons in his application of the sixteenth Psalm in his important discourse in the second chapter of Acts. Let us ask, then, who this nymph must be, whose neck is like the tower of David, builded for an armory whereon there hang a thousand bucklers, all the shields of mighty men. To apply all this finally and entirely to a little Arab girl, would surpass all bounds of Oriental extravagance. Certainly this magnificent imagery was intended to lead the mind to a meaning which would better justify it. And then it seems inconsistent with the rural comparisons connected with it. A simple girl could not be at once like goats, like kids, like sheep, like a piece of citron, and like a tower hung round with shields. We allow the remoteness of Eastern comparisons; they are not nice and squared like those of Coleridge. But the human mind in all ages is essentially consistent; it always seeks real similitudes, and is always governed by a law. If we reflect that the Church is often a temple, a fortress, a city, an edifice built for beauty and protection, we cannot wonder that Solomon himself, with his future kingdom dimly gleaming through his contested act, should slide from the incidental to the general, from the low to the sublime; and still less can we wonder that the Holy Spirit should guide his lips to its great design. We conclude, therefore, with some confidence, that the variety and the excess of these comparisons were intended (certainly by the deeper author) as indications of the allegorical meaning.

Our translation is in some cases disputable, and in some cases free. A translator has two objects; first, to preserve the literal meaning as far as possible, and, secondly, to preserve the poetic shading of the expression and thought; and sometimes one must be sacrificed to the other. Thus, when we say that "thine hair is like that of the goats which hang over the clefts of Mount Gilead," it is true *hanging over* is not the simplest rendering of the verb גָּלְשׁ; but my object was to get the parallel image, — the same picture which the poet designed. I was thinking of Virgil's "pendere procul de rupe." If I have lost the literal idea, I hope I have kept the spirit. The banquet, too, literally speaking, would be sickening; it only becomes beautiful by the allegory.

The spiritual instruction, admitting the allegory, lies on the surface. The mixture of beauty and coercion is found in the Gospel both objectively and subjectively considered, and the strength of the coercion comes from the beauty. As Plato says, οὔτε γὰρ αὐτὸς βίᾳ πάσχει, εἴ τι πάσχει· βίᾳ γὰρ Ἔρωτος οὐχ᾽ ἅπτεται· οὔτε ποιῶν ποιεῖ· πᾶς γὰρ ἑκὼν Ἔρωτι πᾶν ὑπηρετεῖ.* It may be concluded, also, that the beauty of the Church (i. e. regenerated hearts) is an imparted beauty. "I clothed thee with broidered work, and shod thee with badgers' skins, and I girded thee about with fine linen, and I covered thee with silk. I decked thee with ornaments, and I put bracelets upon thine hands, and a chain upon thy neck. And I put a jewel upon thy forehead, and ear-rings in thine ears, and a beautiful crown upon thine head. Thus wast thou decked with gold and silver; and thy raiment was of fine linen and silk and broidered work: thou didst eat fine flour and honey and oil; and thou wast exceeding beautiful, and didst prosper into a kingdom. And thy renown went forth among the heathen for thy beauty: for it was perfect through my comeliness, which I had put upon thee, saith the Lord." (Ezekiel xvi. 10 – 14.) Such, then, is the beauty of the mystic bride, like that of a sheet of water, reflecting from its glassy bosom the splendors of the sky.

Here it occurs to say one word on imputed righteousness, — that everlasting trap for idle controversy, that everlasting source of consolation to the simple Christian. Every one, before he raises a dispute in the Church on this point, should ask himself what is the

---

* Plato's Symposium, CXIX. C.

real issue between those that affirm and those that deny. Both parties agree that there is no literal transfer of our sins to Christ, or Christ's obedience to us. But all Christians pant after perfection, — a perfection never found on earth. When Dr. Watts says, —

> " And lest the shadow of a spot
> Should on my soul be found,
> He took the robe my Saviour wrought
> And cast it all around, —

he means, probably, these things : 1st, that salvation is of grace, — all grace from its commencement to its completion ; 2d, that our justification is as complete as would be that of a perfect man ; 3d, that grace in the heart tends to individual perfection ; and, lastly, that all the deformities of our nature are lost in the subsequent beauty. This he chooses to express in complex metaphor, because the language is addressed to the heart. But how supremely silly to put this language into a crucible, and analyze it until it has lost its meaning!

The meaning and application of the sixteenth verse are so exceedingly obvious, that it hardly needs a comment. It is one of those cases where the allegorical meaning is more obvious than the literal one. An invisible power calls forth the odors and the fruits. What is it ? "The word is nigh thee, in thy mouth and in thy heart."

The first verse of the fifth chapter suggests the freeness of Christ's love for his people, and the rich provisions of his grace. Here is a cup not intoxicating, and we cannot drink too deep. The secret of perseverance in religion is to make our religion our delight. "Where your treasure is, your heart will be also." St. Paul has the prose parallel to this verse: "He that spared not his own son, but delivered him up for us all, how shall he not with him also freely give us all things?" (Rom. viii. 32.)

CHAP. V. 2-8.

SOLOMITIS.

I was in a drowse, with a sleeping eye but a watchful heart. I seemed to hear the voice of my beloved, saying to me, Open to me, my sister, my Love, my dove, my spotless One; for my head is damp with the dew and my locks with the drops of the night. I have put off my robe; why should I put it on again? I have washed my feet; why should I defile them?

My beloved put his hand through the window; my heart fluttered for him. I rose to open to him; my hands dropped myrrh, and my fingers sweet-smelling myrrh, on the handle of the bar. I opened to my Beloved, but my Beloved had turned his back,—he was gone.

I sunk at the thought; I sought him, but I could not find him. I called, but he gave me no answer. Nay, the watch of the city found me. They struck, they wounded me, they tore off my mantle, even the sentinels at the gates. But I adjure you, O daughters of Jerusalem, if you see my loved One, tell him I still languish with love. Notwithstanding the persecutions from his people, my heart is still fixed on him.

This scene, perhaps, is a sort of imagination of the bride, by which she pictures to her fancy a call from her spouse, which she neglects; and, regretting that he is gone when she awoke to seek him, she imagines herself going to the city to find him. She had really been there before, and had experienced the jealousy and opposition of his people. She now reconstructs the scene to her own mind. It is very manifest to my mind, that there is a real history behind all this poetic description. We know from the record, that Solomon made affinity with some of these rural tribes. It is very natural that such a marriage should excite great attention at his own home, especially among the daughters of Jerusalem. They sneer at her beauty, and contend that, though a wife, she is not a legitimate disciple; she contends that in the ardor of her love she does not yield to them. We are informed that in the first preaching of the Gospel the chief persecutions were stirred up by the Jews. (See Acts xvii. 5-9, and other places.) Even the better Jews, the converts to Christianity, were an exceedingly unconformable people. They listened to Stephen until he spake of going to the Gentiles, and then they drowned his voice in their tumultuous cries; and when Paul addressed them (Acts xxiii.), and touched on the same delicate point (ver. 21), " they then lifted up their voices and said, Away with such a fellow from the earth; for it is not fit that he should live." We see, then, in this picture, the beginnings of the same spirit; and the bride, who bears all meekly for her spouse, prefigures the superior love and purity which was found at first in the Gentile Church.

I have heard the words in verses 2 – 6 beautifully applied, and I think with as much correctness as beauty, to the Christian, or the Church, losing for a time a sense of a Saviour's presence, and not watching his return with the vigilance which is required. I was remiss, I slumbered; I sought negligently, I prayed feebly, and the sweet sense of my Saviour's presence was gone from me. He waits to be gracious; I was unwilling; he stood at the door of my heart until his head was damp with the dew, and his locks filled with the drops of the night. What an affecting picture! and surely the whole round of poetry, ancient or modern, does not present a more beautiful periphrasis than calling the dew the "drops of the night." The proneness in a sluggish heart to idle excuses is here delineated. "I have put off my robe," &c.

Perhaps it may be asked, What is meant by the expression in the fifth verse, "My hands dropped myrrh," &c.? Is it a general expression of beauty and excellence, or is it something more specific? And how is it appropriate to the author's design that such splendid imagery should adorn the act, that, when the bride is represented as remiss and sleeping, her fingers should drop incense at the very hour when she opens the door in vain? There is danger of refinement here, I allow. But the object seems to express the sentiment. Though sleeping, though negligent, though I am conscious of much unworthiness and imperfection, yet I have something left; all is not gone; and when I awake to duty and prepare to receive my Lord, I am still acceptable and accepted; my hands dropped myrrh, &c. on the latch of the lock I was unloosing, — the savor of real piety remained.

CHAP. V. 9-16.

[SOLOMITIS *seems to hear the daughters of Jerusalem speak.*]

What is thy Beloved more than others, that thou so chargest us, thou beauty?

SOLOMITIS *answers.*

My beloved is white and ruddy; he bears the banner over all the host. His head is refined gold; his locks are a palm-bough, black as those of a raven; his eyes are those of a dove, perching by the canals of water, washed in milk. His cheek is a bed of spices, a circle of aromatics; his lips are lilies dropping myrrh and balm; his hand is like the gold of a ring, encircled with gems from Tarshish; his breast is ivory work broidered with sapphires. His legs are pillars of marble, resting on polished stone; his form is like Lebanon, like the noblest of its cedars. His neck is delightful, and his whole person formed for desire. Such is my Beloved, such is my friend, O ye daughters of Jerusalem.

The change of persons is very rapid in Hebrew composition. We may suppose the bride to *imagine* she hears this question from the daughters in Jerusalem (ver. 9). When they call her the fairest among women, we must suppose the word ironical, or the word הַיָפָה in its contracted form, must be a meaner one, and express a reluctant concession. I have translated it by a single word, — thou beauty, — which expresses a very short concession, or bitter irony.

In the next verses she vindicates herself. She seems to say, Yes, my rivals, though I meet your objections and sneers, I know how to appreciate my royal bridegroom as well as you. I see his beauty, I appreciate his worth, and I am not ashamed to tell you. Perhaps the novelty of my condition leads me more to feel his grace and condescension. The speech is a vindication.

The permanent lesson is very obvious, and is taught literally by our Saviour in the case of the woman who washed his feet with her tears, and wiped them with the hairs of her head. The more we feel our own deformity, the more the excellence of Christ impresses the heart.

CHAP. VI. 1 - 9.

[SOLOMITIS *still hears the objection.*]

Where is thy loved One gone, O thou fair among rustics? whither has thy loved One turned himself? Let us seek him with thee.

Answer.

My loved One has gone down to his garden to crop his spices; to enjoy his garden; to pluck his lilies. I am my Beloved's, and he is mine; he feeds his flock in the lilied field. Thou art fair, my Beloved, as Tirzah; comely as Jerusalem; admirable as a bannered host.

SOLOMITIS.

O, turn away thine eyes from me; they are terrible in their sweetness.

SOLOMON.

Thy hair is like a flock of goats, hanging from Mount Gilead. Thy teeth are like shorn sheep which go up from the washing; each having twins, none barren. Thy cheek behind thy veil is like a slice of citron. A train of threescore queens, and fourscore concubines, and virgins without number, may follow other brides; but thou, my dove, art the single object of my love; thou art perfect, the only child of thy mother, the select one of her that bore thee. Even the daughters of Jerusalem shall regard thee; the queens shall bless thee; the concubines shall sound thy praise.

This praise of the bridegroom must be very grateful to the modest spouse, conscious of her rusticity, and conscious, too, of her love, but almost afraid to lift up her eyes to hear the reproaches which her rivals are ready to heap upon her. The doctrine of grace, free grace, is here illustrated, and that God is no respecter of persons. The vilest heart and the lowest nations may be purified and raised.

CHAP. VI. 10-12.

Solomon.

Who is this breaks out as the morning, beautiful as the pale orb of night, super-eminent like the Great Warmer of the world, and wonderful like a well-ordered host?

Solomitis.

I went into my garden of nuts, to see the verdure of the valley, to see the vines germinate, to see the citrons bud. Or ever I was aware, my soul bore me away, as on my native chariot.

The periphrasis in the tenth verse I have endeavored to preserve. No doubt the author intended to call neither the moon nor the sun by their direct and prosaic name. He calls the one the whiteness and the other the heat, from their effects and most striking power. I have given the eleventh and twelfth verses to the bride, for I think they must belong to her. She walks into her garden; she sees the vines and flowers, and her soul is ravished with instant love. How many lessons! First, divine love is love of the invisible one, whom "having not seen we love, and whom, though we now see him not, yet, believing, we rejoice with joy unspeakable and full of glory." Secondly, we see that this love is a gift. It is shed abroad in our hearts by the Holy Ghost given unto us. "Or ever I was aware, my soul — my spontaneous affections — bore me away like the fiery courser in the race." And, thirdly, it was in the use of means that this gift came, and very natural means. "I went into the garden; I walked among its shades; I surveyed its beauties; I remembered the owner, and my soul melted with rapture and love." So I should apply this simple paragraph, and fear no mysticism but such as was intended by its inspiring Author.

The last verse is variously rendered. The question is, whether it be a phrase or an expressive name. Ammi-na-dib. Some celebrated charioteer, or, My willing people. I prefer the latter.

CHAP. VI. 13.

SOLOMON.

Return, return, O bride of Solomon! return, often return. Let us contemplate thee; what shall we discover in this bride of Solomon? The chorus of a host.

The Hebrew verb which I have rendered *contemplate* rather inclines to mental sight, — to seeing as the prophets saw, in vision. I cannot but think that this verb, together with the answer, — "The chorus of a host," — gives plain indication of the allegory and the under-meaning. Applied to a mere woman, they are extravagant and absurd.

CHAP. VII. 1-9.

SOLOMON.

How beautiful are thy ankles over thy sandals, O daughter

of a generous sheik! the swell of thy haunches is like that of a cup, the invention of a skilful artificer. Thy front is like a bowl, brimming with wine; thy form like a hill of wheat skirted with lilies. Thy two breasts are like two young does; thy neck is like a white tower. Thine eyes are bright as the fish-pools of Heshbon, at the gate of Bethabbarim. Thy nose is as a tower of Lebanon facing Damascus. The head that surmounts thy body is like Carmel; and its tresses are such that the grandeur of a king might be entangled in them. Thy height is like the palm, and thy bosom like clustering grapes. I will taste that breath like the flavor of apples. Thy throat like sweet wine shall pour its sweetness to my lips and my teeth.

Perhaps there is no part of the allegory harder to manage than this. The reader will see that I have softened and generalized some of the specifics in the original description. But in so doing I have scarcely departed from the spirit of the original. Let the reader consider the literal design of this description; it is to bring forth the image and collection of images as a stepping-stone to the ulterior object. We must see the literal, before we can see the resemblance which leads to the allegorical parallels. Now, among the Orientals, obesity is always considered as a beauty and a perfection. This is the general object in this description. The form of the damsel was healthful, ruddy, plump, and full; and full dresses were very much worn in the East. The expressions שָׁרְרֵךְ and בִּטְנֵךְ are not so much intended to designate the parts as the general roundness of the form. So says Gesenius in his Lexicon. I have, then, with the strictest fidelity to the original, rendered it, "Thy FRONT is like a bowl; thy FORM like a hill," &c. This communicates to the English reader the design of this description.

But what possible lesson, asks the fastidious reader, can be derived from this articulate description of a rustic beauty? I must repeat the remark, that I think these comparisons of towers, &c. are plain indications of an under-meaning. As God hears the prayers he inspires, so he loves the beauties which his grace imparts. His judgment is infallible, and where he approves, there is matter for approbation. The virtue of the world is an outside virtue. The graces of his bride, the Church, are latent beauties; the more they are searched, they are seen. They flow from one fountain, and in all their particular forms they are real.

CHAP. VII. 10–13.

SOLOMITIS.

I am my Beloved's; his affection is fixed on me. Come, my Love, let us go into the fields, let us spend the night in the villages; let us go into the vineyards; and there, amidst germinating buds, opening flowers, and flourishing pomegranates, will I yield thee my love. There grow the mandrakes; and there have I laid up all fruits and flowers, new and old, to invite thy repose.

This is the passion of the bride to retain her lover in the country. It shows her anxious preparation, and her felicity at his presence. She evinces the strength of her affection and the justice of it from his amazing excellence. The Gospel is to make its greatest triumph and show its greatest power in humble life. "The poor have the Gospel preached to them." "The common people heard him gladly." "For ye see your calling, brethren, how that not many wise men after the flesh, not many mighty, not many noble, are called. But God hath chosen the foolish things of the world to confound the wise; and God hath chosen the weak things of the world to confound the things which are mighty; and base things of the world, and things which are despised, hath God chosen, yea, and things which are not, to bring to naught things that are; that no flesh should glory in his presence." (1 Cor. i. 26-29.)

CHAP. VIII. 1-4.

SOLOMITIS *continues.*

O that thou wert my brother, nurtured at the same breast; that I might find thee without; that I might kiss thee without reproach; that when I sigh for thee I might bring thee to the house of my mother, who taught me, that I might give thee the scented wine and the juice of the pomegranate. His left hand is under my head; his right supports me. I adjure you, O daughters of Jerusalem, that no one disturb or wake my love until he wishes it.

It is astonishing that any one should regard this poem as a sensual exhibition. The imagery, I own, is naked and Oriental; but when you have once seen and forgiven this, the passion is uncommonly pure and delicate, even its first application. Hence the bride expresses the purest love. "O that thou wert my brother," &c.; and in verse third of chapter seventh, שָׁרְרֵךְ אַגַּן הַסַּהַר גוי׳, I have no doubt it means, "pelle non corrugata a partu," which was the sign and the proof of chasteness. Everywhere, though the language is primitive, the sentiment is delicate, and every expedient is used to paint the purest passion. It must be granted, however, that the mystic writers delight to express the strength of their feelings by the Epicurean language into which they fall. They are so intent on the higher object, that they fear and feel no contamination from the subordinate illustrations. This we see in Augustine, Madame Guyon, Mrs. Rowe, Dr. Watts, and all the writers of that school. The mind seems to be free from all fetters, and earth is forgotten in its celestial flights. No doubt such a practice may be abused; but, nevertheless, it is so constantly exemplified, it must pass for a general law.

CHAP. VIII. 5-7.

WITNESSES, *Hebrew and Gentile.*

Who is this that ascends from the wilderness leaning on her Beloved?

12

Solomon.

Under the apple-tree I found thee; there thou wast born, there thy teeming mother brought thee forth.

Solomitis.

Place me as a signet upon thy heart, as a signet upon thine arm. For love is strong as death, jealousy harsh as the grave; its coals are burning fire, refulgent flame.

Author *speaks*.

Many waters cannot quench love; nor rivers drown it. If a man were to offer all the treasures of his house for love, they would despise him.

I suppose the words in the fifth verse of the eighth chapter to be very emphatic. They are a general exclamation of astonishment all round; it matters little who speaks them. The amazing vivacity of the Oriental fancy, like the poet's mind in a fine frenzy rolling, glancing from heaven to earth, allows us with a similar effect to put these words into the mouths of several persons. It may be the bridegroom, hearing in imagination the exclamations around him; or it may be the bride, or it may be the author; for not as in the perfected drama is it necessary in this poem for the author wholly to retire. Whoever speaks, (and it matters little who,) it is an expression of astonishment, that a rustic nymph from a heathen land should be led up to Jerusalem by the wise and splendid king. It is a striking picture.

And surely the application is obvious. Long was the contest which Paul had with the Jews before he could peaceably offer the Gospel to the Gentiles. "But when Peter was come to Antioch, I withstood him to the face, because he was to be blamed. For before that certain came from James, he did eat with the Gentiles; but when they were come, he withdrew and separated himself, fearing them which were of the circumcision." (Gal. ii. 11, 12.)

In the seventh verse, I suppose the author to speak. I suppose all dramatic writers, even Shakespeare himself, not to be so lost in the personated character as not to put into their mouths occasionally the general sentiment, — the moral of what they are saying; and the more artfully this is done, the better. Perhaps the general sentiment was never more skilfully transferred from the mouth of the author to that of a personated character than in this seventh verse: "Many waters," &c. It suits either. But as it seems to me the moral of the whole book, I have chosen to mark it as the sentiment of the author.

And the whole application of this part of the book is important, and vastly important in that age, as the prospective and permanent spirit of true religion, underlying all its changes and forms. It is illustrated in 1 Cor. xiii.: "Though I speak with the tongues of men and angels, and have not charity ($ἀγάπην$, love), I am become as sounding brass, or a tinkling cymbal."

We are now coming to a part of this poem which to the English reader is utter darkness, and it must be confessed that the learned critics have shed very little light upon it. I can imagine a neologist, or infidel, taking up his Bible and saying, "In this book you tell me I must expect to find the words of wisdom; in every part I may expect to find the inspiration of God. Now I take the Bible and open at Canticles viii. 8, and read: 'We have a little sister and she hath no breasts: what shall be done for our sister in the day when she shall be spoken for? If she be a wall, we will build upon her a palace of silver; and if she be a door, we will enclose her with boards of cedar.' And then she is made to say, 'I am a wall,' &c. Now," the infidel asks, "what possible lesson can I learn from such inspiration as this? So far is it from being the wisdom of God, I cannot derive from it the least gleam of sense. Is there any revelation made to us by unintelligible nonsense? I cannot be profited by what I cannot understand."

To such an objector I might reply, My fellow-mortal, if *you* cannot understand this passage, just pass on and you will soon find more perhaps than you wish to know. But do you not know that every writer may pass for a weak one until he is understood,—Lord Bacon himself? The very darkness on the surface of these words leads me to inquire into the design,—the under-meaning.

It may be remarked, that there is an hiatus between the seventh and eighth verses; and the great question is, how we shall fill up the transition. It is marked as an hiatus by Dathé and Rosenmüller and others. I cannot pledge myself that I shall satisfy my reader in explaining this difficult portion of Scripture; I will only say, what is obscure now might have been obvious once. But I seem to see a very probable design. Let us consider, first, that the Hebrew poets, bordering on the hieroglyphic period and using a primitive language, are obliged to make rapid transitions, and leave interstices which are only to be filled up by the reader's sagacity; secondly, these intervals are sometimes supplied by what is said in the next paragraph, but sometimes purposely left; thirdly, they are very fond of the enigmatical style, and, fourthly, this style is especially to be expected in an enigmatical poem; and, lastly, from Solomon's splendid temple, the architectural style applied to the Church was very current. St. Paul uses it (Ephesians ii. 19–22): "Now, therefore, ye are no more strangers and foreigners, but fellow-citizens with the saints, and of the household of God; and are built upon the foundation of the apostles and prophets, Jesus Christ himself being the chief corner-stone; in whom all the building, fitly framed together, groweth into an holy temple in the Lord: in whom ye also are builded together for an habitation of God through the Spirit." So Solomon says (Prov. ix. 1),

"Wisdom hath builded her house," &c., and our word *edification* comes from the same source. Now I suppose at the close of this poem the author gives an enigmatical solution of his design. He means to make a pause, a transition; he goes back, he recapitulates, he retraces the whole design. He imagines the family of the bride — and I suppose the little sister to be the Solomitis of the whole poem — to say in the outset, "We have a little sister," &c. The author artfully puts the solution into their mouth. Let us explain the whole in an enigma. "There is to us a little sister; she has no breasts." What is she? "If she be a wall, we will build on her a tower; if a door," &c.; and then she is made to reply, "I am a wall," — that is, I am not a literal being. I am something more productive than King Solomon's vineyard. A further disclosure did not suit the purpose of the writer, or the preparation of the age. Just as the Book of Job, after starting many questions which could only be solved by the life and immortality brought to light in the Gospel, partially solves these questions by inculcating in the last chapters that conscious ignorance which prepares the way for the Gospel. The negative part seems to me very clear, that this wonderful bride was not a mere woman. Perhaps I may add, that one word omitted in the hiatus, or a single corrected error in the present reading, might have made the whole passage plain; or, for aught I know, God may have permitted these dark places in his divine revelation as tests of our patience, our penetration, our reverence, and our love.

It is possible, too, that this passage is not placed at the close of this book chronologically, but because it comes in there best as an exponent. This itself is a source of obscurity.

CHAP. VIII. 8-14.

FAMILY *speak, or are heard speaking.*

We have a little sister; she is not yet mature: what shall we do for her in the day she is wooed? If she be a wall, we will build on her a tower; and if she be a door, her panels shall be cedar-wood.

SOLOMITIS.

I AM a wall; my breasts ARE towers; and by his favor I have found peace (i.e. my religion). Though King Solomon had a vineyard in Baal-hamon, and he let it out to cultivators, and each man brought him the rent, — a thousand pieces of silver, — my vineyard is ever before me; a thousand are for thee, O Solomon, and two hundred for its keepers.

O thou that dwellest in gardens [such as mine], followed by suitors, let me hear thy voice! Make haste, my Love; and be like a hind, or deer, on the fragrant hills.

A riddle is now the amusement of children. It seems a small business for modern sages to be proposing and guessing riddles; but it was once the work of wisdom and the employment of kings. Josephus tells us that Hiram, king of Tyre, sent sophisms and enigmatical sayings to Solomon, and none of them was too hard for his sagacity. (Antiq. Jews, Lib. VIII. chap. 5.) If this seems to be an idle employment, it is because we forget the history of language. In the earlier stages of learning, language is a very imperfect instrument of communicating. As it expresses less, we must guess more. We must piece out its imperfections by our divination. Even now the Hebrew language, with all the vast improvements which ages had introduced on the hieroglyphic symbols, and all the assistance of the Masoretic punctuation, has ellipses and transitions which it requires great ingenuity to fill. How much more when we go back to picture-writing! We have some specimens of the ingenuity of the Iroquois, published among the New York State Papers, to show how far these barbarians had proceeded in recording events by these symbolical riddles. (See the Documentary History of New York, Vol. I. pp. 12, 14.) When they advanced to the hieroglyphic state, the rules were better ascertained, but conjecture was still necessary. But even the phonetic languages in their first formation were very imperfect. The Chinese, it is said now, has no syntax; it takes almost a life to learn to read it. It was essential to all learning in those days to know how to untie a knot and to guess a riddle; and a tincture of this mode of communication lingers long in an improved tongue after its necessity has ceased. How many cases in the Bible are there, in which this sagacity is almost essential to the art of reading, and is certainly the one thing needful in interpretation. (See Psalm xlix. 4; Ezekiel xvii. 2; Ibid., chap. xl., xli., xlii.; Jeremiah ii. 18; Ezekiel xx. 49; Jeremiah i. 11, 12; 2 Kings xiv. 9; 2 Chron. xxv. 18; Matthew xxii. 41 – 46; Mark xii. 35; Rev. xiii. 18; and many other examples.) The dreams of Pharaoh and Nebuchadnezzar were riddles until the holy prophets had interpreted them; and the Bible is full of similar examples, where the first perplexity increases the last impression. Some are explained, some are left to the reader's patience and sagacity. It was in conformity to a long and necessary custom that this book is closed by a riddle, to be discovered only by a persevering attention and a congenial heart. This method exactly suited the design of the poem. The book was probably written for a peculiar taste and a peculiar piety. We are assisted to guess. The negative is at least clear. This wonderful bride, so ardently loved by this representative king, is not an Arab girl. What is she?

The reader will see that there reigns throughout my hypothesis this one principle, that the permanent meaning of this song had an historical origin, and that the fact in history suggests the spiritual import by a uniform analogy. It is true it may be said, — a point which I shall certainly concede, — that it *is* an hypothesis. We have no *direct* testimony that the Song was written on the occasion suggested. What are your proofs? I answer, — and there I rest the cause, — that the supposition of such an occasion admirably explains every part of the dialogue, and, what is more, *I do not recollect a single passage where the hypothesis grates.* Most hypotheses need a little forcing of the phenomena to make them stand. I ask nothing of this to support mine. The rule works both ways. Every passage in the poem suggests it, and there is not a single hint by which it seems to be overthrown. There I rest it.*

But, after all, some persevering sceptic may put to me the question, and ask, Do you really believe that any modern Christian of taste and discernment can read the imagery of this book for purely devotional purposes? Is there not a little pious affectation in that enthusiasm which pretends to see Jesus Christ amidst the gaudy figures and flowers of this Oriental song? Do you yourself peruse this work without any disturbance of the fancy, and feel the spiritual elevation while you read? Lay your hand on your heart, and give an honest reply. Laying my hand on my heart, then, I reply, that I honestly believe all I have said. I have

* I beg, however, the candid reader to make a distinction. The allegorical character of the book, and my *particular* theory of its historical origin, by no means stand on the same evidence.

no doubt of the allegorical character of this wonderful Song. I spontaneously and seriously admire the strain, as an exquisite specimen of Hebrew archaism. I allow, indeed, that I am obliged, in order to feel all its force, to read it as I do Homer, with a perpetual reference to the age in which it was written, and the people to whom it was addressed. How is it that we relish Homer? Is it not by perpetually forgetting that we are moderns, and throwing ourselves back into the conceptions and manners and figures of the Epic age? Is not half our pleasure relative? If we stood directly before the bard's narrative, and weighed his merits in modern scales, he would lose some of his lustre and be contemptible in some of his opinions. We read of πόδας ὠκὺς Ἀχιλλεύς and λευκώλενος Ἥρη, *Achilles swift of foot*, and *the white-armed Juno*, both of which expressions would be misunderstood by a modern reader, — the one would describe a coward, and the other a disproportionate beauty, — but both of which are exquisite specimens of ancient taste. So with regard to this Song, I solemnly say, that, viewing it in this reflected light, I regard it as a most exquisite gem of antique genius; and its piety is made ten times more affecting by its peculiar dress. It has struck a note, however, which has been reverberating ever since; and though I must place myself at an almost infinite distance from that fervent faith that has most relished it, yet I claim, without a fear and without a blush, that *its distant war-*

blings have lessened on my ear. I hope to sing it in my dying moments; and I have no doubt, should I be so happy as to reach the blessed region, the theme will be renewed in Heaven, where the only love will be divine, and the only marriage our espousals to God and the Lamb.

PART III.

THE SUPPLEMENT.

THE SUPPLEMENT.

Thus this book which has perplexed the Christian, been perverted by the Romanist, and excited the sneers of the infidel, is found not to be an impediment, but a prop, to the fulness of Scripture; not a spot, but a gem, in the diadem of revelation.

The fault of the age is want of veneration for the Word of God; and such is the perversity of our thinking, that we call this escaping from Divine teaching by the flattering appellation of progress, improvement; as if, in getting rid of God's wisdom we were sure to increase our own.

This error comes in from various causes: scientific difficulties, exaggerated objections, contempt for ancient wisdom, philosophy, historical scepticism,—for example, the speculations of Wolf on Homer, and Niebuhr on Roman history; the boldness of modern criticism, and the independent spirit it inspires; the love of theory, and especially learned theories; and, more than all, the general pride (I must say it) of the human heart.

The power of revelation consists in two things: first, the information it gives, and secondly, the veneration it impresses, both of which are abated by the criticism of modern times. All the learned speculations of Eichhorn, Paulus, Strauss, and Parker come to one point, — to turn our trembling regard for the Bible into ineffable contempt.

Now, the very genius of the Gospel is faith in a speaking God. We are to distrust our own wisdom on the infinities of religion; we are to TREMBLE at the Divine Word. This gives a revealed religion all its character and all its power.

Remove this, and you destroy the power of the whole system; so the common people will say, and human nature speaks through them.

The peculiarity of the teachings of Jesus and Paul is, that they require faith. The ancient moralists, like Plato and Tully, founded duty on seeing and following nature (*sequi naturam*), by which they meant, not the impulses of the heart, but the laws of nature. But the Gospel differs; it requires faith, and "without faith it is impossible to please God." Now, faith, being an internal act of the mind, implies an objective. "The obedience of faith is, to embrace an obscure truth with a firm assent, upon the account of a Divine testimony." (Bates on the Harmony of the Divine Attributes, p. 102.) "Thy testimonies are very sure." (Psalm xciii. 5.) "Thy testimonies have I taken as an heritage forever." (Psalm cxix. 111.) "Thy testimonies that thou hast commanded are righteous and very faithful." (Psalm cxix. 138.) "Concerning thy testimonies, I have known of old that thou hast founded them forever." (Psalm cxix. 152.)

Faith implies the infallible inspiration of the record on which it reposes. The Gospel is a book-religion. The genius of science is to look forward to the future; the revelations are before us. Here, as Bacon has said, we are the ancients, and our early progenitors are the true children; and the reason is, because the volume of nature is spread out before us, and all her recondite laws are to be discovered by successive investigation. It takes time to exhaust the investigation. But all the considerations which make it wise and safe to look *forward* for the perfection of science, make it wise and safe to look *backward* for the teachings of religion.*
"Jesus Christ is the same yesterday, to-day, and for-

---

* These remarks need a little modifying. So far as the Bible is to be regarded as a profound book, the complement of whose instructions is to be found by a humble and progressive criticism, so far it stands parallel to the less obvious laws of nature, and we are entitled to look *forward* for the full discovery of its information. But still, allowing this, we may say science and revelation are opposites, as it is the distinction of the one to place her fulness of light in the future, and the other in the past. The guide of one is independence of mind, and the other — predominately — submission, — submission to God. The one is like a star, which is so remote in space that its full light has not yet reached us; the other is a lamp which we already possess, whose glorious blaze we must discern by removing obstructions.

ever;" and a religion that meets the wants of man must (in substance and outline) be as permanent and uniform as the wants it meets.

But there is a modern view of inspiration, which, by altering its meaning, vacates its power.

Among the meanings of this many-meaning word, the following are the most important: —

First, reason and intelligence considered as divine gifts; this use is sanctioned in the Scriptures. Job xxxii. 8: "But there is a spirit in man, and the inspiration of the Almighty giveth them understanding;" probably alluding to Genesis ii. 7.

Secondly, the inspiration of poetry and eloquence; as when the poet says, half serious and half conscious of fiction, "Sing, heavenly Muse!"

Thirdly, a sudden impulse on a great occasion; as when a child utters something beyond his years, or an ordinary man makes a happy reply, we say they seemed inspired.

Fourthly, the inspiration of office; as, when Saul was anointed, as he turned from Samuel, "God gave him another heart." Every one, parent, school-master, clergyman, magistrate, no sooner assumes the responsibilities of his new station than he feels a peculiar influence guiding, and often anticipating, his reason.

Fifthly, the light given in common sanctification, such as every pious man recognizes. It may be regarded as a passive inspiration, preparing the mind and heart to receive Divine truth whenever presented.*

Lastly, inspiration proper, — Θεοπνευστία, — the previous meaning of the word which makes all the other meanings a strong expression for a weaker idea. It is such an influence of the Spirit of God on the mind of the writer, that he becomes the organ of infallible truth in the teachings of revelation. It is this last kind of inspiration which the sacred writers claim for themselves. The object of such inspiration is to communicate Divine truth, and place it directly on Divine authority.

But a different theory has recently prevailed. Taking advantage of the ambiguity of the word, and substituting some of the lower meanings for the higher, some have taught that inspiration is a very common gift, claimed by the sages of all nations; that every man that has an inventive mind and a pure heart may be inspired; that modern wisdom has peculiar claims to this inestimable gift; that Pythagoras, Socrates, Confucius, were all inspired as much as Isaiah or Paul; in a word, that every wise and good man is inspired, and that the Scriptures claim and are dictated by no

---

* "Falsum vero intelligere, est quidem sapientiae, sed humanae; ultra hunc gradum procedi ab homine non potest; itaque multi philosophorum, religiones, ut docui, sustulerunt: verum autem scire, divinae est sapientiae; homo autem per se ipsum, pervenire ad hanc scientiam non potest, nisi doceatur a Deo." Lactantius, Inst. Lib. II. Sect. 3.

other inspiration. The celestial vision is open to every higher mind.

One proof of the inspiration of the Scriptures is found in that vast prospective wisdom by which they seem to foresee an unborn error, and by a double proposition, both a negative and positive, anticipate and discard it. So true is this, that an historical commentary might be written of all the wild speculations which Paul and the other writers have virtually overthrown before they existed. Thus when Paul says (Colossians ii.), "Beware lest any man spoil you through philosophy and vain deceit, after the tradition of men, after the rudiments of the world, and not after Christ," how is the wisdom of this caution illustrated in the heresies of the Docetæ, indeed, the Gnostics generally, the Manichees, — all the prominent heresies before the Council of Nice. The Apostle seems to have had a prophetic intimation of the reigning error and the source of the error, and to have watchfully guarded them against it. The whole of the Manichean delusion came from giving the word $\sigma \acute{a} \rho \xi$ in his Epistles a philosophical, and not a Hebrew signification. So the Apostle John is supposed by some (some say he wrote after they appeared) to anticipate the rising errors of the Docetæ. (See the Gospel, xix. 34, and 1st Epistle, v. 6.) Now it seems to me that the sacred writers had the clearest conceptions of the recent laxer views of inspiration; and in the most solemn manner, and repeatedly, in the clearest language, have said, by a double affirmation, that *their* inspiration was *not* the modern kind, but *is* the infallible word divine.

First, our Saviour, on whom the Spirit was poured without measure, did not claim to have unfolded the whole Gospel (as during his life the facts were not completed), but promised his Apostles (John iii. 12) authoritative illumination. "I have many things to say unto you, but ye cannot bear them now. Howbeit, when He, the Comforter, is come, he will guide you into all truth" (the article is used in the Greek, ALL THE TRUTH, i. e. the whole system); "for he shall not speak of himself; but whatsoever he shall hear, that shall he speak; and he shall show you things to come." (John xvi. 12, 13.) We are then to look for the development of the Gospel after the great central fact of his death was accomplished. Christ came to prepare the way,— to give the fact, not to interpret it; just as the God of nature accomplished the creation before he explained it. Accordingly, Paul says: "We speak wisdom among them that are perfect; yet not the wisdom of this world, nor of the princes" (that is, philosophic leaders) "of this world, that come to naught. But we speak the wisdom of God in a mystery, even the hidden wisdom, which God ordained before the world unto our glory. But, as it is written, Eye hath not seen, nor ear heard, neither have entered into the heart of man, the things which God hath prepared for them that love him. But

God hath revealed them unto us by his Spirit; for the Spirit searcheth all things; yea, the deep things of God." (1 Corinthians ii. 6 – 10.) What can be clearer, both on the affirmative and negative side. Inspiration is not *that*, it is *this;* it is not what you say, but what I say. It is not a common vision, arising from a pure and cultivated reason, — though that may be an excellent receptive of elsewhere-discovered truth, — but it is a peculiar gift to us Apostles. We speak wisdom; and what we speak never was discovered to human invention. "Eye hath not seen, nor ear heard, neither have entered into the heart of man, the things that God hath prepared for them that love him;" that is, the facts and principles of the Gospel. "But God hath revealed them unto us," — the inspired teachers; and the reason why they must be discovered by inspiration is, they are " the deep things of God." Can anything be more plain? The Gospel is the righteousness of God (i. e. the mode of justification) revealed. (Romans i. 17.) Hence Paul asserts his title to be a teacher. " Paul, an Apostle, not of men, neither by man, but by Jesus Christ and God the Father who raised him from the dead." (Galatians i. 1.) And again : " But I certify to you, brethren, that the Gospel which was preached by me is not after man. For I neither received it of man, neither was I taught it but by revelation of Jesus Christ." (Galatians i. 11, 12.) Our Lord had foretold, " He that heareth you, heareth me; and he that despiseth you, despiseth me; and he that despiseth me, despiseth Him that sent me." (Luke x. 16.) "For after that, in the wisdom of God, the world by wisdom knew not God, it pleased God by the foolishness of preaching to save them that believe." (1 Corinthians i. 21.) Then we have this natural caution, which certainly implies the superiority of revelation: "Beware lest any man spoil you through philosophy and vain deceit, after the tradition of men, after the rudiments of the world, and not after Christ." (Colossians ii. 8.) Mark the discriminating negative. And again: "Let no man deceive himself; if any man among you seemeth to be wise in this world, let him become a fool," (let him acknowledge his incompetency to forge a revelation, or its truth,) "that he may be wise. For the wisdom of this world is foolishness with God. . . . . The Lord knoweth the thoughts of the wise, that they are vain." (1 Corinthians iii. 18 – 20.) "God, who at sundry times and in divers manners spake in time past unto the fathers by the prophets, hath in these last days spoken unto us by his Son, whom he hath appointed heir of all things, by whom also he made the worlds." (Hebrews i. 1, 2.) The people were astonished at Christ, "for he taught them as one having authority" from Heaven. (Matthew vii. 29.) The same authority is claimed for the Old Testament. It is a literal revelation from God. "Did ever a people hear the voice of God, speaking out of the midst of the fire, as thou hast heard, and live? Or hath God assayed to go and take him a nation from the midst of another nation, by temptations, by signs, and by wonders, and by war, and by a mighty hand, and by a stretched-out arm, and by great terrors, according to all that the Lord your God did for you in Egypt before your eyes? Unto thee it was showed, that thou mightest know that the Lord he is God, and there is none else besides him. Out of heaven he made thee to hear his voice, that he might instruct thee; and upon earth he showed thee his great fire, and thou heardest his words out of the midst of the fire." (Deuteronomy iv. 33 – 36.)

The description the sacred writers give of the Gentile nations is mournful, and from such corruptions we cannot expect prophets to arise. "And we know that we are of God, and the whole world lieth in wickedness." (John v. 19.) "Because that, when they knew God, they glorified him not as God, neither were thankful, but became vain in their imaginations, and their foolish heart was darkened: professing themselves to be wise, they became fools, and changed the glory of the incorruptible God," &c. (Romans i. 21 – 23.) "The prophet that hath a dream, let him tell a dream; and he that hath my word, let him speak my word faithfully. What is the chaff to the wheat? saith the Lord. Is not my word as a fire? saith the Lord; and like a hammer that breaketh the rock in pieces?"

(Jeremiah xxiii. 28, 29.) "And when they shall say unto you, Seek unto them that have familiar spirits, and unto wizards that peep and mutter, should not a people seek unto their God? for the living to the dead? To the law and to the testimony: if they speak not according to this word, it is because there is no light in them." (Isaiah viii. 19, 20.) The triumph of Moses over the magicians of Egypt, and of Daniel over the wise men of Babylon (Exodus ix. 11, and Daniel ii.), expresses the superiority of inspired prophets over the most improved examples of Gentile wisdom.

"When thou shalt come into the land which the Lord thy God giveth thee, thou shalt not learn to do after the abominations of those nations." (Deuteronomy xviii. 9.) And in the eighteenth verse: "I will raise them up a prophet from among their brethren like unto thee, and will put my words into his mouth, and he shall speak unto them all that I shall command him." In the twentieth chapter of Exodus we find that a whole nation heard a manifest revelation, and saw the terrible proofs. "Is it because there is not a God in Israel that ye go to inquire of Baal-zebub the God of Ekron?" (2 Kings i. 3.) Naaman the idolater, after he was healed, confessed: "Behold, now I know that there is no God in all the earth but in Israel." (2 Kings v. 15.)

It is the very purpose of the nineteenth Psalm to contrast a Divine revelation with the light of nature.

Though the "heavens declare the glory of God, and the firmament showeth forth his handiwork," yet it is "the law of the Lord that is perfect, converting the heart; the testimonies of the Lord are sure, making wise the simple."

I need not multiply quotations; the Apostle includes it in a short sentence, when he says (1 Corinthians ii. 16.): "We have the mind of Christ; of Christ who was in the bosom of the Father and hath always declared him."

> "Say, will the Stoic's flinty heart
> Melt, and this cordial balm impart?
> Could Plato find these blissful streams
> Among his raptures and his dreams?"

Such are the claims of some of the chief of the sacred writers. Now they either lie, or were mistaken, or utter the truth. If they lie, let us scorn them; if they were mistaken, we will not take weak men for our inspired masters; if they uttered the truth, we have a Bible, let us bow to its authority.

I have called these views of inspiration modern. They are undoubtedly very old, but called into life by the course of modern speculation. Let us consider their modern origin.

First, they came partly from the course taken in metaphysical speculation. It is well known that Locke taught that experience was the source of all our knowledge. Man had no innate ideas, — his concepts all came from sensation and reflection; and this account generated all the materialism of the French school; also the extravagance of Berkeley and the scepticism of Hume; who taught that experience could never give us the concept of power, or the nature of the connection of cause and effect; and the logic of Hume, considered as an *argumentum ad hominem* to the disciples of Locke, was considered as unanswerable. This mournful scepticism produced a reaction, and threw the German metaphysicians on a different course. They began to suspect that experience, under the forms of sensation and reflection, was not the only source of our knowledge; they thought they discovered a deeper fountain in the pure reason,

> "The vision and the faculty divine."

A direct intuition of necessary truth; that power by which the very perception of a thing shows its necessity. This power makes a great figure in the metaphysics of Coleridge, and all his strict or partial followers. Now it was very easy to extend this vision and faculty divine until it became an extra-biblical inspiration. A wise man had, as some thought, a necessary insight into divine truth. He had the mental sun before him, and a soliform mind; and of course the vision was complete.

Secondly, the *usus loquendi*, the mode of speaking

in the ancient world, was supposed to favor this broad view of inspiration. The word $\Theta\epsilon o\pi\nu\epsilon v\sigma\tau i\alpha$, whose cognate is $\Theta\epsilon o\pi\nu\epsilon v\sigma\tau o\varsigma$ (2 Timothy iii. 16), is well rendered from analogy by *divine inbreathing*, which the Greeks and Latins attributed to their oracles; and the Jews, by the phrase, "the spirit of Jehovah was on me," imparted to all men of superior genius, and especially to poets and prophets. Now, from the common use of language, — the safest guide, — we are taught, by this expression they understood all those earnest speeches and emotions of mind, especially in poets, which they referred to some divine power. There is a remarkable place in Cicero (Pro Archias) : "We suppose the study of other things to consist in teaching precepts and art; but a poet has his powers from nature herself, is excited in his mind, and is moved by a certain divine spirit." So Virgil is quoted (Æneid, Lib. VI. 5, and III. 385), and Horace (Lib. IV. Car. 6). This is the same thing, they allege, as when Peter says, "they are moved by the Holy Ghost" (2 Peter i. 2); that is, borne by a divine impulse, — rapt; to all which expressions the signification is, a strong affection, coming from the divine fountain, making the speaker eloquent; nor do I doubt the expression "taught of God" (John vi. 45, 1 Thessalonians iv. 9) has a similar meaning. In a word, all mental excitement which arises from God, whether by a direct operation, or from an admiring mind, or from truth which providentially comes to man, is called in the common speech of antiquity, inspiration. (Döderlein, Vol. I. pp. 91, 92.)

It is remarkable that some ambiguities in the Hebrew language are adduced as favoring these views. Thus the Hebrew word נָבִיא signifies both a poet and a prophet; the cognate verb signifies to sing, to utter poetry, and to prophesy; and the word in the fifth Psalm which our translators have rendered "foolish," comes from an expression of the highest praise. The argument would be that the very etymology of their language lets out the secret; the words are ambiguous because they confounded divine inspiration with natural excitement; and some would quote, perhaps, what Elisha said when about to prophesy for Jehoram and Jehoshaphat, before their battle with Moab (2 Kings iii. 15) : "But now bring me a minstrel. And it came to pass as he played, that the hand of the Lord came upon him." Now it would not be a prodigy, if some German commentator, educated even before Strauss came upon the stage, should take it into his head to say that the hand of the Lord coming upon him was the natural effect of the music. It would be a very *simple* account of the incident.

But, thirdly, there is another origin, and that is the mythic mode of interpreting which now prevails. This word has recently come into use; and it has wrought wonders both in profane and sacred history, and has had a cognate influence on our views of inspiration.

What does it mean? Is it a lie? No. Is it a truth? No. But a shapeless thing moving between them, and always moving much nearer to the lie than to the truth. In one of our June sunsets you may regard yon tall shadow, lying eastward of yonder oak, as the myth of the tree; or the shade of Cowper, as he describes it when the evening stretches a length of shadow o'er the field: —

> "Mine, spindling into longitude immense,
> In spite of gravity and sage remark
> That I myself am but a fleeting shade,
> Provokes me to a smile. With eye askance
> I view the muscular-proportioned limb
> Transformed to a lean shank. The shapeless pair,
> As they designed to mock me, at my side
> Take step for step; and, as I near approach
> The cottage, walk along the plastered wall,
> Preposterous sight! the legs without the man."
>
> *The Task*, Book V.

This "preposterous sight" which provoked the poet's smile was the myth of himself. But let us hear it defined by one who made the greatest use of it in his historical speculations. "Mythological tales of this sort (i. e. Romulus and the wolf) are misty shapes, often no more than a Fata Morgana, the prototype of which is invisible, the law of refraction is unknown; and even were it not so, still it would surpass any powers of reflection to proceed so subtilely and skilfully as to divine the unknown prototype from these strangely blended forms. But such magical shapes are different from mere dreams, and are not without a hidden foundation in truth. The name of dreams belongs only to the fictions imagined by the later Greeks, after the tradition had become extinct, and when individuals were indulging a wanton license in altering the old legends, not considering that their diversity and multiplicity had been the work of the whole people, and not a matter for individual caprice to meddle with." (Niebuhr's History of Rome, Vol. I. p. 169, Hare and Thirlwall's trans., 1835.)

We have an idea of what a myth is in the samples of Incredibles given by Palæphatus, and of which a selection is in the old Græca Minora, which was formerly studied at Andover Academy; though most of the explanations, perhaps Niebuhr would say, are more incredible than the wonders they defend.

Now it is to be expected, when we have reduced all the narratives of the book to myths, we should conclude the spirit that inspired them to be a delusion.

To these sources of speculation we may still add another, and that is, the pleasure that an iconoclast takes in breaking all the sacred images he finds, however august the temple which encloses them, and whatever the service to which they are consecrated. Gibbon has described (Vol. III. p. 465) the assault of the Roman soldiers on the figure of Serapis, when all the multitude expected that the heavens and the earth would instantly return to their original chaos if the statue fell. It *did* fall, and the thunders were silent, and the heavens and the earth preserved their original tranquillity. Human nature is so made that it loves its own daring; and some go on from one deed to another, until they have blasted all the sublimity in the universe. They sit rejoicing on their own black thrones, and contemplate exultingly the ruin they have made.

The falsehood of this new doctrine is just as manifest as the truth of the Bible. It is ingeniously false; false in fact and false in spirit. It is not simply wrong, but it is a complete reversal of the sacred design. The aim of the sacred writers is to draw a line between divine and human wisdom; to give us the declarations of God instead of human philosophy. The great object of modern heresy is to confound that line. The Bible demands faith; this system produces distrust; nay, it renders the Pauline faith forever impossible. It takes away our confidence in the word, and puts it on human idealism. It weakens what God strengthens, and strengthens what God weakens. It is a false fact, producing a false influence; and even the intermingled truth which makes its absurdities plausible, becomes an error in its influence and connection; even as a stone which a young tree encloses and covers in its bark, perverts its growth, impairs its beauty, and produces its ruin.

We may illustrate this point by the view we take of most of the superstitions in the world. Superstition is generally the relict and distortion of a perished revelation. Superstition has always been considered what the new interpreters pronounce the Bible to be, and, with a revelation to guide our selection and to help us to discriminate, its various forms teach us *something*. But without a higher light how dark its pages, how latent its truth, and how utterly contemptible its authority! Take the Hindoos as an example. Their system assumes the guilt of man, the need of purification, and a host of errors and imbecilities in the mode. Repentance with them is swinging on hooks; sanctification is washing in the Ganges. The ray of light mingled with their darkness is so feeble as hardly to be seen, and so associated with vaporous delusion as to have no authority.

The folly of this system may also be seen in the contrasted example of Socrates. He was just in the condition in which the Novelists say Moses was, Isaiah, and Paul. He was an honest man, wishing to enlighten his age. He must have had three kinds of consciousness. First, he must have been conscious of his own superiority; secondly, he must have been conscious of his own non-inspiration; and, thirdly, that the world needed authoritative teaching. All these were present to his mind. What does he do? Does he choose a salutary fiction to supply the vacancy, or does he fall into a partial delusion as to his mission? Not at all. He acts as a good man would act; he confesses his ignorance; he is everywhere looking round for some revelation to lean on; he sees how desirable such a revelation would be; he owns its vast importance. He is looking round and catching at each reed of hope that his own traditions present him. Because he has no Bible, he turns some of the verses of Homer into the voice of God; he makes the oracles speak from heaven, and he appeals to the traditions, — $\tau \grave{a}$ $\lambda \epsilon \gamma \acute{o} \mu \epsilon \nu a$, — and $\grave{a}$ $o \acute{\iota}$ $\pi o \iota \eta \tau a \grave{\iota}$ $\dot{\eta} \mu \hat{\iota} \nu$ $\dot{a} \epsilon \grave{\iota}$ $\theta \rho \upsilon \lambda o \hat{\upsilon} \sigma \iota \nu$, — the intimations of the poets, — show how he longed for Divine instruction, how firmly he rejected any personal claims to it. Even his Demon he explains to be only the voice of Providence. Now compare his conduct with that imputed to the prophets in an imputed similarity of condition, and how he shines over them! How much greater his truth! How much wiser his discrimination! If the Apostles had his honesty and wisdom, could they have turned a false inspiration into a true one? Would they not have copied his example? The only possible solution, consistent with the least respect for their hearts or heads, must be, with equal integrity they were truly inspired. They had a different consciousness.

The nature of this opinion is seen in its influence. As it opposes the prime design of revelation, — that is, to diminish our confidence in independent speculation, and carry to the highest point our veneration for the Word, — its influence is seen in the havoc it makes on human faith. Men now venerate nothing; they are like the unjust judge (Luke xviii. 2), "which feared not God, neither regarded man." They have lost their Bible and deified their reason. The first form of this innovation had this peculiarity, that it drew an indefinite line, which moved along, swifter or slower, like the edge-shadow of a cloud over the field; one bold step was sure to lead to another, when boldness was regarded as the only wisdom. The Scripture often presents us in single passages an alternative of a very sublime meaning or a very mean one, and the duality of choice is a guide to the interpretation; thus, in Luke x. 42, "One thing is needful," you may say, our Saviour intended only, "One dish is enough for my frugal table;" or you may take the common interpretation: True piety is what we principally need; "seek first the kingdom of heaven and its righteousness." But how immensely different the grandeur and importance of the two meanings! and can a spiritual man lay the two side by side, and compare them, and not see the right choice? So in 2 Timothy iii. 16: "All Scripture is given by inspiration of God, and is profitable for doctrine, for reproof, for instruction in righteousness." The English reader sees that the word *is* is supplied in the translation, and the question is, Where shall we place it? Shall we say, as some say, All

Scripture that is profitable for doctrine, for reproof, for correction, for instruction in righteousness, is given by inspiration of God; or shall we take the old arrangement, and consequently the old meaning? Here comes the instructive duality. The old meaning gives us a clear rule, and we may be sure that, knowing what inspiration is, it must be useful. The other meaning throws us out on a vague sea; we are to trust our own sentiments. We are to judge first, what is profitable for our instruction and eternal benefit, and then to say it comes immediately or remotely from a divine revelation. We are to take the Bible itself, and to say, Whatever I think profits me, I allow to be inspired; the rest I reject. Who does not see that this construction reverses the design of the first; it reverses the very design of inspiration? Here are two paths; one leads you from your feeble self to the throne of God; the other leads you from the throne of God to your feeble self. Which, now, is most suitable to the tone of authority in which Paul generally speaks? To my mind, the very stating of this choice gives the answer. If I find a broken reed driven by the gale, I know it is not a weaver's beam or a giant's spear; it is certainly not the sword of the Lord and of Gideon.

And see the consequence of abandoning the certain line for a vague one. Some time in the last century, Farmer respectfully and timidly suggested that the temptation in the desert (Matthew iv. 1-11) is a mental conflict, a kind of allegory to describe vividly the thoughts that revolved in the breast of Christ when he was about to begin his ministry. The suggestion went over to Germany and set their fertile minds at work, and now, in less than half a century, we have their improvements floated back. The temptation, according to Strauss, was a myth, written after the alleged period of the transaction. As an historical fact it has no consistency, — no possibility of existing. What is its design as an historical incident? It has none. It grew up afterward from a personated devil, and the Jewish idea that he must be the adversary of the Messiah. Christ must be invincible to the strongest temptation. He must have no worldly ambition, no internal weakness. As a fact, what infinite difficulties! How could he see the kingdoms of the earth from a mountain? How was his divinity peccable? Did the Devil know who he was? and if he did, how could he hope to prevail? There is no end to such questions, and therefore the whole history is expunged. Christ himself, with all his miracles and teachings, vanishes into a sublime idea; and humanity and divinity are united in some fictitious personage, invented by some lying benefactor of our race in the second or third century. Such are the sublime discoveries of modern wisdom. Such is the new religion.

Of course a central truth removed and a falsehood substituted in its place must be dangerous. The danger is, destroying the power of revelation, — the truth, the faith, the reverence, the hope, the joy, the final salvation! Revelation reveals nothing. We never, with these views, tremble at the Word of God. We never make even the mistake of the disciples of old, at the voice from heaven, when they said, "It thundered." (John xii. 29.)

The danger of withdrawing our veneration from the divinely great, and putting it on the human, is everywhere apparent. The experiment has been made. The Word of God has never been too much respected. When we cast away these cords, we become prisoners to a tyrannical superstition, or to a noxious liberty. In rejecting the Bible, the first effect, of course, is infidelity; but this is seldom permanent. The popular mind cannot rest there. Men pass through unbelief to priestcraft. If we lose the infallible book we go to the infallible pontiff, or some kindred delusion. The state of Europe is now an illustration. Since the French Revolution there have been thousands and thousands panting for civil liberty. The effort has been made, but it fails, because anarchy is the result. Napoleon III. is now kept on his throne by fear of anarchy. The first Napoleon rose to power over the evils of anarchy. The Pope holds his power because he rules over a population that have not proved their competence to self-direction. It is the perpetual argument of all despots, that the people are incapable of salutary freedom. The hierarchy of the Romish Church rose on the obscuration of the Bible, and lost its supremacy when the Bible was restored. Man is capable of freedom just in the degree that he understands and submits to the revelations of God. Spread over France a people like the old Puritans, — let every pulpit be filled with kindred spirits to Dr. John Owen, Dr. Bates, Mr. Nye, John Bunyan, Dr. Watts, Dr. Evans, Dr. Doddridge, — and representative government is the only practical wisdom. Nay, I will go further, and confidently add, that whereas it is said by certain reasoners, and said with plausibility, and, as I think, with much truth, that progress is impeded by a servile devotion to the dead past, our revelations are in the noble future, — I maintain that a hampering respect for this dead past, in philosophy, in government, in history, in political economy, is best prevented by a boundless veneration for the old revelation. It is the very thing to make us free in all the other lines of thought; as, if I am approaching a dangerous coast and see the real lighthouse flaming on the promontory, I shall not be deceived by the little flickering lights which are found in the villages, and but for the contrast might be mistaken for the nobler guide.

The Bible teaches a moral perfection, and shows the inferiority of the world around to its own standard; hence it produces the love of innovation in everything except its own principles. Pascal, Newton, Boyle, —

their watchword was, submission in religion, independence in philosophy. On the other hand, China is an example of the most doting conservatism, but it has no Bible. Nay, in the inductive philosophy itself, it is a kind of revelation that produces the free investigation. Galileo despised the decrees of the Church and the conclusions of the old philosophers, because he saw the certainty of the laws of nature.

THE CLAIM AND THE PROOF.

But are we to believe the Scriptural writers inspired merely because they claim inspiration? Is not this to assume the very point to be proved? Are there no false pretences under the mask of religion? If these holy men of old did not mean to deceive others, might they not be deceived themselves? Yes; we allow it would be weak reasoning to place the evidence of inspiration on their own claims. The true proof of their inspiration comes from the general evidence of the truth of the Gospel. The two things are inwoven and cannot be separated. It is not my purpose here to go into the general evidence for our holy religion. But if it came with signs from heaven,— with wonders, with the accomplishment of a long line of prophecies; if the kingdom of God was early predicted and long expected,— nay, was always found to some extent in the world,— and was the only fulfilment of an intelligible design in the universe; if man has always sighed over the inadequacy of his earthly existence, and panted for something nobler and better; and if the Gospel has filled the vacuum and met his wants, — then its general truth is inseparable from its essential record. Without a reliable record, the Gospel would be, as Florus says of Rome, "res unius aetatis." St. Paul, in the beginning of his Epistle to the Romans, professes to gather his knowledge of Judaism from the Old Testament. He sees the truth of its facts in the fidelity of its history. "Separated," says he, "unto the Gospel of God; which he had promised afore by his prophets in the HOLY SCRIPTURES." Christ, in Luke xxiv. 44, appeals to the sacred record, and supposes it equally valid in his age as when first given: "And he said unto them, these are the words which I spake unto you, while I was yet with you, that all things must be fulfilled which were written in the law of Moses and in the prophets and Psalms concerning me." And in the next verse we are told, "Then opened he their understanding, that they might understand the Scriptures." Now we may depend upon it, that this reference to the Hebrew books implies an authority adequate to prove the prediction of Christ's mission; and, more than this, a well-known canon, for Christ never would have mentioned the record in this loose way, (i. e. without a specific enumeration of the books,) had not the canon been settled and perfectly well known. But surely if

T

the old religion was thus linked in with the inspiration of its law, prophets, and Psalms, much more the perfection of the new, so essential to the salvation of the coming ages. The miracles, the prophecies, the internal evidences of the Gospel, the grandeur of its design, and its efficacy on the nations and on the heart, are so many proofs of the inspiration of its consecrated books. Inspiration is one of the necessary concomitants; nay, it is an all-important one. If this were denied, we should be compelled to say, We cannot *believe*, because we cannot *know* the Gospel. As we now stand on similar ground as to relishing the beauties of Homer with the audience of the old rhapsodists who recited his verses, so we have the perfection of Christ still teaching us through inspiration. It is a great, standing miracle. The proofs are, — first, the book answers to the alleged design; secondly, the history of its preservation is satisfactory; thirdly, translation preserves its essence, — it was prepared to pervade all careful translations; fourthly, the common evidences of Christianity imply and prove its preservation in the world.

The chief part of the dogmatic Gospel (i. e. its principles, independent of its facts) was written by the Apostle Paul, and Paul was a *chosen vessel*. (Acts ix. 15.)

We are sufficiently guarded against imposture. When Moses went to the people, he gave proof of his commission (Exodus iv. 30); he gave his proof, also, to

Pharaoh. Christ, also, came with all the perfection of his teaching, and the signs and wonders which accompanied it. The Apostles, also, wherever they went, carried their proofs with them; the voice of nature was appealed to, conscience and her moral laws, the testimony of the soul, as Tertullian calls it, the coincidence of all the parts with the grand design, as supporting the assumption that they came with a message from God. They assume the past inspiration of their great book, and they prove by involution the future inspiration. Indeed, how can we have confidence in the facts, and not believe the essential conditions of perpetuity? We know the existence of the distant planet by the chain of beams which connect the glittering orb with the observing eye.

Some of the messages of the prophets were probably never delivered to the idolatrous people addressed. The burden of Babylon in Isaiah xiii., the address to Moab (ch. xv.), the burden of Damascus (ch. xvii.), the dark message in chap. xviii., the burden of Egypt (ch. xix.), and certainly the message in the thirty-eighth chapter of Ezekiel, never reached the people specified; they were probably written for more lasting purposes; they were a sign to God's ancient Church of the security of his protection, and the terrible ruin that awaited his enemies. The force of these declarations was ripened by time.

Indeed, the first verses of the Epistle to the Hebrews suggest at once the need and the certainty of inspiration. "God, who at sundry times and in divers manners spake in time past unto the fathers by the prophets, hath in these last days spoken unto us by his Son, whom he hath appointed heir of all things, by whom also he made the worlds," &c. It is not an incident; it is the essential effluence of the celestial light.

I do not say — let me be understood — that the prophets and Apostles are to be believed because they *say* they are inspired; but I contend that no man can suppose they were the accredited organs of revelation to one age, and not believe they are the same to all ages, *if they claim it*. This is impossible. We may reject them totally, and then we are infidels; but we cannot receive their claims in one department and not in another; for suppose a man to make to us a speech which we believe to be a message from God, and suppose he sends the same speech to a distant friend, does it lose its authority by being committed to paper? Inspiration is only the necessary means of perpetuating to all ages what in one age, or in various ages, was actually done.

The proof, then, is certain, and the security against delusion is complete. (See 1 Corinthians x. 11.) God is no respecter of persons; as the equity of law demands that, if a man has a field, he shall have access to his field, — the very design of property being that we might use it, — so when God gives his own instruction to mankind, the very design of the gift implies its preservation. He did not light up the sun for one day only. Christ is the Saviour of all ages. Though literally crucified at Jerusalem, he was set forth as crucified among the Galatians (Gal. iii. 1.), and through the immutable record to all mankind.

This high view of Divine inspiration has been met with many objections, as indeed what truth is there to which objections may not be made? It is said, for example, it is not obvious to our senses and not known by experience, — *nostris sensibus haud obvia nec per experientiam cognita,* — and this may be said of the law of gravitation, yet its laws and results are not the less certain. It does not impair either the proofs or the benefits of Divine instruction, because we cannot define exactly *how* the spirit moves over the instructed mind. If I see a signal from the Admiral's ship, and know the sign, it is not of the smallest importance to me how they hoisted it to the mast-head, — whether by a rope, or a sailor carried it up and nailed it to the staff. There it is, flying to the wind, with all its significance. Besides, we *do* know, in some degree, the mode; the prophet often saw emblems in visions which were interpreted to him. The incapacity of language to be a vehicle of certain instruction — its vagueness and uncertainty — has been objected to the claims of inspiration. "There is no man," says Thomas Paine, " that believes in revealed religion stronger than I do." " That which is revelation to me exists in something which no human mind can invent; no human hand can counterfeit or alter. The word of God is the creation we behold." We will not depreciate the light of nature. It has its lesson, and speaks the builder, God. But surely it is within the compass of the infinite power of God, if he can make himself manifest in his works, to make himself understood by his Word. Why not? Language is certainly the most perfect image of our reason. Does any one really doubt whether Plato, Thucydides, Cicero, or Tacitus, notwithstanding all the dangers of ambiguity in language, transcription, &c., have substantially communicated their systems and their narratives to the admiring generations which have followed them? Much has been said about translation; that the authority of a verbal inspiration is lost in the first translation. They do not consider, with respect to the adequacy of a translation, the difference of subjects. Plato, for example, in some of his dialogues, is almost untranslatable. The later Platonists, in one point of view, are very difficult to translate; in another, very easy. It is very difficult often to get their exact meaning (if they had any), and, in another view, it is very easy to preserve a parallel mysticism. See the writings of Emerson, Bunsen, Hegel, Feuerbach, &c., on whom the Alexandrine mantle has fallen, and whose writings (at least some paragraphs, nay, whole chapters) are as good a translation as the dark day in 1780 in New England was a good translation of the darkness in Egypt. Poetry and eloquence, Homer and Cicero, the coloring of the imagination, the force of satire and the niceties of manners, are not easily represented. A work on law, a statute, are easy. Euclid is as perfect in English as in the original. The question is, Where do the topics of revelation rank as to the facility and perfection with which they can be presented in a modern version?

Now it is curious to see the provisions made by the wisdom of God, to make his Word, like his sun, a common light. The Hebrew language had reached that development above the hieroglyphic, above the Chinese, below the Greek delicacy, whose finer shadings are hard to preserve, — it had reached a development to which every other tongue looks back as a standpoint. It is the most translatable language in the world. Then its subject is the most simple elements of moral thought, — God, hope, fear, repentance, faith, love, obedience, heaven and hell, — eternal ideas and eternally recurring. Its writers, instead of appealing to a metaphysical background, as modern theologians are too fond of doing, appeal to a sacred history, — a body of facts which shed light on every principle. They appeal, also, to our inner breasts, the active and passive elements of our moral being. Then, as Lowth observes, "the Hebrews not only deduce their metaphors from familiar or well-known objects, but preserve one constant track and manner in the use and accommodation of them." In Lect. VI. he instances the case of light and darkness used for prosperity and adversity. Then the Bible avoids the ambiguity of an abstract, single word; the passions are often pictured, — as repentance in Psalm li., gratitude in Psalm ciii., adoration in Psalm civ. The omnipresence of God is pictured in Psalm cxxxix., and his majesty and his mercy in Isaiah xl. Who can doubt that the first chapter of Genesis is adequate in all the translations? "In the beginning God created the heavens and the earth;"— what an important preparation for the whole book, and how easily transferred to every tongue and people through the whole earth! The Apocalypse is a very curious book, — so very dark, and yet almost nothing depends on the translation. The emblems are the same, in Greek, English, Mohawk, or Irish. Wherever there is a material similitude, there is to be found an adequate word. In fine, a wonderful provision is made to produce an identity of instruction amidst a diversity of translation. Dip the water of the river of life in any vase, wood, glass, marble, gold, Wedgewood ware, or terra-cotta vessels, it is still the water of the river of life. No such sample of predominant thought over every form of language is found (out of the mathematics) in all the writings of antiquity. It seems like the foresight of its Author.

It is surely an idle question to ask of such a book, coming from such a source, whether the inspiration was verbal. Here is an omniscient God, who foreknows all contingencies, and without whom a sparrow does not fall to the ground; he selects his chosen vessel — Paul, for example — to communicate his revelation to mankind. He knows his instrument, he knows his turn of thought; he encompasses his path while he is writing, and surveys the work when it is done. All contingencies fulfil his design. Now, with such an inspirer, and such an instrument, can there be any questioning as to the perfection of the work?

THE CANON.

A WORD must be said respecting the canon of Scripture. The word *canon* means a rule; and when applied to Scripture, it means that authorized list or catalogue of the books truly inspired and having Divine authority. How was that list formed, and whence did it derive its authority? Every one sees, if there is such a thing as inspiration pervading certain separate compositions, they must form an important class; they must differ from other books, as a constellation differs from a collection of lamps hung up in a tree in an illuminated garden. They are likely to have much to distinguish them, as Divine wisdom, subject, manner, purity, authority, influence, testimony; and as successive ages have agreed in not confounding the stars of heaven with illuminating lamps, so earnest men would be likely to mark with definite limits the books that guided their faith and imparted their consolation. The objective, i. e. the real existence of such books, acting on collective observation, would create a law. It is well known there was a controversy between the Papists and Protestants concerning the formation of the Canon. The Papists said — desirous of supporting ecclesiastical power — that the canon depended solely on the authority of the Church. "I should have no more faith," said one of their writers, "in Matthew than in Titus Livy, were he not sanctioned by Church authority;" and they quoted the famous saying of Augustine: "Non crederem Evangelistis nisi auctoritas Ecclesiae me ad id faciendum commoveret,"—"I should not believe the Evangelists, unless the authority of the Church moved me;" — and again: "Auctoritas librorum nostrum confirmata est, per successionem Apostolorum, episcoporum, et conciliorum,"—"The authority of our books is confirmed by the successive judgments of Apostles, bishops, and councils." From this position the Protestants started back; they were afraid of the consequences; they charged the Papists with reasoning in a circle. You say the Scriptures depend on the authority of the Church: must not the Church depend for its authority on the Scriptures? The Protestants put the authority of the Scriptures on the private spirit;

that is, on the enlightened reason of every good man, who felt that every sacred book spoke with a peculiar power; and here the Papists in turn charged them with absurdity. For, said they, if you are enlightened enough to know which book is Scripture, you do not want its information; and if not, how do you know that it is the Word of God? (See Andrew Rivet's Summa Controversarum, Vol. I. p. 206.)

The fact is, we have nothing to do with this controversy, which has long since become obsolete. The question lay deeper in the recesses of fact than either party saw. It was not the authority of the Church alone that settled the sacred canon, — though the Church must have been the chief depositary of these important writings, — but it was the influence of the Church acting on the broad surface of human opinion, and all the laws of influence and probability that govern it. Just as the Jews were a chosen nation, to whom were committed the oracles of God (Romans iii. 2), and our Saviour without the least hesitation says, "They have Moses and the prophets" (Luke xvi. 29); and again, "Search the Scriptures" (John v. 39), a perfectly well-known catalogue of books. The Jews had no difficulty in knowing what these Scriptures were; nay, in verses forty-sixth and forty-seventh of this chapter, he equals the writings of Moses in point of authority to his own personal presence. For had ye "believed Moses, ye would have believed me; for he wrote of me. But if ye believe not his writings, how shall ye believe my words?"

Moses lived about 1500 years before Christ; and if the old canon is not questioned by our great teacher, preserved as it was through the long period, the insulated literature, and the various commotions and captivities of the Jews, how much more have we reason to trust the new canon, formed as it was in a comparatively enlightened age, quoted by a host of friends and enemies, loved, hated, assaulted, defended, and producing such a thrilling interest amongst mankind. Consider the law; here is a short list of books, consisting of narratives, letters, and prophecies, written, as one party believe, not by Plato or Homer, but indited by the Supreme Wisdom, by which thousands live, and for which they are ready to die, (and numbers did die,) faith in which perpetuates the instruction of their Saviour, and constitutes the hope of their salvation; these books are written in a style as different from other writers as the addresses of Bonaparte to his soldiers differ from the style of Dr. Johnson. Now is it wonderful that the laws of human action, among friends and foes, should mark the books and hand them untainted (as to their substantial parts) to future ages? There is no wonder about it; it is what the world has done for Plato, for Cicero, and even for Mahomet himself, — or whosever genius it is that reigns in the Koran.

It should be remembered that the sacred writers formed a school, actuated, as they claimed, by one object and having one aim, — to enlighten the world. "I am a debtor," says one of them, "both to the Greeks and Barbarians; both to the wise and unwise; so as much as in me is, I am ready to preach the Gospel to you that are at Rome also." (Romans i. 14, 15.) To this people, to whom the Apostle was so ready to preach, he sent an elaborate epistle; it is a kind of system of his divinity. It was addressed, no doubt, through Romans, to all mankind; for he says (Colossians iv. 16): "When this Epistle is read among you, cause it to be read also in the Church of the Laodiceans, and that ye likewise read the Epistle from Laodicea." The Epistles from such a sacred hand, no doubt, had a cyclical character; and if they were what they claimed to be, and if human nature was then what it is now, both in believers and unbelievers, there is no difficulty in accounting for the discriminating veneration with which the writing was preserved; for love never forgets, hatred never forgets.

God made a promise to preserve his Church, — to found it on a rock, and that the gates of hell should never prevail against it. (Matthew xvi. 18.) Now, if we look at this promise, or the law by which he probably executed it, we discern the way in which the canon was known. The design of revelation, also, seems to warrant a similar confidence. The Gospel is not a gift for a passing generation; a written language is not less certain than a spoken discourse. If Christ promised his disciples, when brought before councils, to give them the aid of the Holy Ghost, (Matthew x. 20, "It is not ye that speak, but the Spirit of your Father that speaketh in you,") we may well conclude that, when they gave instruction for all ages, the inspiring spirit would not forsake them.

It is observed by Thomas Paine, "The Councils of Nice and Laodicea were held about 350 years after the time Christ is said to have lived, and the books that now compose the New Testament were then voted for by yeas and nays, as we now vote a law. A great many that were offered had a majority of nays, and were rejected. This is the way the New Testament came into being." No doubt these councils might be atoms among the causes that settled the canon. But had the Church been strictly one, had these councils been strictly œcumenical, had no one rejected their authority, it is obvious that legislation *follows*, rather than *makes* public opinion. Had not public opinion uttered its voice, the Laodicean Council could not have spoken. They were the very organ of their own age.

The fact that some books had a suspended claim before they were received is significant. It is well known that, in Eusebius's canon, the Second Epistle of Peter, the Second and Third Epistles of John, the Epistle to the Hebrews, and the Apocalypse, are numbered among the books to which objections were made; but these objections were overcome, and the books ultimately received. Two inferences may be made from this fact: the care and deliberation with which the canonical question was considered,— the deliberation was careful and conscientious; and, secondly, the strong objections are greatly diminished, perhaps entirely removed from the books, by their ultimate reception. At any rate, were they rejected, it would not alter the foundation of the Gospel.

The preservation of the Apocryphal books, both those often bound in our common Bibles between the two Testaments, and the Apostolic Fathers, translated and published by Archbishop Wake, is a remarkable fact, and serves, I think, an important purpose. As to the Apocrypha of the Old Testament (commonly called by the name Apocrypha), it serves the same purpose that a counterfeit bill does when compared with a true one. The very existence of this collection (i. e. the Apocrypha) starts a question in the common mind which we must look at. "The Church," says Jerome, "reads them for edification, but does not receive them as inspired." But how is this? How can these books hold this middle place? If they are forgeries, why are they not indignantly rejected? and if they have any authority, why are they not reverentially regarded as divine? What is the chaff to the wheat? This natural question demands an answer. First, there is no proof that the books were intentional forgeries; secondly, they are so linked in with real Scripture, that they serve the important purpose of illustrating it; they were most of them written before the time of our Saviour, and have been preserved by the special providence of God. Thus the First Book of Maccabees is real history, — is the only real history of the period; for Josephus owes his information to it, and it is necessary to illustrate the fulfilment of an important part of Daniel's prophecies. Paul probably alludes to it in Hebrews xi. 37, 38: "They were stoned, they were sawn asunder, were tempted, were slain with the sword; they wandered about in sheep-skins and goat-skins, being destitute, afflicted, tormented (of whom the world was not worthy), they wandered in deserts and in mountains, and in dens and caves of the earth." It is our only authentic record for verifying these portions of acknowledged inspiration. Then the beautiful books of the Wisdom of Solomon and the Wisdom of the Son of Sirach, are like the second rainbow on the cloud, whose diluted lustre must be compared with its brighter origin. They bear all the marks of a redundant imitation. The story of Bel and the Dragon, cut off from the end of Daniel, though childish enough, is an expressive picture of priestcraft. But the great use of the Apocrypha is to give us A CONTRAST; to give us an imitation that cannot reach its original; to show what the Jewish genius was without the leading-strings of inspiration. Thus the story of Judith is the painted paradise of a Jewish imagination, suggested by real history, exaggerated by their own unregulated fancy, — the ideal heroism that floated before the minds of a people inured to captivity and unfamiliar with conquest. Had the Old Testament been a myth, as the destructives say, it would probably have been in the same style as the Book of Judith. Even the highest flights of Jewish wisdom, improved as it was in the Alexandrine school, as seen in the beautiful compositions, the Wisdom of Solomon and the Wisdom of the Son of Sirach, (and they are beautiful, and in some respects more artistically beautiful than the Proverbs themselves,) yet these remarkable books reflect light on the authority of real revelation; for, first, they are manifest imitations; they both draw their character from the old Proverbs of Solomon; secondly, they are *too* eloquent; they lack the majestic simplicity of their prototype; thirdly, they are too subtile, too refined, too much human speculation; fourthly, they are manifestly tinged with Platonism, nay, the mysticism of the Alexandrine school; and, lastly, one of the authors allows that he is one ὃς ἀνώμβρησε σοφίαν ἀπὸ καρδίας αὑτοῦ, that poured out wisdom from his own heart. Thus both the baldness and the excellence of these books (it seems to me — it is a matter of taste) serve to reflect light on the Scriptures. The same may be said of the Epistles of the Apostolic Fathers, — some more mean and despicable while others rise to a higher rank; — but the best of them, the First Epistle of Clement to the Corinthians, serves to show the Divine finger-marked line; for what is it? A cento of quotations from other scriptures; it is conscious weakness leaning on previous strength. We have in Eusebius an alleged Epistle from Christ to Abgarus, king of Edessa; and it is written with all the marks of an author conscious of his task, and conscious of his inability to execute it. It is wisely short; and the writer walks in cramping-irons. In a word, these feeble and even better imitations show the unapproachable character of their pattern. The greatest minds (and much more the poorest) are often thrown into a condition when their selected work chills them and imposes a want of spontaneity; just as Milton, when he puts speeches into the mouth of God the Father, or God the Son, loses the ease of his own boundless invention, and makes them talk the sentiments of the most established theology.

> "Milton's strong pinions now to Heaven can bound,
> Now, serpent-like, in prose he sweeps the ground;
> In quibbles angels and archangels join,
> And God the Father turns a school-divine." — POPE.

It is often said, that, because we find the books of the canonical Scripture bound up in one volume, it is no proof that they are all inspired; they are a *collection* of pamphlets, each to be examined and each standing on its own merits. It must be allowed that the *mere* fact of these books being collected into one volume is of small importance. But it is not a mere fact; it is a significant fact; it is a fact which has a cause, — a chain of causes; and it expresses a result which is vastly important. As the geologist finds in a certain location a piece of conglomerate rock, and from its structure argues the causes of various periods, the origin of the harder rock, its separation, its rolling for ages on the shore, its being imbedded, and the hardening of the imbedding formation, so the reflecting mind takes up the Bible and asks the history of its formation. Why are these books always printed together? and whence come their union and authority? In that simple fact (i. e. being enclosed in the same covers) there is the discussion of ages; there is the testimony of the Church, the objections of her enemies, the cross-examinations of later literature, the investigations of Origen, Jerome, Augustine, Erasmus, Luther, Calvin, and the later critics; and, finally, the decision of the thinking world on a question in which they are most deeply interested. The union is significant; and one is tempted almost to excuse some of the old Puritans, in their popular works, when they slid over the question of the canon, and argued for the authority of the Bible as if it had always been one book. The fact is, its parts flow together with a sublime unity, if not always with a dove-tailed exactness. The minute discrepancies do not impair; they rather serve to show more strikingly its *one reigning spirit*.

Thus we see that everything in the Christian revelation tends to bring human guilt and ignorance in contact with divine purity and teaching. God is THE ONLY WISE; and his voice is heard in nature only when it is interpreted by revelation. Without this interpretation, IT thunders, IT rains; but when God is disclosed, then "the voice of the Lord is powerful; the voice of the Lord is full of majesty. The voice of the Lord breaketh the cedars; yea, the Lord breaketh the cedars of Lebanon. The Lord is upon many waters." (Psalm xxix. 4, 5.)

I have spoken of the destructive interpreters. The reader may wish to know who they are. They are men who boast of a free inquiry; some of them have great learning; but all their investigations tend to diminish our veneration for the sacred Scriptures, and look to other sources for direction in piety and wisdom. They are such men as Paulus, Strauss, Theodore Parker, &c. Their path is always a free one, but it never returns to the veneration of the past.

The reigning sophisms in all their speculations on the Bible are two:—

First, assuming tacitly their point that the Bible is not a Divine revelation; that it comes from the old mistake, the mythic spirit, which they say is the common genius of antiquity.

Second, seeing and showing all the *conformities* to their assumption, and not seeing or reducing to a minimum all the discrepancies. Here they are truly ingenious. They never see the golden thread, the Divine unity, the unfolding design which runs through the Old Testament and the New, which shows the harmony in the kingdom of God. The sun itself would probably lose its lustre if shivered into fragments.

The difficulties arise when each incident is torn apart from the general design and history. Spots on the sun can only be estimated when seen in the sun. Suppose I assume that a miracle is impossible, or make a maxim that what is impossible (by impossible meaning some event which flows not from some regular law of nature) is not to be believed; of course my rule of interpreting becomes affected by my assumption. Or suppose I assume that inspiration is only the natural impetus of genius; of course, I shall read every page discolored by my theory. Every logician throws his conclusion into his major proposition. This is sound logic, but often bad reasoning. How different all this is from the wants of a humble sinner going to his master for instruction and rest!

In one way these destructives bear a strong testimony to the truth they oppose. Somehow or other, sooner or later, thay postulate to themselves the very authority they deny to the Bible. They feel the need of divine instruction, and they find it in their own self-assumed, *adequate* conceptions of God. They care not what he says, because they know what he must say. They often begin very modestly by saying, of certain doctrines on the surface of Scripture, we know that they cannot be true; they are inconsistent with the wisdom and goodness of the Deity. This inconsistency is a question which we can judge. For example, the justice of eternal punishment,— this is inconsistent with all our moral apprehensions of justice. We know God enough to know he cannot create a being to be forever miserable. We know Divine justice enough to know that such a terrible penalty cannot be consistent with it. But, ah! my enlightened friend, if you know this, you know a great deal more. How can you stop there? You have taken into your hand a most difficult question, and, by analogy, it draws a whole series of questions after it. You have entered the circle of celestial light; you have got behind the eternal throne. Hence the destructives, having taken this ground, boldly go on. Hence Kant says: "Religion is (subjectively considered) the acknowledgment of all our duties as Divine commands." In the same spirit Fichte says: "Since all religion sets forth God only as a moral lawgiver, all that is not commanded by the moral law within us is not his, and there is no means of pleasing him except by the observance of this moral law." (Mansel's Limits of Religious Thought, p. 239, notes.)

Even the modest and sober Dr. Channing, in his Moral Argument against Calvinism, assumes, I think, if we examine it narrowly, this formula: God can give us no commands which do not conform to the previous dictates of our moral nature. And Theodore Parker, the Marshal Ney of the religious world, the bravest of the brave, says with an untrembling consistency: "This we know, that the Infinite God must be a perfect Creator, the sole and undisturbed Author of all that is in nature. . . . . Now a perfect motive for creation, what will that be? It must be absolute love, producing a desire to bless everything which he creates. If God be infinite, then he must make and administer the world from perfect motives, for a perfect purpose, and as a perfect means, all tending to the ultimate and absolute blessedness of each thing he directly or mediately creates; the world must be administered so as to achieve that purpose for each thing. Else God has made some things from a motive and for a purpose not benevolent, or as a means not adequate to the benevolent purpose. These suppositions are at variance with the nature of the Infinite God. I do not see how this benevolent purpose can be accomplished unless all animals are immortal and find retribution in another life." (Theism, Atheism, and the Popular Theology, pp. 108, 109.) This assumption is well answered by Plato; he traces knowledge to the one and the many, — that is, the all-inclusive one and the all-included many,— in other words, the archetypal world, all whose ideas are perfect, clear, and fixed. But this philosophy postulates omniscience; for everything is related to all things, and it cannot be understood in its relations until all things are known.

Take your choice, then. You need infallible teaching; you need certainty; that is, you need faith. Men seek it somewhere. They find it either in an infallible book, or an infallible pontiff, or their own infallible minds. The worst idolatry we can be guilty of is to set up our own partial knowledge as a substitute for omniscience.

Let us then restore this holy book to the supremacy it once held, and which it must hold when religion lives in the earth. Religion rests on authority; our ignorance of lower causes drives us to the first; we depend on the Bible, not only for the instruction it imparts, but for the veneration, the quickening power it gives to the soul. The Bible has not only words, but charmed words; and approaches our natures with the boundless variety which different ages and dispositions require.

If the book here translated does not meet the wants of any particular reader, he needs not pronounce it superfluous. Divine truth has many other forms. Let us decide the question whether we have a Divine authority to walk by or not. Let us have no half-rule; let us think what a thrill of attention and fear would pass through the soul, what a charm would attend the reading of the Divine Word, what a glory would gild the sacred page, if we could restore the sacred impression felt when the glad message was first brought from Heaven to man! Our faith would then be operative, because it would have something to rest on; and "the Word of God would be quick and powerful, and sharper than a two-edged sword, piercing even to the dividing asunder of soul and spirit, and of the joints and marrow, and would prove a discerner of the thoughts and intents of the heart." (Hebrews iv. 12.)

THE END.

www.ingramcontent.com/pod-product-compliance
Lightning Source LLC
Chambersburg PA
CBHW021157230426
43667CB00006B/441